Listen for a Lonesome Drum

A York State Chronicle

New York Classics
Frank Bergmann, *Series Editor*

End of Lake Skaneateles

LISTEN FOR A
LONESOME DRUM

A York State Chronicle

Carl Carmer

Decorations by
JOHN O'HARA COSGRAVE II

SYRACUSE UNIVERSITY PRESS

Copyright © 1936, 1950, 1978 by Carl Carmer

All Rights Reserved

First Syracuse University Press Edition 1995

95 96 97 98 99 00   6 5 4 3 2 1

This book is published with the assistance of the John Ben Show Foundation.

Originally published by David McKay Company, Inc., in 1950.

The paper used in this publication meets the minimum requirements of
American National Standard for Information Sciences—Permanence of
Paper for Printed Library Materials, ANSI Z39.48-1984. ∞™

Library of Congress Cataloging-in-Publication Data
Carmer, Carl Lamson, 1893–
    Listen for a lonesome drum : a York State chronicle / Carl Carmer :
decorations by John O'Hara Cosgrave II.
        p.   cm. — (New York classics)
    ISBN 0-8156-0261-8 (alk. paper)
        1. New York (State)—Description and travel.   2. New York (State)—
History, Local.   3. New York (State)—Social life and customs.
4. Folklore—New York (State) I. Title. II. Series.
F124.C36   1995
974.7—dc20   94-42361

Typography and format designed by Leonard W. Blizard

Manufactured in the United States of America

FOR

Katharine Carmer Bailey

Contents

Part One

Genesee Fever   1

Part Two

Look Down to Honeoye   57

Contents

Part Three

The World on the Turtle's Back

Part Four

"Truth Shall Spring out of the Earth"

Contents

Part Five

Part Six

Part Seven

Contents

Decorations

Genesee Fever

Bailey House, Geneseo

What there is about the Genesee Valley of upper New York State to invite witches, I don't know. . . . Something about the land induces people to arise and prophesy and cock their ears toward the invisible powers.

Paul Horgan in *Harper's Magazine*, April 1, 1936

1

Foreword

YORK STATE IS A COUNTRY THAT ENGAGES THE spirit, summoning strange images. It is a land of near horizons, lifting high-angled screens between its folded valleys. Its days are full of clouds that drift over green summits and throw evanescent figures on the tilted fields, of sunny elms inexorably darkened by the march of shadow from the straight-edged slopes.

I was born among these hills and when I was a boy I knew what it was to lie in a meadow and wonder what kind of life there was above the crests and beyond them. Returned to it after many years I can understand more clearly than ever why this stretch of wrinkled land has held in the near past more of man's mystic and psychic receptivity, perhaps I should say creative imaginings, than any other region in America.

In these hollows the Onondagas kept their sacred fires, interpreting to the Iroquois nations the messages of the Creator and of those warriors who had found the Paradise at the end of the right fork of the Milky Way. And when the Indians had been exiled the white pioneers, raising their eyes to the earthen walls of their cleared lands, found spiritual release above them in those skyey reaches where men

· 3 ·

have often fancied the gods walk. And so it happens that in almost every lowland today people tell the story of someone who saw visions few may see, heard voices meant only for appointed ears.

The little winds that wander the labyrinth of York State valleys sometimes bring with them, however, a sound that is not a voice. It is the beat of a drum. The roar of cities overwhelms it but there are few upstate farmers who have not heard at some time or other that faraway tattoo. When it sounds in the southern sections of the state people say, "The Britisher is walking to his death again," and tell the tale of an English officer who deserted his country's service for love of a Yankee soldier's daughter—only to be captured and to march up the steps of the scaffold to the slow rhythm of a muffled drum. Farther north the sound is louder. There the listening housewives shake their heads, saying "Poor Willie," and tell of a mad boy who often carries a bass drum to a hilltop "where the sound will spread all ways," flailing into the sky the rhythms of his tortured brain. Among the Finger Lakes to the west the sound is greater still—so loud in fact that it is sometimes mistaken for that of firearms. I have heard the professors of the universities and colleges of the region speculate learnedly on the causes that underlie "The Guns of Cayuga" but none has given an explanation any more reasonable than that offered by an old fisherman who said, "It's the sound of drums beneath the water."

Perhaps Chief Jesse Cornplanter of the Seneca Nation was right when he told me, "The York State drums are the death drums of my people. When the British fought the Colonies my forefather, Chief Cornplanter, was a friend of General Washington. But many of the tribe joined with the English armies in the fighting against the white man who had taken their land from them. And so toward the end of the war the American Congress sent a revenging army against the Senecas and the other Iroquois nations. They destroyed our villages, they burned our granaries filled with harvest, they killed our women and children. When they had gone the Senecas who were left, starving and homeless, beat on their water drums and sang their death songs. Now the drummers are dead, too, but sometimes they come back to the places where their villages were and beat their drums again and sing the death songs for the Senecas killed by the cruel white army."

Whether or not they accept my Indian friend's interpretation, the people of York State are emphatic in declaring that the phenomenon of the drumbeats exists. When the first hot day of the new summer has come, they say, when the apple trees on the orchard slopes lift yellow-green branches above the tops of the hills, a steady rhythm, first felt rather than heard, pulses through the sun-drying air. It grows slowly into a recurring liquid note—as if the hollow of the drum on which it is beaten were partly filled with water—and it dies away gradually as though the distant drummer had moved still farther away, had passed a summit and begun a descent on the other side.

And likewise, they say, when the first snow has fallen and the clouds make a wide gray blanket above the white one they have laid—out of the horizon where the gray and the white meet comes an insistent murmur, then a repeated resonant thudding that swells and dies away again in the wind-swirled drifts.

The miraculous voices and the beat of the invisible drum are both, I think, part of one mystic quality. What their connection is I do not know, but they form a fitting background, certainly, for the spiritual exaltations that have come to dwellers in this country. Here men, wondering at words spoken from the bodiless air, listening for a lonesome drum, have sent their minds beyond the realm of experience, where like eager hawks they have seized on shining prey and brought it triumphantly to earth. Let theologians and philosophers weigh the trophies. It is enough for some of us to know the hunters and to hear the tales of the hunting.

2

Homecoming

FIRST THE WIDE HUDSON, ITS WATERS IN THEIR deep-cut course throwing sun-sparkle through the morning mist, then the rolling shadowed Catskills cut by the sudden valley of the silver Schoharie, and, as the noon cicadas began to sing, Sharon and the long swelling slopes of the York State hills. I reached a summit and saw water below me—Cazenovia—the beginning of those slim blue lines that stripe the green of home country.

I passed another lake, Skaneateles, and rolled to a stop at

a curb where dozens of cars had already drawn up. Eagerly I sought the door of a pleasant white house set in a row of others a quarter-mile away from the water. In front of it hung a simple sign—but all habitual travelers of York State know that here is the spot where the poetry of the countryside is to be forsaken for that of cuisine. Krebs provides upstate food cooked the upstate way—thick soups that are hot, creamy, fragrant; roasts whose juices flow evenly and generously within their crisp fat walls, pies whose crusts are stiff and flaky and golden brown. In the airy rooms filled with tables I heard people talking York State—with short *a* sounds extended (not clipped as in New England) and with definite *r*'s. It is a hearty dialect though not a beautiful one.

Sleepily I climbed back into my car. The lakes beyond were covered with a soft bluish haze—Seneca lying below the graceful gray city of Geneva—Canandaigua whose white sands line the dignified old town from which it gets its name. The shadows were lengthening a little over East Bloomfield and Lima but the turn-off was near. A white wooden horse stood in the yard of a pillared red brick tavern, and I swung to the left beyond it on the Long Beach road. A few miles, a right turn toward Geneseo, and the hills were gentler. Suddenly the valley of the Genesee opened before me, I was descending an easy slope toward the wide flats, and on the other side I could see the steady rise toward the far rim. All the atmosphere above the green and brown fields was yellowed by the afternoon sun.

My sister's home stands on a little knoll silhouetting the green whips at the tops of the fruit trees against its white sides. I could see it almost a mile away and I increased my speed.

"We're all glad you've come," said Katharine, embracing me, "and I especially, for now you can carry this tub out to the barn. There are fifteen gallons of lemonade in the tub and there are sixty thirsty currant-pickers in easy radius of the barn. Let's put it on your running board and I'll keep it from turning over while you drive."

We could see the pickers straighten from their positions over the currant bushes as we progressed and the glad news of lemonade soon had them converging behind us on the road to the barn. Guy Bailey, my brother-in-law, shook my hand.

"Glad you're here," he said. "After this lemonade is gone, would you mind the scales while I help George load the new truck? This fruit must be delivered in Washington in the morning—and George has to get some sleep before two when he begins the drive."

"Sure," I said.

"You pickers," said Guy. "This is my wife's brother, Carl Carmer. He's the foreman in charge of the scales now."

"Yes, Mr. Bailey," they said, crowding around us. They were mostly children between the ages of twelve and sixteen —sunburned despite their big straw sun hats.

"Hello, Carl," said one of them and then they all chorused, "Hello, Carl."

I was a little embarrassed. In the South where I had been living for seven years children spoke respectfully to their elders, called me "Mr. Carmer," and only on long acquaintance used the slightly less formal "Mr. Carl." I soon realized, however, that these York State children were not meaning to be disrespectful. On the contrary, their use of my first name was intended to be complimentary, signifying their acceptance of me on an equal basis as another worker.

The other foremen went by their first names as well. Only my brother-in-law as owner of the farm and their employer was "Mr." Gradually, as my living upstate continued, I once more became aware of the independence of life there and its natural acceptance of equality. Children and servants and landowners all use the same greeting, "Hello"—and there is no implication of differing social status anywhere save in conversations with the owners of the great estates when both children and adult farmers are likely to get tongue-tied and shy.

The lemonade was all gone and there were two tons of crated currants on the new truck when the pickers, shrieking their good-byes, climbed aboard the old one to be delivered to their homes. The far edge of the plate-like valley was turning a deep blue as the sun dipped below it and a cool fragrant dampness was beginning to gather into the slowly fading twilight.

"One of the Italian pickers left a bottle of wine for you," said my sister as I came up the steps. "You must have credited him with overweight. You'll find it in the pantry."

"Later," I said. "I'm feeling tired and sunburned and healthy and I like being back upstate again and I'm going to have a bath."

When I came to dinner I shouted for joy. My sister said, "I remembered how much you used to like salt pork and milk gravy and baked potatoes, so I thought we'd have it for you. We're real farmers in the summer—don't have to be faculty members at the Normal until October. And here are your rather hastily cleaned niece and nephew. Children —your only uncle."

An hour later we were sitting out on the broad veranda and gazing off toward the slanting open fields of the upper valley where tall elms in the white moonlight looked like dark half-open fans.

"We have read what you have written about Alabama," said Katharine. "It must seem a long distance from us here."

"Yes," I said, contrasting lush beauty under a red moon with the silvered economy before me, remembering hundreds of sweet night noises that would seem cacophonous in this clear stillness.

"We have our typical and individual traits, too," she said. "Had you ever thought of trying to picture York State as a country, York Staters as a people?"

"That's why I'm here," I said. "But it's more difficult to characterize home folks. It takes perspective."

"Some things about us upstaters are pretty obvious, though," said Guy Bailey. "And the main one is that we have a good many interests and whatever we're interested in we're likely to get excited about."

"He means fanatic," said my sister.

"Now take Bobby Green, for instance. He's a colleague of mine in the science department at the Normal. You try to find him and he's either in the garden growing the most remarkable peony yet on record or in the attic cutting costumes for his puppets. Once he gets started on puppets and——"

"And he's almost as bad as Guy Bailey on birds," said his wife. "Who risked life and limb and ptomaine above the Arctic Circle last summer to photograph the nest of a Harris sparrow?"

"The only one ever taken," said Guy, "and if your brother would like to see it——"

"Later," said Katharine. "He's coming with me now and

I'll show him some things about a characteristic upstater, born and reared up here—and his father before him as well."

"This is his laboratory," she said a moment later. "And *he* talks about a puppeteer."

In the center of the room a pillar of stone rose to the height of about four feet from the floor-boards which were cut out around it.

"What's this," I asked, "a pagan altar?"

"Practically," said Katharine. "He got the idea the floor shook under the violent treadings of his family so he had this built to hold his microscope steady. It descends into the earth four feet and it weighs three tons and it costs I don't know how much. But that isn't all. Come out in the yard."

Beside the sundial in the moonlit rose garden she reached down and pulled on an iron bar. Suddenly it seemed as if she had tilted up a square plot of land. A hinged cover big enough to allow the passage of a man rose upward. There was the sudden click of an electric switch and I found myself gazing into a light-flooded cement-lined pit. It contained a cot and a table and on the table sat an apparatus supporting a large camera.

"That camera is pointed out of a window just above the level of the ground," said my sister. "He sprinkles various kinds of bird food outside and when the birds come to eat he takes their pictures. Once he gets down there he's likely to stay indefinitely and the children have to bring him his meals. The only way I've been able to get him out is to tell him the tractor is busted. He's nearly as crazy about farm machinery as he is about birds. We have only a few acres but you'd think he was cultivating Soviet Russia."

"Well, I'm not the only one," said my brother-in-law, joining us. "Most everybody up here has a hobby that seems to occupy more of his time than his job does. We might take up a very popular one in these parts if you'd open that bottle in the pantry."

"Bill," I called to my small nephew sitting on the porch, "how about bringing me that bottle on the pantry shelf—the dark one?"

"I drank it," said Bill. "I thought it was grape juice."

"What?" said his father and mother and I at the same moment.

"I drank it," said Bill. "I thought it was grape juice."

Three adults rushed to the porch to regard the twelve-year-old who was rocking calmly in his chair.

"Don't you feel funny?" said his uncle.

"No," he said.

"Don't you want to go to bed?" said his mother.

"No," he said.

"Well," said his father, "your report cards don't show you to be much of a scholar but from this evidence of control I'd say you were likely to turn out to be a gentleman anyway."

3

Geneseo

AT GENESEO THE GENESEE IS A TINY STREAM AS IT crosses the flats. The sides of the valley slope very gradually and the whole impression from a sufficient height is that of a beautiful plate of floral design with a crack running through its center. In histories of early times it is recorded that men avoided this place. Visiting it, they said, was sure to bring on a disease they called Genesee fever. And even recently a prominent Roman Catholic divine informed his Geneseo hostess that he could feel the presence of an evil spirit in this valley.

Life in Geneseo, with minor exceptions, is very like life in any of the upstate valley towns. It is simple and unexciting, and it has an idyllic, pastoral quality that makes it remembered. The people of the town and its immediate environs have more intellectual quality than most of the little villages south of Rochester. The Geneseo Normal School, a state institution, has brought to the town to instruct the schoolteachers of the future a faculty that includes men and women of real achievement and distinction. These, with their variety of interests and their ambitions, have a decided bearing on the town's mental quality. They and other college graduates have formed a Liberal Club that occasionally lives up to its name, and whose monthly meetings are sometimes delightful, sometimes boring to its members. The proportion of people of intelligence and character, merchants, craftsmen and teachers, in the town itself must be unusually high. The circle of their influence, however, is a small one. Once the village limits are left behind, rural life becomes what it is in most sections where people live lonely among the hills.

Only a short distance to the south lies the weird valley of the Calebogue with its shut-up little houses and its air of empty desolation. Only a few of the people who gave it its name—the Caleboguers—live there. Calebogner has been a none-too-savory epithet in the Genesee country for a long time. I had difficulty finding out its origin and meaning. A scholarly old gentleman told me that Calebogue was an

Cliffs on the Genesee River

Indian name meaning "end of a valley." But an elderly physician had a more likely suggestion. Over a hundred years ago, he said, a man named Caleb Bogue built a mill back in the hills and imported his employees from down around the Hudson River. They were a tough lot and unpopular with their neighbors who called them, after their boss, "The Caleboguers."

They have moved back, now, where the hills are higher and living is more primitive. Somewhere below those summits that circle Springwater and Webster's Crossing lives the man who, according to the elderly physician's story, borrowed another man's wife during his own spouse's recovery from childbirth and lent the man a cow as security for her. There, too, lives the "family with the claw hands," people who are born into the world with stiff hooks for fingers, "makin' it easier for 'em to steal than to work."

From the Caleboguers, too, comes the most remarkable murder story of the Genesee country—the tale of the bloodless corpse. They say a housewife talking over the telephone to a friend employed as a domestic in the home of a well-known man heard her scream, then a crash—then nothing more. When, at the behest of the housewife, the police investigated they found no trace of the woman, and the man who employed her said she had left his house without informing him of her intention of doing so. Some weeks later her body floated ashore on the coast of Lake Ontario near Watertown. It had made a long journey. Possibly the waters had rolled it down the Genesee to the Great Lakes and then it had been borne along by the current that sets toward the St. Lawrence and the Atlantic. But this corpse was not like other corpses that drift in from deep waters. It had a peculiar leprous color. An autopsy showed that someone, probably the murderer, had made an incision in one of the legs and withdrawn through it every drop of blood in the body. No sufficient evidence has ever been adduced to indict a suspect, and the tale of the bloodless corpse will probably remain an unsolved mystery.

The Caleboguers are a wild lot, inbred, uneducated, their tempers undisciplined by any kind of law, and when a trial of one of them takes place they fill the Geneseo courtroom. They are the hillbillies of upstate. I saw one of their women brought to juvenile court once for failure to send her little girl to school. She could not have been more than eighteen years old and her daughter was about five. The mother seemed to be wearing but one piece of clothing, a sacklike dress that fell to her bare shins. Her hair was long and matted with burrs. She looked sullen and fierce and she was quite as lacking in comprehension as any wild animal. But she moved with the grace of a bobcat.

Ministering to these people, protecting their interests, caring for their sick, teaching them what religion they could understand was the most enigmatic and inexplicable character of the valley, the squat sturdy white-haired man known to all the region as Father Flaherty. Himself in the most humble circumstances, this priest-without-a-parish served the hill people gratis. Once enrolled in a medical college, he prescribed for their illnesses; an eager student of the law, he advised them in their conflicts with it; a former shepherd of a Roman Catholic flock in the valley, he administered spiritual advice and, when death came, extreme unction. In his clerical garb, a big broad-brimmed black hat over his white hair, a stout thorn-stick in his hand, Father Flaherty was a familiar sight on any road in the country. He had been a storm center for many years and, like many another man, he was not always right.

It is difficult to pick the truths of his biography from the mixture of fact and legend his neighbors spoke of him. There is the story of the dramatic morning when both Father Day and Father Flaherty arrived to hold Mass at the same time and Father Flaherty was restrained by a cocked pistol in the hands of a Father Day supporter. And Father Flaherty himself once told me of his days as an involuntary resident of several York State prisons. He was working on a book on prison life with recommendations for changes in the penal system. He was an educated man and a good talker, though at the time nearly eighty years old. I tried to get him to relate to me the story of his life—including those strenuous days that led to his incarceration—but he courteously refused. He said a man's career may best be judged by whatever of his work lives after him when he has left this life, and I agreed. Father Flaherty has grown to heroic proportions in the folk tales of the valley.

Just west of the Genesee and near the tiny village of York live another group known to their neighbors as Covenanters. For over a hundred years they have been in the valley, a peaceful prosperous agricultural people, letting the current of time roll over them without moving them from the bedrock of their way of life. Their principles and many of their practices, established for them by the Second Reformation in Scotland between the years 1638 and 1649, they hold to with all the perseverance characteristic of the Highlander. Best known of their exceptional customs has been their steady refusal to swear allegiance to, or to vote or hold office under, the provisions of the Constitution of the United

States because that document "is radically and willfully defective in that it does not recognize the existence of God . . . and the Word of God as the supreme law." They have never refused to pay taxes or to recognize the authority of the government or its right to legislate but they claim that because "these glaring defects, with the denial of any religious qualification, the absence of the name of God from the oath, and the license of immorality and crime upon which it sets its official seal, give the document called the Constitution such a character of infidelity and irreligion, no true Christian ought to give it his full sanction."

In their religious meetings the Covenanters use no hymns, confining their singing to the Psalms, and they do not allow any instrumental accompaniments. Christ and the Apostles in their worship sang only Psalms and never used an instrument of music, they say, and so they will do likewise. They exclude from membership all members of secret societies "on account of their blasphemous oaths and irreverent use of God's titles and attributes." On the Saturday before a communion service cards are given out to members in good standing and on the following day only those who present these cards are allowed to take communion.

The last time that I went to see any of my Covenanter friends across the valley the night air was very warm and the stars seemed to hang in the branches of trees that lined the road ahead. I could smell the rich earth, the sweetness of cut grass as I passed the meadows, the pungency of the barnyards as I came upon the angled masses of farm buildings.

I stopped outside a large frame house, yellow where the clear light struck in between the tree shadows. There was a lighted lamp in the big kitchen at the side and through the window I could see a large pan piled high with white eggs.

The farmer had heard my car and came to the door. He greeted me pleasantly, though I could tell that he was surprised at my arriving so late—it was nearly nine. I went in and sat a while with him and his wife, a sweet-faced woman who mended while she talked. They told me about their religion and what it had meant to them—and it seemed to fit the emotional needs of their isolated existence in an unfrequented corner of an upstate valley.

When I left, my host came out on the porch with me.

"Have you seen the Ford star?" he said.

"Why, no," I said. "I hadn't even heard of it. What is it?"

He guided me to the edge of the porch and pointed out a spot of light that flared like the end of a torch not far above the western horizon.

"It burns," he said, "it doesn't twinkle like the other stars," and though I knew it to be Venus I agreed.

"It's really a balloon," said the farmer. "Mr. Ford has it put up every clear night an hour or so before now and it's reeled in a little after eleven. It's wonderful these days what people will think of for advertising."

As I crossed the little river on my way back and saw the stars reflected in the slow smooth water I thought how the gods had changed since people first looked into a night sky.

Geneseo

Most picturesque of the groups of valley dwellers is the scant circle of landowners. For over a hundred years a large share of the country near the river has been owned by a few families. It is a legend that at one time the head of one of them could ride all the way from Geneseo to Rochester without leaving his own property. Though their estates are fertile the owners have not cultivated them, preferring to keep them for pastures and for their hunting. The valley families, as they call themselves, like to picture their environs as the equivalent of an English county with its squires and villagers and rustics. To foster the impression they have filled the region with beautiful animals—grazing kine, clean-limbed hunting horses, packs of eager foxhounds. In the hunting season the valley distances echo the sound of the horn, the pink coats glow through the morning mists.

Among themselves the valley families, the Wadsworths, the Chanlers, the Stowes, the Chandlers, and a few others have great fun. Those who happened to witness it will not soon forget the dark night of the nightgown steeplechase when white-clad figures like mounted ghosts rose above or fell below the sticks of the valley fences. The fox hunters make every effort to subsidize their victims by urging the valley farmers and sportsmen not to shoot the foxes and by offering to pay for whatever damages the barnyard may suffer from their depredations. Though at times it might have seemed probable that a mink or skunk was responsible for the loss of a farmer's chickens, the idea that it was not a fox has seldom occurred to the farmer and the hunters have always paid up promptly.

The heads of the valley families are widely known for their personal charm. There is no better evidence of this than in the fact that, though they are rich men, the voters of the section have returned some of them to political offices in the state and nation year after year, generation after generation. And like their British prototypes these men, of broader background and better preparation for public life than most politicians, have had a strong feeling of responsibility to their constituencies though it has been partially vitiated by their ever conservative, often reactionary thinking. Indeed, one of them was so anxious to keep Geneseo a little English-type village that he bitterly opposed its being lighted by electricity.

Within the bounds of the artificial British class-pattern, all concerned act loyally. The landowners bow from their motors, they are generous to a fault with their old retainers and with any local public enterprises. Those economically less fortunate praise them for their liberality and their democratic ways, and gossip about them with the kind of affection English housewives reserve chiefly for the royal family. And every so often in the democratic fashion of merry England the squires invite the villagers to lawn parties at their manors which, to keep the *vraisemblance*, bear the names of Hertford House (built over a hundred years ago and an almost exact reproduction of the famous English house), The Homestead, Bellewood, Hampton, Sweetbriar, Bleak House. The local press helps in the game with paragraphs that have a strangely British country-life ring:

"If any were uneasy lest they forget the rules of etiquette, their fears were instantly dispelled by the cordial greeting of the Congressman and his charming wife" (Livingston County *Leader*). The relationship between the landed gentry and the countryside is cordial and amusing—but a little as if it were a creation of Gilbert and Sullivan. Perhaps it could better be compared to an English high comedy in which neither the leading players nor the character actors are very sure of their lines or the stage business. It could never be reconciled to any conception of American democracy.

The owner of the land over which Center Street in Geneseo now runs deeded it to the town "from the first coming of Christ to the second." It is doubtful, however, that even the arrival of the millennium would cause residents on the street to give it up gladly. For it would seem that every plot of ground not only on the street but throughout the whole valley creates its own unique *nostalgie* in the hearts of those who once lived there. It creates a memory of elms standing alone in empty places and reaching for the mass gold of a sunset or the scattered coinage of stars. It calls back on the mind's shining screen vivid images of sturdy, kindly men, fleet horses rising in swift parabolas over their pasture bars, frantic, big-eared, snuffling hounds. Perhaps the most lasting impression is one of divorce from the rest of living. In a deep quick-cut valley one feels that there are hills and lowlands next door. But the very slowness and gentleness of the long upward arc from the wandering waters toward the horizon would seem to identify that far line against the sky as the last rim of a separate world.

Like every other section of York State, the Genesee country has its favorite tall tales. One of the tallest, that of the Silver Lake sea serpent, was considerably affected by the later discovery of the barrel hoop and papier-mâché remains of its horrible protagonist in the attic of the old Silver Lake Hotel. However, Tim Roscoe's story of how he got rid of the starlings that pestered the life out of him at his farm over in Hoehandle is still unquestioned. Tim says the birds were eating up his chicken feed, snatching silage from his cows, and drinking his well dry. It made him so mad he got out all the different paint pails he had on the place and made the side of his barn look like a granary stored full of corn and wheat and oats and rye. As soon as the starlings saw Tim's painting they lit out for it full tilt and came up against the barn wall so hard they broke their —— —— necks. Guy Comfort reported in the Perry *Herald* that all other starlings, "incensed by the hoax," avoided Tim Roscoe's place and that Tim wrote to Washington to the Department of Agriculture to recommend his scheme for ridding farms of bird menaces.

HERMAN STRUTTER, WHO LIVES OVER NEAR THE BEAVER colony at Hermitage, did not have so happy an experience with invaders. He woke up one night on his first-floor sleeping porch and saw that the outside door was open. He jumped up to close it and fell headlong. His wooden leg, which he had left on when he went to bed, was missing. When he looked at the stump he found teeth marks and when he looked at his bed he saw it was littered with chips of wood. Later, limping on a crutch, Herman found beaver tracks leading to a hole in the ice in a nearby pond. Just where Herman's leg is in the beaver dam has not been ascertained.

4

The March
of the Lambs

AT DINNER ONE EVENING GUY SAID: "OLD JIM
Feathers has been picking here a few days but he says he's got
a job at real money in the mushroom cellars at Akron if he
can get there. I thought we might take him over after our
coffee."

"Bill has a scout meeting and Doris and I are going to the
movies," said my sister.

"Then we three'll go," said Guy. "I thought we might
stop in at the big camp meeting over there. It's the middle
of the week now and it ought to be pretty well steamed up."

"I didn't know they had 'em in this part of the world,"
I said.

"More York Staters have gone crazy on religion than on
puppets or peonies," said Guy.

"Or peewees," said his wife.

"This country is full of the relics of religious enterprises,"
he continued, "some of them pretty alive, too. There's the
Mormons and Shakers and Spiritualists and Millerites, not
to mention the Covenanters and the Brotherhood right here
in the valley, and all the evangelistic churches as well."

We were sitting on the porch sipping coffee and watching the moon rise when we heard a slight cough beside us and there stood Jim Feathers. The dim light showed me a short, wiry man in dark clothes and white shirt and tie which seemed to carry out the color scheme of his deeply tanned face and very white mustache.

"Hello, Jim," said Guy. "We're going to take you over and we're ready when you are."

"I won't never be readier," said Jim and we three men walked around the house and climbed into my open car.

The smell of locust blossoms seemed pressed down into the bowl of the valley as we sped through it. The moon was high and alone and it covered the meadows with a white radiance and made the upper waters of the Genesee into a glimmering belt across the flat bottom land. We rode in silence for a while but at last Jim Feathers said:

"I hear you're thinkin' of lookin' in at the camp meetin'."

"Yes," said Guy.

The old man chuckled. "I used to be quite a hand to go to them things," he said. "Not that I took much stock in 'em but some mighty pretty girls used to go and the preachers'd get 'em so excited that they'd cry and carry on and somehow they always seemed easier to handle afterwards. I recall I was standin' outside a meetin' once, a circle meetin' they called it and it was a humdinger, a whippoorwill if you ask me, and here comes the prettiest little girl all wrought up and not knowin' where she's goin'. So I takes right hold and begins luggin' her off to the grove when a great big preacher from Monroe County who'd been waitin' around too saw me an' he steps up and says:

" 'This little lamb belongs to God. You may not place your hands on the chosen of the Lord.'

The March of the Lambs

" 'The hell I can't,' I says and I hauls off and plugs him on the nose. He come back at me and we had one whippoor-will of a fight. It lasted an hour and all the folks from the circle meetin' come out and made another kind of a circle and yelled at us. He was big but I was a tough little cuss and I tired him out. When he couldn't get up no more I went lookin' around but I'd lost my little lamb and I never found her no more."

We had dipped into the valley that hides the town whose gay name is Pavilion and climbed out again finally to reach the first street lights of the city of Batavia.

"Now it's a wide three-car highway until we get to the Akron turn-off," said Guy. It seemed only a few minutes to the traffic light that marked the turn.

"Tonawanda Indian Reservation is off to our right just a few miles," said Jim.

We crossed a railroad track, turned left by a big octagonal house, and were in the midst of the business section of a little town.

"I get out here," said Jim. "I'm much obliged to you, Mr. Bailey. Hope I'll see you folks again before long. To get to the camp meetin' you go right down to the end of the main street and turn left. You'll see a sign soon enough."

We climbed a long slope after our left turn and then saw a wide white banner above us. "Camp Meeting" it read, and we turned into a field where many cars were parked. Our headlights picked out a poster on a tree in front of us: "Tents may be rented from the Committee of Ministers in Charge."

As we climbed out we heard the sound of many voices singing in the distance and we hastened toward it. Soon we

· 27 ·

were picking our way through a grove of high maples and hemlocks. Here and there the light of a lantern, hung on a front center-pole, showed a canvas tent with wooden flooring. There were a few outside stoves and fireplaces. Clotheslines, stretched from one tree to another, held odd assortments of apparel.

A glare ahead made us quicken our steps and we walked into a great circular clearing in the middle of the grove. At the end opposite us stood a wooden platform protected by canvas sides and back and illuminated by a string of electric bulbs. Across the platform and facing us sat nine men in a straight row. A tenth had risen from his chair and was speaking. Between us and him stretched a long series of plain lumber benches on which sat several hundred people. Above them dangled three more strings of electric bulbs.

Most of the men were wearing dark suits and white shirts topped by the glossy white of stiff collars from which either black or white cravats, narrow and spiritless, drooped to the cover afforded by their vests. The women wore dresses of figured cotton, long-sleeved and long-skirted. Some of them were partially covered by black coats that extended to below the knee. Down in front there were several rows of children, sunburned of face, shaggy of hair, fidgeting about in what were evidently their Sunday clothes.

The speaker was a tall man who moved about the platform with a lithe, slinky grace. He was apparently in his late thirties and the huge curling forelock that crowned his wide forehead was streaked with white. His eyes, deep-set and gray, roved incessantly, settling for tiny moments of concentration, then moving on. He opened his large mouth wide and seemed to extend his chin at the same time. His voice was deep and had a smooth, soothing quality which he accentuated by his confidential, apparently unpretentious method of delivery.

"I want to hear testimony from some of the children now," he said, a half-smile on his face. " 'Suffer the little children,' Jesus said and we want all the children to know Him and the peace that He brings to troubled lives. Suppose we start at the right end of the third bench with the boy in the blue suit."

There was a twisting and turning, and the boy wriggled as he got to his feet.

"I used to tell lies and once I took a boy's marbles," he said, "but now I've found Jesus and I don't do them things no more."

The leader's eyes had been searching about the crowd while the boy spoke but they returned just in time.

"That's right," he said gently. "We cast the burden of our sins on Jesus and He bears it for us if we only believe in Him. Now the little girl, next——"

While the girl's shrill recital of petty misdeeds about her home was going on the leader began again his endless, restless looking about.

We had sat on one of the rear benches, and now I noticed a couple seated two rows in front of us. The man was in clean blue overalls and a blue shirt, the woman in a white dress of a limp material that hung loosely. She was rocking back and forth a little and I saw as she turned to the man that her face was working as though she were about to weep. The leader seemed to see it at the same moment, for while the girl was still speaking his hand, forefinger extended, whipped out toward her. "And *you*, sister," he called. "At last you are realizing the wages of sin and the joy and peace of salvation. Can't you hear Jesus pleading in your heart?"

His own voice took on a deep, urgent, desperate note. "He is knocking at the gate. Will you turn Him away? Oh, hear Him, hear Him."

The woman rose and tried to speak but tears suddenly seemed to overwhelm her, making shiny drops on her cheeks as they rolled from her eyes. Still standing, she began to sob and speak alternately but her high-pitched words were not understandable. At this moment a stout, bald, ruddy-faced man rose from a chair behind the speaker. "Praise God," he cried. "Let us march on to victory. Let us begin our marching service while the army of evil is in retreat," and stepping up beside the leader he began singing in a tremendous voice:

"We're marching to Zion——"

Instantly the other eight ministers formed in a column of twos behind them and all ten marched off the platform bawling the hymn lustily. All the congregation rose and with the exception of Guy and me and a few others, evidently spectators also, fell in behind the marching men.

> We're *march*ing to Zion
> *Beaut*iful, *beaut*iful Zion
> We're *march*ing upward to Zion-n-n
> The *beaut*iful city of God.

Outside the clearing they stepped and now they were marching in the half-light among the tall trees—a long procession of stumbling figures dwarfed by the great trunk-pillars of an outdoor cathedral. They were singing with all the strength of their lungs and the accented syllables of the hymn smote our eardrums in rhythmic percussion. The ten ministers at the head seemed to make a focus of sound as, stepping with military precision, they threw their heads back and hurled baritone notes at the treetops. The long line marched in a wavering curve through the grove, turned to pass back of the platform and reappeared on the other side, singing louder than ever. The ministers were heading them back now to the benches. They climbed the steps of the platform shouting lustily while their followers once again filled the seats. The rhythm took a faster beat as the leader again took his place in front of the line of chairs.

"Keep singing," he shouted. "Help some wandering lost lamb to find the shelter of the Saviour's arms." He struck a higher pitch while the song made a weird obbligato to the pleading solo music of his voice.

"You cannot know peace with out Him," he said. "Confess your sins and come to the sweet rest of His arms. Once you have acknowledged wrongdoing and turned to Jesus nothing can destroy your happiness. Oh, come to Him—can't you hear Him—see—He stretches out his arms to you——"

There was a shriek from one of the middle benches. Two girls who seemed to be about seventeen years old, one tall, thin and blonde, the other small and dark, were struggling with each other.

"I *will* go," screamed the tall girl, "and you'll *have* to. I've got it at last. Come with me and be saved." Her face was tense, her eyes blazing beneath her frowzy short-cut yellowish hair. The other girl wept bitterly and gave way slowly as her companion dragged her by the hand down the aisle toward the platform. As they climbed the steps I saw they were both dressed in middy blouses and dark skirts.

The blonde girl pulled the other down to the front and held her there with her left hand while she gesticulated with her right. She spoke excitedly, sobbing sometimes between her sentences.

"We've been saved," she said. "We've found Jesus and perfect peace. Just last night after the meeting we met two boys out by the gate and we went for a walk in the woods *and*" (her voice rose in a hysterical shriek) "we did things we shouldn't *do*."

The ministers and the people on the benches sat motionless and staring. There was a silence that must have been shorter than it seemed. When it grew unbearable the tall leader spoke:

"Amen, sister," he said soothingly. "Jesus is strong to forgive. No matter what our sins we can find rest in Him."

"Now we've confessed," shrieked the girl, still hanging to the hand of her companion who stood beside her with her head bowed, "and now we have the peace that passeth understanding and have entered into the fellowship of the saved." Then suddenly she turned and bursting into loud weeping led her silent friend down the steps to the front bench on which they both collapsed into each other's arms.

The leader looked a little taken aback and uncertain but the bald fat man who had started the marching stepped forward and began to sing in his heavy, powerful baritone:

"Shall we gather at the river——"

Everybody began singing at once and the volume increased until it seemed that the clearing was a great well of sound that swept upward along the dark tree-walls.

As they finished, the leader held up his hand. "We have just witnessed a magnificent thing," he said. "If this great camp meeting with its ninety tents in the grove and its hundreds of people accomplishes no more than the saving of these two souls it will have been well worth while. But this I hope is only the beginning. We shall carry on here and at our meetings in Chautauqua County next week and in Tompkins County the week after, until this whole great state has felt the power of Jesus."

"Let's go," I said to Guy and we began walking away toward the tents.

As we reached the field where the car was parked I saw that two men were following us. We stopped and they hurried to catch up.

"Aren't you Carl Carmer?" said one of them, a well-set-up young man. "I think I met you at a meeting of the National Folk-Lore Society. I'm William Fenton, Government anthropologist at the Tonawanda Indian Reservation, and I want you to know my friend Chief Jesse Cornplanter of the Seneca Nation."

As introductions were completed I looked curiously at the Indian who was before long to become my close friend. Jesse Cornplanter is over six feet tall and his body is stocky and powerful. His face is round and full, failing to emphasize the characteristic high cheekbones of most Indians, but it has the slanting eyes, the light copper color of an Oriental. His voice is strong and his manner straightforward and easy. He moves gracefully and with an air that somehow suggests belief in himself.

"What are you doing here?" I asked. "Making sociological studies?"

"Not exactly," said Fenton. "We wanted to see a Christian ritual that might be compared with those of the Long-House People."

"Did you find it?" I said.

Cornplanter laughed.

"I wish you would come to the Reservation as my guest and judge for yourself. Any time you like."

"I'll do it," I said. "You can count on my coming before long."

5

Through Learning's Golden Gate

I REMEMBERED GUY'S REMARK, THAT WHATEVER upstate people are interested in excites them, late one morning when I was on my way to Chautauqua. I had stopped for lunch at the dignified old red brick building on the side of the great hill that rises above Dansville. It is one of the earliest recollections of my childhood, this long many-windowed institution which adults called the Jackson Sanitarium.

I had found the lobby full of young men and women, most of them in shorts and very obviously in a gay mood and I was reflecting that the patients of the old days would have been shocked by this group and by the statue of a healthy young nude girl which faced the main doorway, when a young man came up to me and spoke persuasively:

"The song-meeting is still going on," he said. "They need some more voices and you'll enjoy it." Without waiting to hear my protest he took me by the arm, and in a moment I found myself in a large room crowded with chairs, most of

which were occupied. A blackboard stood high in front of
this assembly and a man with a long pointer was leading in
song while he indicated the words of a chalk-written lyric:

> Gee, but I'm glad I'm alive
> I'm always glad I can strive
> Each daily effort is one step toward the goal
> Set for my body, my mind and my soul.
> I'll make good use of my mistakes
> I'll make every effort it takes
> To lead me to mastery
> Onward to victory
> Gee, but I'm glad I'm alive.

Everybody in the room was singing lustily and as soon as
I recognized the tune as that of a popular ballad of some
years ago—*I Get the Blues When It Rains*—I joined in. My
guide smiled approvingly and darted out the door, evidently
in search of more voices.

> Gee, but I'm glad for the sun
> I'm always glad in the sun
> Each ray of sunshine that permeates the air
> Always reminds me of health so good and rare,
> I sit and wait for the sun.
> It cheers me as my health docs come.
> It shines as I seek health
> It shines as I gain health,
> Gee, but I'm glad for the sun.

When we had finished this second stanza, the leader, a
smiling, lusty-voiced fellow, passed out a leaflet entitled
*Songs of Health and Success, As Sung at the Physical Cul-
ture Hotel.* From its contents he selected several which we

sang with great volume. The first was *I'm Aware that I Am the Master*, to the tune of *When the Moon Comes over the Mountain*. Then we did *Breathe, Breathe, Breathing in So Deeply* to the tune of *Tramp, Tramp, Tramp, the Boys Are Marching, I Can Achieve What I Believe* to the tune of *The Trail of the Lonesome Pine, Perfect Health, Wealth of Health* to the tune of *Over There*, and we wound up with a rousing chorus to the tune of *Alice Blue Gown:*

> A band of good fellows are we,
> In this helpful club of P. C.
> We pursue here our health
> And our troubles they melt
> And orders we get to be slim or be fat.
> Our consultant does guide us each day
> The masseur rubs our toxins away,
> And we all stick together
> And we don't care whether
> The world is now round or is flat.

Flushed with our endeavors and with the praises of the leader, we filed out of the room and downstairs into the big light dining hall.

As I ate my solitary meal in a corner of the well-filled room, I looked over a booklet I had found near the hotel desk. On its first page was a picture of a bushy-haired gentleman and the caption below it read "Bernarr Macfadden." Opposite the picture was a letter which began: "Dear Friend: Dynamic powerful health is indeed a precious possession. It fills life with dramatic and romantic experiences"; and ended: "As you read, let me reach out through space, dear friend, and grasp your hand. . . . Imagine that I am sitting beside you, explaining the undying principles that are here so ardently advocated. And if you come to Physical Culture Hotel, my thoughts will hover around you, encouraging every effort toward a triumphant return to health of mind and body. Yours for health, Bernarr Macfadden."

On my way out I stopped at a book booth where I further identified the versatile and famous Mr. Macfadden as the author of *Womanhood and Marriage*, *Manhood and Marriage*, *Predetermine Your Baby's Sex*, and *Married Sweethearts*. On a page of the Physical Culture Hotel *News*, kindly presented to me by the keeper of the booth, I saw the picture of a smiling young lady and above it a headline: "I Consider Bernarr Macfadden a Miracle Man."

I drove westward wondering what the ghosts of the Jackson Brothers, old-fashioned physicians both, think when they come back to their sanitarium.

The four-track cement highway that runs south from Buffalo toward Erie, Pennsylvania, is alive with the speeding traffic of many states. Cars flash by each other in long unbroken lines and the great truck caravans labor mightily as they climb the almost imperceptible grades. The business of America carries on here at breakneck pace and it makes a lot of noise about it.

A sudden turn at Westfield and a plunge into the quiet

rolling vineyards behind it brings still loneliness. A half hour of passing grapevine-necklaced hills and the blue strip of Lake Chautauqua lies below. I rolled along the white road beside the water and stopped at a widespread gatehouse over which great letters read "Chautauqua."

You must pay to enter the fenced-in grounds of Chautauqua, even for a few hours. Fifty cents will admit an applicant for a half day or an evening. Twelve dollars is the price for the season, with a half-rate to ministers and octogenarians. The college boys working at the gate office are very friendly and efficient in seeing that visitors are welcomed and settled. The Athenaeum, elegantly modern when it superseded the Knowers' Ark and the Palace Hotel in the middle eighties, still offers the characteristic atmosphere of the enclosure through its name, its wide verandas, its rococo decoration, its spacious hallways, its tremendous dining room. In the latter, after luxurious York State custom, no meat course is complete without a half-dozen side dishes, including a sherbet, and the popular choice for Sunday night supper, after the replete grandeur of the midday dinner, is corn-meal mush and milk.

The Athenaeum commands a view of Chautauqua Lake from three of its ornate sides but from only a few of the hundreds of Victorian cottages of the settlement can occupants see the water. Chautauqua is not primarily a summer resort. It is an institution of learning for adults. Many a summer resident since the founding in the early seventies has been willing to build his cottage on a block far removed from a water vista if only he might have the opportunity of partaking in the feast of reason presented by the program committee. In some sections of Chautauqua the visitor would not know that he is near a lake. The cottages, moreover, are closer together than houses in most small towns. But Chautauqua is a quiet place, both through community regulation and through the inclination of its people. Automobile traffic is discouraged by special laws here, and while the old curfew rule is no longer in effect, public opinion is strong against late talkers and the streets are still at ten o'clock at night.

A few steps up the lake bank from the Athenaeum lies the Amphitheatre, center of the intellectual and artistic activities of the summer. In this sloping bowl of wooden benches, every day and every night of the summer season, Chautauquans listen to sermons, lectures, music. During an evening concert long loops of electric bulbs beneath the high roof shed a yellow light on what seems to be a field of white chrysanthemums, really the silvered heads of the listeners, a field interrupted here and there by the dark morning-glory of an ear trumpet. For Chautauqua's ardent experimentalists in adult education at the turn of the last century have been coming back to their laboratory for many years now and the great majority of those who listen are past middle age. Down at the big boathouse on the lake, the college student employees are dancing with the listeners' grandchildren and not caring at all for the religious, intellectual and artistic dishes served in the Amphitheatre bowl, but the listeners hold fast to their ideal.

Chautauqua began with religious teaching. Then it expanded to take all knowledge for its province. For seventy-five years it has served the cause of adult education. But it is no longer a place of experiment. It has fought to keep up with the changing times but the progressivism of the last century is the conservatism of today.

Chautauqua has softened its rules and one may now leave

the enclosure on Sunday, dance or go to the theater on every night but Sunday, stay up late. But when a symphony orchestra plays music more modern than Debussy, Chautauquans walk out. They are shocked by even the more innocuous plays performed by the Cleveland Playhouse Company. They want their educational lectures to be nondisturbing and well mixed with humorous anecdote. Naturally they get what they want. Most of the lecturers and artists who reach the Chautauqua platform can be counted on to draw in their horns before a charming elderly audience who want to hear their own opinions eloquently rehearsed.

Moreover, the program committee—possibly influenced by that part of public opinion represented by the women's clubs—has begun to lose its sense of values. For in its lists of ex-Presidents of the United States, great scientists, distinguished educators and divines there occasionally appear the names of people of no remarkable achievement, pretenders to fame—speakers who depend on ingratiating themselves by "cute" platform tricks or by dressing themselves in fanciful or "appropriate" costumes to deliver a "recital," rather than by the quality of their thought.

Chautauqua living is well organized. With the aid of a season program printed well in advance and the *Chautauquan Daily*, a pleasant sheet given to accepting the self-valuations of visiting artists and lecturers without critical estimates, the resident knows for weeks in advance what he will do with every hour of each summer day.

For the college student, young or old, and many high-school and grade teachers, New York University provides credit courses of a value unquestioned. For the religious, thirteen denominations provide separate buildings in which their creeds are interpreted, and nearly every day there is a devotional Hour at the Amphitheatre. For the musical there are operas, concerts, recitals. And for the social there are the water sports, the theater, and the clubs.

Clubs are legion at Chautauqua. There are the Bird and Tree Club, the Chautauqua Woman's Club, the Chautauqua Literary and Scientific Circle, the King's Daughters, the Golden Belles, the Horse-Shoe Club, the College Club, the Sports club, the Pier Club.

The first-named of these began in a campaign to make cats unpopular at Chautauqua. All or nearly all the members sacrificed their family pussies to make the shaded retreat safe for birds. Once this had been accomplished, the members of the Bird and Tree Club devoted their energies to beautifying the grounds of the enclosure, arranging for lectures on natural science within it, and presenting dramatic fantasies such as that recently given in memory of a fine old tree. "A priest officiated at an altar of unhewn stone and the spirit of fire freed the tree from its maimed physical life. Spirits of the wind, the soil, the seasons, came in light and graceful dancing up over the slope to the music of a violin and the breeze stirring in the vines."

The Woman's Club combines in itself most of the virtues and vices of American women's clubs. While its intellectual ideals are high there is a frequent cuteness, bathos, soft-mindedness about the programs that hardly does credit to an institution whose object is the higher learning. I attended a meeting at which a well-known woman of pleasant appearance and charming manner read very badly poems by Shakespeare, Browning, Wordsworth, Blake, Byron, Emily Dickinson, Walter de la Mare, Carl Sandburg, Elinor Wylie and without comment interspersed them with poems by personal friends in the audience (including one rhymed tribute to herself) and with such arrant sentimentalities as an effusion which, if my pained memory serves me well, was called "Did Jesus Have a Little Black Dog?" This program the club accepted enthusiastically under the blanket title "An Afternoon of Poetry."

For about seventy years the Chautauqua Literary and Scientific Circle has been recommending home reading to its members. It is America's oldest book club. It urges that all members keep abreast of the times by reading the *Review of Reviews,* and its book choices for 1935-36 were *The Life and Times of Rembrandt, R.v.R.* by Hendrik Van Loon, *Tolerance* by Hendrik Van Loon, *Goethe* by Emil Ludwig, and *The Meaning of a Liberal Education* by Everett Dean Martin. The Circle has hundreds of subsidiary reading circles throughout the nation. All members, upon completing the recommended reading over a four-year period, are eligible for "graduation" at Chautauqua on Recognition Day. Many who have never visited the assembly before journey long distances to join their classmates for this ceremony. Clad in white, preceded by little white-clad flower girls and flower boys who scatter blossoms at their feet, the class marches four abreast behind its shining banner through the Golden Gate, opened only on this day of all the year. While a massed choir sings

> Sing paeans over the past!
> We bury the dead years tenderly . . .

the graduates march over the woodland way through St. Paul's Grove to the Hall of Philosophy where the recognition exercises take place. Then they march to the Amphitheatre where the president of the Chautauqua Association delivers to each graduate a diploma, prized reward for having read and discussed at least sixteen books and the *Review of Reviews* during the past four years. The procession is led this time by a brass band, then the flower children, the banner with its feminine guards, the Inner Circle (graduates with fourteen or more seals, each of which is an indication of continued work on the reading courses), the Guild of the Seven Seals (whose members, after they have won seven double seals, are initiated at a ceremony called Candle Lighting), the League of the Round Table (graduates with seven single seals), and other alumni. After exercises a graduation banquet is served at the Athenaeum.

The taste for ceremony at Chatauqua is, I suppose, a relic of the nineteenth century and the early 1900's. It is evident not only in the clubs I have mentioned but it pervades the whole enclosure and is at no time more striking than in the annual Old First Night exercises. Here the Chautauqua Salute, a waving of white handkerchiefs above the head as a sign of approval, must be a picturesque sight to the speakers on the platform of the Amphitheatre. So, too, must be the ceremony of the Drooping of the Lilies in which, in memory of "all departed Chautauquans," the same handkerchiefs are held high in the air and allowed slowly to descend in drooping fashion. After that comes the Community Gift Ceremony, in which, of late, vast sums have been raised for the continuance of Chautauqua, and later there is a Roll Call by counties and by states, by years of attendance, by C.L.S.C. classes and by generations of Chautauquans.

Chautauqua is a sweet, wholesome, quiet place. In order to have these qualities in a world where adult education is a vital necessity, it must limit itself to presenting only a few commendable phases of adult education. Pretty generally it is forgiven for turning its back on those phases which most of its elderly members would regard as unpleasant. They would, I fear, be shocked by adult education as practiced at the New School for Social Research or the Rand School in New York, or by the work done in the same field by Alexander Meiklejohn on the Pacific Coast. But they are happy all summer long in their crowded little streets of cottages, shaded by lovely trees, cooled by breezes from the lake, entertained and stimulated—slightly stimulated—by lecturers on politics and economics and religion and sociology, by speakers who bear famous names, by music and poetry, all in an air of respectable serenity which America remembers with nostalgia as last experienced generally in the first decade of the century.

It was a sunny day when I left Chautauqua. The Devotional Hour had just begun and as I tiptoed by the Amphitheatre on my way to the big gate I heard the minister announce his title—The Cheerios of Jesus.

6

Cities of the West Land

THE GENESEE RIVER QUIETLY WANDERING NORTHward from its steep canyon at Mount Morris gathers momentum as it passes a painfully new unshaded college and, just before it reaches the Rochester business district, hurls itself down in a foam-spattered fall. The water darkens as it leaves the froth and quick bubbles below and it moves swiftly until it slants suddenly out of sight through arches that hold high gray buildings on their backs. Once more before it leaves the shadow of the shops it dives to a lower level but few inhabitants of the city know as they go about on Main Street that beneath their feet swirling waters are racing toward a sharp-cut ledge to leap out and drop in a green and white curtain. The town has kept its own level—letting the river roar downward as it will.

For Rochester is a sane city, disciplining alike the madness of nature and of man. It is a fine rich municipality lying flat on the plain that borders Lake Ontario, a city of homes, of schools, of churches. Just as it would keep its buildings on the same high level above the Genesee it would keep its citizens on a plateau of intelligence and unquestionable conduct. It has the kind of prosperity that politicians are always promising the entire nation if they may be elected to power. Its people have worked in well-equipped, well-lighted factories, in well-equipped, well-lighted offices. Its community-chest drive goes "over the top" every year amid much good-fellowship and self-congratulation on the part of those who, having taken a more than sufficient share of material wealth from other people, expect to be praised for giving some of it back. It has many parks for the recreation of its citizens, each carefully laid out and filled with a great variety of well-cultivated trees and plants. It is a city of successful luncheon clubs—the Ad Club, the City Club, the Rotary Club and many others, thousands of men listening behind their cigars while professional luncheon-club speakers contrive to make themselves sound like relentless logicians and their conservative ideas like venturesome and daring attitudes.

"Social Problems" are extremely popular in Rochester and are solved by committees. Never has there been a commonwealth with a higher percentage of men of civic interest. Committees are its army, "Service" is its banner.

Rochester has often called itself the state's best-governed city. For many years it rested somnolently under the tyrannic rule of a rather unpicturesque leader named George Aldrich. He gave the city a smoothly running government by boss rule. After he died the citizens got up courage enough to try a city manager. This, involving abandonment of old methods, proved altogether too honest and radical a regime. Rochester is back under a benevolent boss rule again.

Only the university and the press have stood out against the anesthesia of conservative mediocrity in Rochester. While the former has initiated little in the direction of ridding the city of its inertia, it has frequently stood out against the pressure of a stupid public opinion. It fought valiantly to keep the services of a professor of German during World War I—and lost. When a church which had employed a young professor of history to lecture on current events before its "Men's Class" on Sundays canceled his contract because he spoke of the Soviet regime as "too idealistic," the university stood off a demand for his dismissal in which even some of its own trustees joined. It refused to take disciplinary steps when a group of its students, including the son of its wise and able president, formed a Society of Atheists. As for the press, the healthy disillusionment that descends upon the newspaperman as soon as he becomes one has made no exception in Rochester. Despite a pressure from the outside greater than in many localities, the city's newspapers remain independent and, most of the time, unimpressed.

The people of Rochester are friendly. They try to help each other. They gladly sacrifice for their children. They are earnest, pleasant, kindly, lovable. Psychiatrists could well point to Rochester as a city of normal people. But it pays the price of being normal. Its gods are respectability and mediocrity. Its bugbears are radicalism and any kind of strong feeling.

When George Eastman became fabulously wealthy he had McKim, Mead and White build him a house of which that firm has not since been very proud. It contains twenty-eight bathrooms, and a pipe organ on which a professional organist used to entertain the solitary bachelor owner during his every breakfast. On his death Mr. Eastman left the house to be assigned to each president of the University of Rochester as living quarters during his administration. Up and down East Avenue on either side of it are other houses built by Kodak profits, by profits of the Bausch and Lomb Optical Company, by profits from Hickey-Freeman, Adler Brothers, Stein-Bloch, Society Brand coats and suits, from Sibley Lindsay and Curr's Department Store. Elegance is the aim. The society reporters find East Avenue an easy assignment. The residents of the Norman châteaux, the English manors, the Georgian mansions believe in the society pages and see nothing ridiculous or un-American in their pretenses to rigid social classifications in imitation of long-established British social life. From time to time a woman of wealth and ambitions assumes a dictatorship of social activities. One of these conceived the project of hiring a theater in the business section of town and there having society girls and men perform the best one-act plays free of charge in order to give shopgirls of the town an opportunity to acquire culture instead of food during their lunch hour. Another tried for years to bring society and the university faculties together in a brilliant salon—achieving only the most desperately self-conscious and inordinately stupid parties. A third decreed that there should be no smoking in the dining rooms of the leading women's club and encouraged hostesses to report guests who broke the rule.

Rochester has made the world's greatest experiment in attempting to exchange money for culture. Aided by Mr. Eastman's fortune, its citizens have spent more than fifty millions in the effort to bring "appreciation of the right things" to the populace. Mr. Eastman dreamed of a theater in which the motion picture would reach its highest development, showing only artistic films with an accompanying concert by a full symphony orchestra. Its foyers would acquaint patrons with the best in modern painting through their murals and the hanging from time to time of traveling exhibits. All the arts should be represented at their best in it. But the murals were by Maxfield Parrish and Ezra Winter, the traveling exhibits showed only third-rate work, the patrons did not always find themselves in the mood for a symphony at the same time that they wanted to see the cinema, and there were not many artistic motion pictures anyway—and so the project failed.

Mr. Eastman dreamed of a great music school that would make Rochester into an American Milan. He built the buildings, invited Sibelius and many another great artist, and the city waited for results. Nothing exciting happened. Most of the artists reported that they could not work well in Rochester, there was something about it that dulled and deadened them. As the symphony orchestra went on functioning it became more and more identified with uninspired conductors, until it became known more for sound craftsmanship than for creative achievement. Its concerts are well attended by well-dressed people who applaud politely and walk with becoming pride round and round the main foyer during the intermissions. A player in the orchestra told me that while the orchestra is performing the musicians can feel the weighty blanket of misunderstanding over them. "Rochester seems to *try* to achieve mediocrity," he said. "It would embarrass our audience if we played the *Tristan und Isolde* music with Toscanini conducting. Everything must be correct, sound, sure—never passionate or abandoned."

Rochester is a temperate city, satisfiedly walking the middle of the road, always circumspect, prudent, discreet. It has never had much of that quality which for want of a better name is called color. Its one picturesque citizen was Rattlesnake Pete—Pete with his big hat and his twin St. Bernards and his saloon with all its snakes and guns and games of chance and rough male atmosphere. But Pete is dead and his place is gone and he left no influence behind. The German population threatened for a while to make Rochester a more amusing town—with a fine big restaurant called Odenbach's that knew how to serve Wiener Schnitzel and Apfelstrudel and an orchestra called Dossenbach's that knew how to play Viennese waltzes—but there weren't quite enough Germans. And now the Italians are helping a bit. The grand dames who undulate about the main foyer at the symphony as if it were a goldfish bowl sometimes open their mouths in surprise to see beside them a gaily-decorated olive-complexioned Neapolitan housewife, enthusiastic about herself, her escort, the crowd, and willing to be enthusiastic about the orchestra if it will let her. Perhaps she is the saving leaven.

Rochester has obtained what it has wanted most. Its people are much too able to fail of their goal. They have wanted security, friendliness, educational institutions, disciplined moderation in all things. Believing in culture theoretically, they have attempted to buy it and have swindled themselves because they really have no irrepressible yearnings for it. Save in occasional groups, they do not care passionately about music, poetry, painting. To do so and admit it would betray a lack of balance—and that a typical Rochesterian will never do. They have built the temples of art but they are only formal worshipers. Theirs is as beautiful a city as man can make with his hands and his brains. It is dull because it has been handicapped by the failure of the spirit of man to cooperate.

The country between Rochester and Buffalo is a fertile plain beside the blue water of Lake Ontario. Its level roads run through miles on miles of low, wide-spreading apple trees. In the spring hundreds of acres of blossoming orchard perform ballets in the wind and the bluebirds, the Baltimore orioles and the orchard orioles are quick spots of color against the pinky-white of the swelling treetops. A few weeks later the cedarbirds with wax-red chevrons on each flirting wing are crested bandits among the cherries and the cicadas have begun their long summer grind.

In the autumn this country is invaded by an army of pickers, following the harvests north—hired men with tall tales for an October evening beside a pitcher of cider on the kitchen table. Then in the villages along the slow water of the Barge Canal—once the Erie—Saturday night often sees a fight between a drunken picker and a "Polack," one of the quarry workers in the Medina sandstone pits. Sometimes there is a wedding made noisy by the soft-eyed Italian truck farmers who are covering the black earth of the Tonawanda swamps, a few miles south of the orchards, with a green carpet. The section is becoming a rural melting pot of peoples of many nationalities.

In the old days this was as much of a Yankee region as if it had been a part of New England. The oldest inhabitants of Albion, maple-shaded center of the apple country, still laugh over the tale of how their village won the designation as county seat over the neighboring village of Gaines. When the towns began making their claims to the legislators at Albany, Gaines had won a signal advantage by pointing out that the Oak Orchard River gave it water power while Albion had none. The shrewd citizens of the latter community, however, invited a committee from Albany to visit their town and see for themselves. They then went to Hart's Creek which occasionally in moister summers had been able to summon up enough water to provide a swimmin' hole for their sons, erected a dam, and waited. When a small lake had formed they built a grist mill. And when their distinguished visitors arrived they were met by a group of genial gentlemen who filled them with hard cider and then drove them out to observe the town's newly developed power. As they came within sight of the mill its operators sent the water swirling through the race, the great wheel began to turn, there was a bustle and a shouting, a busy display of bags of flour. Before the little lake had run dry the committeemen were back in town being refilled with cider and Albion was the county seat.

Buffalo is a place of contrasts—of big and distinctly different communities bound together into a huge blustery city beside the tossing waters of Erie, stormiest of the Great Lakes. All day long Buffalo receives the treasures of the lands that lie west and north along the shores of America's chain of inland seas. On the waterfront the long, low lake freighters carrying ore and grain and meat make port under the shadow of towering elevators, their navigators happy to reach haven without that most dreaded of lake catastrophes—a shifting of cargo and capsizing. Here weather-beaten old fishermen, veterans of many a hissing squall, put out each day in their stained craft whose hulls have never felt the slap of brine. And as the boats come and go there is a running about and a shouting, usually dimmed by the steady rush of wind. The port of Buffalo exists apart, hardly aware of the city depths behind it.

And the people in those depths are equally indifferent to the lake shore. To thousands of its people Buffalo means the golden glow and desperate drudgery of a steel furnace, the stuffy interior of a flour mill, the bloody stench of meat packing throughout the day, and then a bed in one of the ugly, one-pattern houses, dreary gray and drearier brown, that cover acre after acre of the city's extent. The Poles live here, numbering a third of the population and not yet so thoroughly Americanized that they have forgotten the language and the customs of the country whence they or their immediate ancestors came. Only in their churches with bulbous spires and elaborately decorated interiors does the average outsider see the influence of a European background. An occasional newspaper reporter or social worker has attended in Little Poland an Old World festival, a wedding or a birthday celebration, to return with a gay tale of the colorful ceremonies which the drab walls of the houses sometimes hide. And not even the Poles are yet aware that Buffalo is preponderantly a Polish city.

The casual wanderer through Buffalo's residential streets will not walk far without coming upon a corner redolent with the smell of beer and sauerkraut, cheese and apple dumplings. In more solid comfort than the Poles, in roomy, over-decorated houses, the Germans have built hearty communities that own a quality and a culture the city could ill afford to be without. These people are big and round and jolly. From the cool sawdust-strewn depths that are hidden behind the swinging doors of their saloons comes the sound of heavy male voices united in Gemütlichheit. There is fancy and sentimentality in this German society and the stolid conservatism of civic-minded burghers.

Last and most powerful of the groups that make up Buffalo are the rich old families living in heavy elegance behind the respectable excesses of the scroll saw that line Delaware Avenue. Safely immured in their wrought-iron trimmed castles and their mansard-roofed mansions dotted with stained-glass windows, these conventional and conservative people have pretty much forgotten that it was harbor tolls which long ago established them as Buffalo institutions. They know neither Poles nor Germans nor do they recognize the smells of fish and grain and meat blowing from the water front. Though they are not as rich as the moneyed people of Rochester, though their homes are not as expensive nor as new, they are complacent in the knowledge that they have been well-to-do longer. They do not recall the pioneering crudities of their fortune-founding ancestors.

The four chief strains of Buffalo's population become aware of each other only at City Hall and in the downtown business section. In both places they meet with representatives of less well-defined groups. Though smaller in number than the Poles and the Germans, the Irish continue to exercise their talents for politics. The best-known figure of twentieth-century politics in Buffalo is the late "Fingy" Conners, more colorful though less successful as a boss than Rochester's George Aldrich. "Fingy" was a water-front product, a poor Irish boy who became a longshoreman before opportunity and ability conspired to place him beside the folk of Delaware Avenue. Buffalonians tell with affectionate relish varied stories of his speech at the dinner to honor him as elected head of an exclusive city boating club. The version last told to me went: "It's a big jump from longshoreman to commodore of this club—but I done it."

The Irish, the Germans, the rich old families have kept Buffalo on the conservative side politically through most of its later history. Bosses who could deliver the Polish vote have prospered mightily. The Poles have not yet learned the lesson which the Minneapolis Swedes could teach them. But in other respects Buffalo is much more like the cities of Missouri and Ohio and Michigan than Rochester. In the downtown business streets men from all sections are having so much fun making a living that they forget to organize all the committees for civic betterment which the more homogeneous Rochester affords. There is a rush and a boom in Buffalo's market place. The newspapers are dynamic, excitable, spurred by a healthy rivalry. Hotels are busy and too full of a spirit of genial cooperation, service and camaraderie to suit a quiet traveler. Buffalo is a broad, gusty, powerful city. Only in a few old ways is it characteristic of the country that lies to the east of it. This sprawling, bustling town is no longer upstate. Buffalo is the beginning of the Middle West.

Part Two

Look Down to Honeoye

The Bristol Hills

So and no otherwise—hillmen desire their Hills!

From *The Sea and the Hills*, by Rudyard Kipling

7

The Bristol Hills

I DROVE EASTWARD FROM GENESEO. I SAW THE shores of Conesus and the gleaming mirror of Hemlock. A few miles farther east I passed a weather-blackened farmhouse, its front door barred and sunset-light reflected from the few small squares of glass left unbroken in the upper windows. A mile beyond it stood a wind-cracked frame with staring windows and gaping doorway. Then close beside the road I saw foundation walls supporting nothing now save clambering vines. This was what they had told me I would find in the Bristol Hills—forgotten farm land, lost orchards, long-unused wells, unpeopled houses. A far glimpse of another lake and I looked anxiously along the sides of the road —turned suddenly left up a narrow brown streak of dirt. It was a long climb, but there was the schoolhouse, as they had said. A half-mile more and on a knoll far over to the right I saw gray-white pillars and knew I was near my journey's end. I dipped into a muddy glen and my tires slipped dangerously as I tried to bring the car up out of it. Inch by inch the whirling wheels advanced me, then caught hold and I was beside the house. A girl in a light blue dress came out of the back door.

"Hello," she said, smiling.

Her eyes were lighter than the dress and somehow bluer

and she was little. In wooden shoes and a cap, I thought, she would fit into a Dutch print.

"You're Maud."

"Yes," she said, taking my hand. "Coley's out in the barn milking the goats. Bring your bags in—or perhaps you'd like to enjoy our view first." For a mile below us the land sloped downward in alternate fields and woods, then turned flat in a gentle gesture and edged the darkening waters of Honeoye. A cluster of yellow points of light showed a distant town. The surface of the water was like a pewter tray reflecting candles.

"It's perfect," I said. "And so is the house." I turned to look at the finely proportioned porch with its four tapering fluted columns beneath a widespread gable, at the little wrought-iron lattices of the lie-on-your-stomach windows up under the eaves, at the long line of the one-story wing projecting from the back.

"Do you mean it?" she said. "You don't think we're a little queer to live in exile like this?"

"I do not."

"Well," she said, "I've had my doubts about entertaining a professor of my husband's college days. You've made a good start. Now don't spoil it by crying for cow's milk instead of goat's, or getting effete enough to demand a hot bath."

"Hey!" came a hearty voice from the barn, and Coley walked toward us—a shining milk pail in each hand. He set them down and we looked at each other.

"New York's made you flabby," he said. "A little farm work will do you good."

The last time I had seen him his curly hair had been black around his smooth high forehead, his naturally slight figure had begun to grow sturdy beneath his khaki uniform. Now the curls were streaked with gray, the smooth forehead was seamed, and his figure was slight again, with a mature wiriness. But the old earnest manner was the same, and so was the quizzical look in his light brown eyes. He had said to me once, in his college days, "Some think I'm lazy. It really isn't so. It's just that I want to be doing nothing while I think about what I'm going to do next." I was reminded of that remark when he said:

"For literary purposes you should have come at least a year earlier. I might have had some perspective on this country then. Now I'm part of it, just like my neighbors. I'm good material for you, but a damn poor interpreter."

"Don't put him to work so soon," said Maud. "Let's show him the ark we chose to ride out the depression in. You have to come in through the woodshed because that's where we lived first. We haven't reclaimed the front rooms yet."

The woodshed was a low wide room with walls of paneled pine. In the center was a huge brick fireplace. A map of the Honeoye region was built into the panel above it. A window seat large enough for a man to sleep on lay beneath the window that looked out over the lake. The floor was evenly-laid flagstone, save for a large round millstone in the center.

"There are advantages in having a contractor-husband even if contractors don't get a chance to work any more," said Maud. "This is my blue kitchen."

The stove was large and a stew bubbled and steamed on it. The blue walls shone, so did the blue dishes. I looked at Maud.

"You're Dutch," I said.

She laughed. "Only the Pennsylvania kind," she said. "German really."

"She works too hard keeping the place like this," said Coley. "It's a wonder she doesn't have white sand on the floor."

"Come into the dining room," said Maud. "We like it—and it's as far as we've gone. The bedrooms—even yours—are terrible. But we'll get to 'em some day."

Framed by the wood panels above the high wainscoting of the dining room was a wallpaper whose chief motif was a large urn of classic simplicity. Its colors had once been mellow brown. Now the fading of many years had given them the delicacy of pastels. I exclaimed over them.

"That paper hung in strips from the ceiling of the front hall," said Maud. "On the sides it had been crumpled under plaster and dirt. I tore it down, cleaned it and pressed it with a warm iron. I spent most of one winter putting it together so that the patterns joined—like a picture puzzle. Then we fitted it into the panels and Coley pasted it on so that you can't see the seams without a magnifying glass. I was really bored for something to do after we finished—till I started hooking this rug."

In the corner stretched on a frame was a huge field of rainbow-striped squares. "It's taken up the lonely evenings for almost two years now," said Maud, "and I could finish it in no time if Coley would only realize that spring is here and take off those old red flannels. They're just what I need."

"What's a husband's pneumonia to her art?" said Coley.

After supper we put on our coats and went out on the pillared porch for a little while. The spring moon had risen, almost full, and the waters down below sent messages of light up the long slope. The semicircle of gnarled locusts that edge the patch of lawn in front of the house made grotesque shadows that reached toward us. A purring cat crept into my lap.

"That's Tammany," said Coley, "born in an uninstalled water-closet bowl on Park Avenue, New York City, in the days when contractors had jobs."

"She was a pampered kitten on a silk cushion in the Prohibition gin period," said Maud, "so she's had her problems of adjustment, too."

"And she's solved 'em all," Coley said, stroking the cat's ears. "She rode the truck to Rochester when we went broke and set out for home—and she rode it up here when we decided that this was our way out. We took her with us to visit Ezra Winter on the way up from New York and she walked into a room filled with three cats and two police dogs. Not one of 'em moved while she promenaded around, her tail in the air, taking a good look at each one."

"But when Ezra brought one of those dogs up here," said Maud, "and Mike (he's Tammany's present husband and as mean a tomcat as there is) started to claw hell out of him, Tammany stepped in between and beat Mike off. She's very loyal to her friends."

"She has a thoroughgoing philosophy now," said Coley. "It consists in not being surprised at anything. I think she got it when I drowned her last batch of kittens and put three baby squirrels to suck at her. I was sure she'd kill 'em but she didn't—she brought 'em up the best she knew how."

"She took it too seriously," said Maud. "She'd put 'em in their box and the minute her back was turned they'd be gone. She'd go after 'em and they'd run up the window curtains and chatter at her from the curtain rods while she miaowed at 'em from below. One day she went and got Mike and I thought that was the end—but no. He batted

the children this way and that but he just seemed puzzled
—and a little amused."

"But what became of them?" I said.

"They're in a laboratory of the University of Rochester
and several earnest young scientists are taking daily notes
to prove that squirrels brought up on cat's milk act differ-
ently from other squirrels—or vice versa; I forget which."

"No wonder you don't get lonesome up here," I said.

"Tammany helps," said Maud. "So do the goats and the
lambs—and we had a setter once, but Coley sent him away
when some dogs around here began killing sheep. We were
afraid somebody would think he was one of 'em and we'd
have to kill him. We do get lonesome, though. You see that
wide glow in the sky over there? That's Rochester where
Coley was brought up and where we both went to college.
There's good music over there, and hot baths, and the
houses of friends with servants to wait on you, and parties
galore and——"

"I know about Rochester," I said. "I've lived there, too."

"Most of our friends think we're crazy to prefer this to—
to that," said Coley with a wave of his hand toward the
horizon glow.

"I don't," I said.

"You may before long," said Maud.

The legend about the house we three lived in that spring is that its builder, an officer in the War of 1812, had so disgraced himself by ferocity and cruelty in a Canadian campaign that his superiors had tried to banish him from the society of the civilized. Glad to exile himself from companions he despised, the veteran had chosen this lonely hilltop on which to build a house that would reflect his own good taste and be a comfortable dwelling throughout his days. Some of the oldest inhabitants denied this story. They said "The General" got his title merely from being an important officer in "General Training" days when citizens who believed in preparedness got together to drill much as the National Guard does now. All narrators were agreed, however, that the old fellow's daughter, Miss Julia, who was the last member of his family to live in the house, had kept her father's regimentals and hat all laid out in the downstairs spare bedroom as if their former owner were still in them. Many a caller was frightened to pass through and see them there.

Coley's is the one house of beauty and dignity in the region. The farmers whose high hopes led them to construct homes in the strange loneliness of the Bristol Hills built without regard for line and mass. Only in their ruin, with sagging roofs and leaning walls, do these houses take on a sort of pathetic beauty. Families with ambition and ability found in the swelling curves of this land only bitter disillusion and moved on, leaving behind the shells they once inhabited. The people who remain, only about a sixth of the former population, have long accustomed themselves to ask no more than a bare living from the soil. They do not think to increase that living, even when it is possible.

They are a kindly people, chiefly of Scottish and English ancestry. Though most of their families have lived in America for generations, they still frequently compute prices in shillings. Another peculiarity of language is the use of the word "gull" for gully or ravine. Each farm has its gull lot to which the owner refers with bitter humor as "good only to hold the soil together" or as "so steep ye can plow both sides at the same time."

Long ago the people of this land lost the sense of fine distinction in morals and religion which characterized their grandfathers. Incompatibility between husband and wife is frequently settled much less expensively than by divorce. The wife goes to "keep house" for another man and the forsaken husband employs a "housekeeper." No one sees anything inconsistent or funny about the euphemism, nor about the fact that housekeepers sometimes bear the children of their employers. As for churches, these people have little interest in them—and the chief use of a parson is for a funeral sermon.

Death in the Bristol Hills receives no undue emphasis. It is accepted as casually as birth and the succession of the seasons. Coley and Maud and I called on a bereaved widow the evening after her husband died. We found her sitting on her front porch in the moonlight, plucking at her guitar. She asked us what we would like to hear and she played and sang for about an hour. Finishing up with *Buffalo Gals* and *The Scottish Hornpipe* she said, "Would you like to see him?" and rose to get her flashlight from the kitchen shelf. I shall not soon forget the procession of the four of us moving singly about that coffin with the flashlight throwing an unsteady beam on the dead man's face.

The Bristol Hills

I learned more about the people of the region from our nearest neighbor, "Let" Washburn, than from anyone else. Let, at seventy-four, had more energy and ambition than the great majority of the Bristol Hills farmers. He was a powerful man, straight and sturdy, and did not look over fifty. He had been moderately successful on his farm and would have been more so had it not been for his main weakness—a sincere desire to help other people.

When a neighbor went on a week's drunk, a not uncommon occurrence, Let would sneak down to the dissipator's barn each morning to see that his horses and cows were fed. And he kept an antiquated set of dental tools for the purpose of helping afflicted friends. The accepted procedure was for his patient to arrive at any hour of the day or night bearing a quart of native whisky. Both surgeon and sufferer indulged in this until their courage was sufficiently aroused for the operation. By this time, however, a certain degree of uncertainty had been generated and Let had been known to pull three teeth before he extracted the real malefactor.

Let lived alone. He had a wife, Ellie, but they didn't get on and she went away. Let got a housekeeper but she died. He and his wife were on good terms after they parted. He gave her several thousand dollars when she left, and she spent the money in a very short time. She lived about two miles down the road from Let's house and she kept Let's name. Her place was infested with rats and mice because she couldn't stand cats. Let said her favorite method of getting rid of mice was to grab them by the tail as they were running into their holes and paint them a bright yellow or a vivid blue, any color she happened to have in the paint pail. Then she let the mouse go and, according to her telling, his appearance so startled his family that they all ran away. One day a particularly large rat so objected to being incarnadined that she stuck the meat-fork into its back to hold it steady while she wielded the paint brush.

Ellie was fond of society and the social graces. At sixty-five, she still curled her bobbed hair about her plump face with a curling iron heated over a lamp chimney and added to the effect thus created by wearing earrings. She had small feet of which she was very proud and she squeezed them into short-vamp, babyish pumps, a procedure that puffed out her instep enormously. When she and Let had been married twenty-five years she astonished the whole community and raised its respect for her to a high degree by suing him for divorce, naming her sister Dory as corespondent. She lost the suit but the trial is still reported with great gusto throughout the Bristol Hills. It reached its high point when Ellie's lawyer, cross-examining Dory on the stand, said:

"Did this man have improper relations with you?"

"Not since he's been married," said Dory.

Ellie was having a shindig for her children and grandchildren, of which there are many, and the fiddler had just got started when she heard of the death of Let's housekeeper. She stopped the party at once and the whole lot of them went over to Let's to condole with him and gossip with relatives and friends far into the night.

Everybody in these hills always has time to stop for a little chat. I can still see Let bringing a load of wood up to the side porch, his ill-matched team settling into the last sharp pull.

"Morning, Let. Nice day."

"Yep. Sun shinin' both sides o' the fence."

"Feelin' all right?"

"As well as though I was in my right mind. Glad the rain's over, though. Weather's been sort o' ketchy all winter."

"I saw some new country yesterday. Drove through Hickory Bottom and up over Baptist Hill, came down by Whetstone Brook and ended up at Swindler's Gap. Came back by Mayweed, Vine Valley, Gulburg, and Brag Village."

"Ye'd oughta hit Cold Spring and Cobbler's Knob while you was over there. Mighty sightly places. Did I ever tell ye 'bout the time I was workin' over that way on a hay-pressin' gang? Thunderstorm come up and we jest got to the barn 'fore it bust. Well, we got to talkin', you know the way a gang will, 'bout women an' such. 'Most everybody'd had his brag at it includin' the boss when Henry Orlin spoke up. He says one time a feller hired him to go over to Lima Seminary to get his daughter that had jest graduated an' bring her home. On the way back a storm 'bout like this 'un come up. The gal got scared an' he stopped the horse 'n' buggy under a tree to wait fer better weather. She was so scared one thing sort o' led to another an' 'fore he knew it he'd took what he wanted. Well, jest when Henry finished tellin' that the dinner bell rang an' we made a break fur the house. We'd all got washed an' took our seats when the boss's wife come in with an extry platter o' fricassee chicken an' says. 'Ye know, Henry, this storm reminds me o' the day ye brought me back from Lima.'

" 'Pass the butter,' the boss yells, 'and the beets an' squash an' everythin' ye got.' "

THE GOLDFINCH WAS MAKING HIS UNENDING SERIES OF
yellow down-turned parentheses over the lake slopes when
I had arrived at the old house. Day after day Coley and
Maud and I drove through the land while I listened to people who lived on it. They spoke of weather, of seed, of soil—
and then of neighbors and roads and towns. And almost
always before we said reluctant farewells there was a story—
such a story as tells the quality of mind of the teller and
betrays the sort of snare that catches his imagination.

Sometimes we dared the threatening brook that runs
through Burpee's Hollow and, emerging on the far side of
that ravine, stopped at Frank Drown's propped-up log
cabin, as bent and weather-beaten as the lone man it houses.
Some day the cabin will fall in on Frank while he lies asleep
in his built-in bunk. But cheerfully he says it never has and
tells us to buy our ax helves only from him, for he has cut
them from white ash when the moon was dark. Just beyond
Frank's cabin a mountain rises—Gannett's Hill they call it—
dwarfing the countryside. Tennessee or Kentucky sees no
wilder landscape—the leaning cabin, the mountain, the narrow rutted road called Stony Lonesome that runs along the
foot of the steep side toward Naples and Italy Hill.

And sometimes we skirted Allen's Hill to hear good talk in West Bloomfield and North Ionia, or made off along Jason's Gull to hear a tale that somebody in Tabor's Corners knew better than anybody else. More often Let or Ellie or any one of the neighbors stopped in to swap yarns.

It was a motley collection, my bag of stories, by the time the autumn breezes were blowing up from Honeoye and the brown burrs of horse chestnuts had burst in falling to the ground to show the varnished spheres within. But the stories seem to me to fit, like the many-colored fragments of a kaleidoscope, into a unified whole. Singly the three tales I have chosen to tell here reveal but little of the atmosphere and tone peculiar to this land. Taken together they help to an understanding of its unique quality. Like practically all folk tales, each of these stories has a factual basis. One of them has been labeled history. I am relating it, however, not as it is found in books but as I was able to put it together from information given by people who have never read it. Sometimes more of truth sifts through the years that way than can be found on printed pages. The other two tales reveal something of the savagery and cruelty of rural creeds, qualities too often neglected in studies of a smiling countryside, and I am telling them as they were told to me.

8

The Curtained
Carriage

WHEN WILLIAM MORGAN CAME TO BATAVIA AND asked for work as a stone mason he was disappointed and bitter. Behind him lay pride of birth and the glory of the victorious soldier; ahead only poverty and the drudgery of manual labor. Morgan was a Virginian, born in Culpeper County in the year that another Virginian took command of the colonial armies at Cambridge. By 1813 he was a fire-eater true to the traditions of his birthplace, a captain gallantly stemming the tide of British grenadiers as they charged the cotton-bale redoubts at New Orleans. Then, like many another soldier before and since that fateful New Year's Day, he found it hard to adjust himself to a postwar world. Education, European travel, the faithful service of his country proved scant recommendations in a commerce-crazy nation. Married to a girl who believed in him, he sought vainly for employment consistent with his record and background. With characteristic courage he left the United States and invested all that he had in the operation of a brewery in Canada. Before he could get the business under way it burned to the ground. Crushed by circumstance, humiliated by failure, he moved to Rochester, New York, to take up the trade of a stone mason. And as an anesthetic for his suffering soul he took up drinking hard liquors in excess. A few months later, out of work and without funds, he came to Batavia.

Then for a little while the clouds lifted. He found employment and the comfort of association with men who admired and liked him. In the Masonic Lodge he made friends. Self-respect returned to him, and nursed his injured pride. As a Master Mason he joined the Royal Arch Masons of the nearby town of LeRoy and then, with several fellow members, presented a petition for a like chapter in Batavia.

But among the recipients of the request there were men who suspected this hard-drinking Virginian of not being as qualified in Masonry as he claimed to be. They put aside the petition and circulated a new one on which Morgan was not allowed to place his name. No rebuff could more have aroused his rage and hatred. All the accumulated bitterness of his life welled up in him. Such an insult to a man of his spirit and character could mean but one thing—revenge, and he immediately devoted his whole energies to accomplishing it. He had not far to look for its instrument.

In Batavia he had met a former comrade-at-arms, Colonel David Miller, publisher of the weekly journal, the Batavia *Advocate*. And Colonel Miller had also had his difficulties with Masonry.

The two ex-soldiers in the privacy of Miller's office were not long in planning a stroke that would avenge their wounded feelings and at the same time provide them with money. One day all upstate was stunned by the glaring headlines of the Batavia *Advocate*. They stated that Miller's presses would soon print for public distribution and sale a complete exposé by William Morgan of the secrets of Free-masonry. Those headlines were the beginning event in a murder mystery that a century of research and speculation has never solved.

Response to the announcement was volcanic. At midnight on the eighth of September, 1826, a band of forty masked men, strangely apparelled, appeared on the streets of Batavia, marched silently to Miller's printing offices and set them afire. Then they marched away. Only the alarm given by "a wayfaring man who had taken late lodgings in a stage-coach left in the middle of the street" saved the presses from destruction.

This gave Miller opportunity to launch venomous attacks on Masonry as advocating loyalty to itself over loyalty to law and order. The answers to these onslaughts were threats from the Masons. They were not idle boasts, for three days after the attempt to burn the presses Morgan was arrested in Batavia and taken to Canandaigua, fifty miles away, where, it was alleged, he had stolen a shirt from an acquaintance some time before. On pleading that he had merely borrowed the shirt he was released but was immediately rearrested and clapped into jail on a charge of not having paid his hotel bill on a previous visit. This served to keep him incarcerated until another link in the sinister chain of events which was to excite the whole nation was forged.

Indian summer had brought heat greater than that of the mid-year months to western New York. The moon was very bright through the still air when at midnight three men appeared at the Canandaigua jailer's door. They said to the jailer's wife who opened it that they had come to pay the debt of William Morgan and procure his freedom. The woman demurred at first. It was irregular to release a prisoner so late at night. Couldn't they wait until morning? A prisoner for debt, they argued, should be released when the debt is paid. Finally she acquiesced, went to Morgan's cell and told him he could leave. But as Morgan strode from the jail door a curtained yellow carriage drawn by a team of grays approached the curb. A cry of "Help! Murder!" rang through the deserted streets. Then there was only the swift clopping of the grays as they trotted briskly westward.

By dawn they had covered the thirty miles to Hanford's Tavern, near the village of Rochester. A black carriage, drawn by a team of bays, was waiting, its curtains gleaming dully in the light of the sultry morning. Three men lifted a heavy sagging burden from the yellow carriage to the other. Two of them sat beside it as the other climbed the driver's seat and turned the bays down the dusty Ridge Road. All day the black carriage rolled westward—past the great orchards redolent with the fragrance of ripening apples, the cobblestone houses, the pillared taverns of the old pike. A lone rider was out ahead—and fresh teams of horses were waiting at Clarkson, at Gaines, at Ridgeway. The heat must have been suffocating behind the closed curtains. Curious wayfarers marveled that men should prefer to ride so enclosed on the year's most humid day. Sunset was ahead of them when the driver turned off the road at Wright's Tavern near Lockport and drove into a closed shed. A few men carrying rifles drifted toward it in the twilight, leaned lazily against the walls. The tavern was ablaze with light. Horses stood beside every hitching post outside, and the long "drive-barn" was filled with carriages. Inside at tables loaded with steaming food sat many guests who had been awaiting this moment. They greeted the men from the carriage eagerly. Until ten o'clock then there was eating and drink-

ing, interrupted by expeditions of small groups through the
moonlight where the armed men stood, to the darkness of
the shed there to gaze at the silent man slumped in a corner
of the carriage, bound, gagged, a white handkerchief-mask
across his eyes.

The whole crowd watched the carriage get under way
again. They talked in low tones as it became a distant vague
shadow on the white dust of the road. At one o'clock in the
morning the carriage was in Lewiston and the last lap of the
journey had begun. It ended on the banks of the Niagara
River. There the helpless man was bundled into a boat and
his abductors took the oars. On the other side waited a
group of Canadian Masons to whom they tried to deliver
him. There was a misunderstanding and the Canadians refused to accept him. The resumed creaking of the oarlocks
must have told him of the return to the American side. For
a day then, while Masonic initiation ceremonies went on at
Lewiston and men swore violently-worded oaths of secrecy,
the man who had threatened to publish those oaths was
kept a prisoner in the powder magazine of Fort Niagara.
What happened to him after that no one knows. The story
most often told is that with throat cut from ear to ear, feet
weighted with heavy stones, his mortal remains were rowed
out into Lake Ontario and there heaved into the deep
waters. Whether or not this is true, it appears certain that
the pride of the Virginia war-hero had ceased from trou-
bling. William Morgan was never seen alive again.

Readers of American political history know the immediate consequence. The next few months saw mobs attacking
Masonic processions, an Antimasonic political party established, New York State's four hundred and eighty Lodges
with their twenty thousand members dwindle to seventy-

five Lodges and only three hundred members. And when the outcry of a shocked nation was at its height, when Anti-masonic governers and senators were being elected to office and Masonry in America was in chancery the badly decomposed body of a man was found in Lake Ontario at the mouth of Oak Orchard Creek. Believing that it might be the corpse of the kidnaped man, a committee of twenty-three citizens had it disinterred and brought Morgan's widow to the spot. Before looking on the body Mrs. Morgan, and others who knew her husband well, testified to certain physical peculiarities of Morgan, including a broken tooth in one jaw and a missing tooth in the other. The fact that these marks were identical in the exhumed body made Mrs. Morgan's positive identification of it as that of her husband seem entirely reliable, though she stated that she had never before seen the clothes in which it was clad. The body was taken to Batavia for a burial service that still remains a legend in the eulogistic annals of western New York.

By this time, however, the Masons had found a woman in Canada, a Mrs. Timothy Munroe, whose husband was said to have been drowned in the Niagara River at about the same time Morgan disappeared. Again the body was dug up and again a weeping widow identified it as that of her late husband. Moreover the woman, before she looked upon it, had described the apparel of the corpse with minute exactness, including the location of the patches she had made. But her pre-sight description of the body was mistaken in many ways, even as to height and as to the color of the hair and whiskers.

And so with both sides claiming that it proved their contentions, the body was for the third time laid to rest.

Whether or not those who buried it were gazing on the remains of William Morgan no one can ever know.

The trials of Morgan's abductors extended over a period of five years. Some confessed, others were convicted, several served prison terms. No sufficient evidence was ever found to prove anyone guilty of murder. But in a corner of the Batavia cemetery stands a tall granite shaft surmounted by the carved figure of a man. Inscribed on that monument are these words:

SACRED TO THE MEMORY OF

WILLIAM MORGAN

A Native of Virginia
A Captain in the War of 1812
A Respectable Citizen of
Batavia, and a Martyr
To the Freedom of Writing,
Printing, and Speaking the
Truth. He was abducted
From near this spot in the
Year 1826 By Free Masons
And Murdered for revealing the
Secrets of their Order.

Erected by Volunteer
Contributions from over
2000 Persons residing in
Canada, Ontario,
And twenty-six of the
United States
And Territories.

The Morgan Monument, Batavia, N. Y.

The families who live along the old Ridge Road do not often see this shaft. Few of them know of its existence. But they remember William Morgan and his fate in their own ways. They say that sometimes even yet beneath the apple-blossoms in the orchard a lamb is born with a thin red line about the white fleece of his throat—as all lambs were born in the spring that followed the fearful murder over a hundred years ago. And they say that after a hot September day of toil they sometimes wake to hear the beat of hoofs (muffled by dust though now the road is paved) and that if they dare to look out they may see by the moonlight a carriage, curtained, black, drawn by a steadily trotting team, rolling westward through the night.

9

The Big Party

MOST EVERYBODY IN THESE PARTS'LL GO TO A PARTY sooner'n they'll spit. They've had some high times off 'n' on. Ever since a year ago last May, though, it ain't been quite the same. Folks go but they don't put no life into it. Seems like they feel they wa'n't no use tryin' to come up to the Big Party. Like that little dog o' mine that's part fox terrier, part Boston. Ever since he mounted Jim Massey's collie bitch he ain't been interested in nothin'. He's done the best he *can* an' so he's takin' it easy.

Nobody expected the Big Party to turn out the way it did when they give out word t' come t' the summer openin' o'

The Big Party

Henry Mastin's beer place down in Tiny Town. Course folks said they was goin' an' when the day come an' it was hot fer the first time that spring ye could see they was gettin' a little excited. More'n you'd think quit plow' 'fore sundown, 'n' chores got a lick 'n' a promise. By eight o'clock buggies an' autos was linin' up in the lot behind Henry's place. Quite a crowd was around outside waitin' fer the fiddler to show up when the Raders drew in. They couldn't get their Model T started so they jest hitched it up to the sorrel team an' Joe sat on the top an' drove the horses while Jule steered inside. Some o' the boys had brought jugs along an' they sure whooped t' beat hell when Joe an' Jule rolled up. They had Herb Gulick, the fiddler, in the back an' so everybody whooped again an' went inside an' ordered beer though it didn't set so good on top o' what was in the jugs. Vi Harley, Henry's housekeeper, was sellin' tickets for the dancin' an' she says, anybody that don't buy no ticket gits throwed out but before I throw 'em I'm layin' 'em on the floor an' settin' on 'em. Vi'd run to about three hundred without no extrys an' it aint all fat neither, so folks laughed but they bought tickets.

Henry had cleared away all the tables so they was room to dance but all the drinkin' had to be done at the bar, less'n you had a jug. Herb set his chair up on top o' one end o' the bar, spit in the cuspidor over by the mirror an' let fly on *Yankee Twostep.*

Well, sir, from that minute y'could tell things was goin' t' happen. 'Twa'n't no time at all 'fore George Smith got lickered an' when Herb hollers "Swing Your Partners" George swung Abbie Barkeley so hard he couldn't hang onto her an' she went through one of Henry and Vi's big glass windows right into the junk yard. Didn't hurt her none but it made Vi so mad she grabbed George by the seat o' the pants and throwed him like a bowlin' ball right through the hole Abbie had made. George landed smack on top o' blacksmith Jackson's old anvil an' it broke his leg an' he had to go home.

By that time Vi'd had as much beer as she could hold an' a lot more. She didn't want to go out back 'cause somebody might get in without buyin' a ticket so she fetched a tall tin pail from behind the bar an' goes about halfway up the stairs with it. Well, she sort o' overbalanced an' the first thing anybody knows they hear a crash and Vi turns a complete somerset down the stairs and lands, forty acres o' bare bottom up, on the dance floor, with the tin pail a-clatterin' and bangin' behind her. You could 'a' heard folks laughin' from here to West Bloomfield.

But what made the Big Party was the woman-fight. They was a feller named Ryan lived over Baptist Hill way with his housekeeper. One day he come back from Rochester with another woman an' when folks asked him about it he said, "They ain't no law against a man havin' two housekeepers, is they?" He was a pretty mean cuss an' nobody said much to him nor him to them. So everybody was surprised when he drove up to the party bringin' both women. They got there late an' went inside an' first Ryan'd dance with one of 'em while the other took a suck at his jug an' then they switched around. You could see them gals didn't like each other none from the start. One of 'em was a big woman with black hair an' looked sort of like a fat Indian. The other was sandy-haired an' tall and scrawny an' she had a lot o' gold teeth.

Toward the end of the evenin' when folks was all pretty lickered Ryan finished up one dance with the sandy-haired woman an' when the fiddlin' started again he went right on with her. The big black-haired one stepped up to the two of 'em an' says, "It's my turn." "The hell it is," says the other one.

"You give up that man," says the black-haired one, "or I'll kill you. I was his housekeeper 'fore you an' I know where he got you in Rochester."

"Git away from here," says the tall one, "or I'll tear you apart."

"Quit your talkin'," says Ryan all of a sudden. "You're always sayin' what you're goin' to do to each other. Why don't you do it?"

At that the fat one grabs the scrawny one by the throat an' starts to tear at her hair.

"Wait!" yells Ryan, grabbin' 'em both. "This has got to be a fair fight an' we're goin' outside where we won't hurt nothin'."

Everybody made a rush for the door an' when they got outside Ryan began orderin' folks to make a circle with their autos. They did a lot o' backin' an' turnin' and pretty soon they had a circle o' headlights around a little plot o' ground an' all of 'em was turned on. All the time the two women was screamin' an' cursin' an' tellin' what they were goin' to do to each other. Then Ryan had a couple men take the fat one to the other side o' the circle while he held the scrawny one. "Ready," he shouts. "Let's go!"

The women started runnin' toward each other an' they come together in the middle of the circle. They was scratchin' an' screamin' and clawin' at each other an' their hair come down an' their faces were bleedin'. Then their clothes began to tear an' come off like feathers at a cockfight. First thing you know they was both stark-naked an' still goin' at each other. They was game all right, them two. Sometimes they'd get tired an' just glare at each other not sayin' or doin' nothin' an' the next minute they'd both be screamin' an' tearin' handfuls o' hair out by the roots. First one'd fall down an' then the other, but they'd get up an' keep right at it. Their hair was all streaked with blood, blood was pourin' from scratches on their sides and backs. They was nasty teeth marks on their shoulders an' breasts where they'd bit each other. I never seen a worse mess.

I dunno how it would have come out if Henry hadn't heard his phone ringin' an' answered it. He come runnin' out in a minute hollerin' that the state troopers had seen the circle o' headlights an' wanted to know what the hell was goin' on out there an' said they was on their way to find out. At that Ryan says the fight's over an' walks between the two women.

"Ye better git into my Ford," he says, "or they'll run ye in sure."

The women just stood there for a minute lookin' at each other.

"Go on," says Ryan, " or I'll belt hell out of ye."

But they wasn't payin' him no mind. They jest stood there—all mud an' blood an' hair. Then all of a sudden they tipped forwards, throwed their arms around each other's necks and begun cryin' and kissin' each other.

"Here, what the hell is this?" says Ryan, and he grabs 'em and shoves 'em both in the back seat of his sedan, naked as the day they was born, an' druv off with 'em.

Folks've called it the Big Party ever since. They jest don't expect they'll have a time like that again.

10

The Womanish Man

A CARNIVAL COME TO HONEOYE ONCE. IT HAD A merry-go-round an' a Ferris wheel. An' a lot o' small-size tents with gamblin' games under 'em. You could toss hoops at prizes an' you could have what you ringed. Or you could throw baseballs at a nigger's head an' get cigars for it. An' Miz Simmons tried what they called a Wheel of Chance an' got a funny-lookin' long doll, kind o' slimpsy in the middle an' with a look on his face like he had the bellyache. She's got four gals but she wouldn't give it to none of 'em —keeps it on her bureau in her bedroom an' won't let nobody touch it. Bet it could tell plenty by now if it could talk.

Well, the first time I seen the womanish man, he was sellin' tickets outside the tent where the feller begins by shoutin': "Now women an' children'll find a lot o' instructive an' worth-while exhibits further on down the street. This here show's for men only an' believe me it oughta be." I pushes up my quarter an' this feller looks down at me, an' fer a minute I thought it was a woman. Damn if I don't believe he was wearin' a little paint on his cheeks. Anyway they was sort o' pink an' white an' his hair was yellow an' curly an' he wore it sort o' long.

"Thank you very much," he says, an' his voice is sort o' prissy an' womanishlike. I was goin' to say, "You oughta be in there dancin', too," but I got shoved on by the crowd. By the time I got inside I plumb fergot about the feller. Boy! That was some show. An' after it was over the talkin' feller says: "Now just a few of us is goin' to stay on in here fer a little somethin' extry special. It's goin' to cost a dollar but it's goin' to be worth it—there ain't goin' to be no limit this time." So I stayed on fer that an' I tell you I never hope to see more for my money.

Well, when I come out it was jest beginnin' to get dark an' most the crowd was home to supper. I was jest about t' set out myself when I seen a fat man with a cigar in his mouth talkin' to the curlyhead. He'd got down from the ticket stand an' he was fidgetin' roun', swingin' his hips like a woman, an' complainin' in his woman's voice.

"But I can't be leavin'," he was sayin'. "You told my friend I could have the job."

"I hadn't seen you then," says the fat man. "Serves me right fer bein' a sucker. I'm tellin' yuh, you're through," he says, shakin' his fist at the feller. "I don't want nobody like you in my shows. Gives 'em a bad name. You want to make trouble about it?"

"No, no," says the fella, shakin' his head so's his long hair fell in his eyes. "I don't want no trouble. Jest give me my fare back to New York."

"You'll play hell gettin' it," says the fat man an' walks off chewin' on his cigar.

I went on home t' supper an' didn't think no more about it—that is, till about three days later when the carnival was gone and I goes into Woods and Bogue's flour an' feed store t' get some alfalfa seed. I was sort o' lookin' round when by God up switches curlyhead.

"May I be of service?" he says in that high prissy voice.

"I ain't no cow," I says, "an' you couldn't service me if I was—'cause you're a mighty long way from a bull," I says an' busts out laughin' fit to kill. I could see that got his goat, for he turned sort o' pale an' got twitchy round the mouth an' walked off. When Vic Woods come out to wait on me I says: "You must be goin' t' put in a line o' flowers, too. I see you got the young lady to sell 'em all hired," an' I breaks down laughin' again.

When I got m' seed I stepped over to the Elite Poolroom for a few minutes an' it wasn't no time 'fore I had the boys in there plumb near bustin' their sides over what I said about the cow an' the bull, an' about Vic sellin' flowers. I had so much fun at it I begun thinkin' up somethin' else to tickle the boys with.

"Listen," I says, "I've heard tell about these womanish guys. Ain't nothin' they like so much as a good-lookin' young boy. I got an idea. We'll each put in a quarter an' we'll hire George Woods, Vic's boy, to get him to go fer a walk in the moonlight tonight. We'll get George to lead him around to the vacant lot behind his pa's store an' we can be hidin' behind the barrels back there an' listen an' if he starts anythin' we can jump out an' beat the livin' Jesus outa him. We don't want no such bastards in this town anyway," I says.

All the fellers said sure, that was a great idea—so we waited till George come by the store after school an' called him over to the poolroom an' told him what we wanted. He said he wouldn't do it at first but after I went over to the barber shop an' got two more quarters from fellers over there, that wanted to be in on it—makin' two dollars in all —why, he says he guessed he would. He went over to the store an' stayed a little while an' then he come back an' says it's all fixed. He says the feller jumped at the chance o' goin' fer a walk after supper. So I says: "Jest as soon as it gits dark, 'round eight, you tell him how nice the moon looks from that lot behind your pa's store an' get him over there. You lead him on," I says, "an' don't be afraid 'cause we'll be just waitin' to get a chance to knock hell outa him."

So after supper an' gettin' my chores done, I walks down to town an' picks up the other fellers an' all eight of us sneaks out behind Vic's store an' waits. The moon come up early that night an' it was big an' yellow. We didn't dast talk much 'cause somebody on the street might hear us and want to be in on it an' spoil it all. So everythin' was damn quiet except the peepers over by the marsh was raisin' hell.

Well, sir, it got to be eight an' nothin' happened. An' it got to be quarter past an' the boys began gettin' restless. Jim Butler was jest sayin', "Aw, t'hell with it," when we heard 'em comin'. "Duck," I says an' we all got down behind the barrels jest in time.

They come into the lot walkin' arm in arm an' curlyhead was talkin'. "I never knew anythin' more beautiful," he says. "The air is full of moonlight an' that crying," he says, pointin' toward the marsh. He kep' still fer a while. Then he says, "You know I'm glad I stayed on here after I got fired. I've got along good here, an' I've found a friend." At that he unhitches his arm from the boy's and puts it around his shoulder.

I riz up from behind the barrels an' walked right over to him.

"Take your dirty hand off that boy," I says, "you stinkin'

womanish bastard," an' I let him have it on the nose. He went down like an empty feed bag, didn't seem to be nothin' to him. Then he sort of screamed an' got up an' started to run. But the boys by that time had got in a circle round him an' no matter which way he run somebody fetched him a clip that stretched him out again. Finally he jest laid there on the ground an' begun to cry, makin' a high noise jest like a woman. I reached down an' grabbed him by the collar an' yanked him onto his feet. His watch fell out of his pocket an' he reached down to pick it up but I stomped on his hand.

"My father give it to me," he says between sobbin' and carryin' on.

"I don't give a goddam *who* give it to yuh," I says. "You get the hell out of this town or *we'll* give you somethin'. This ain't no place fer any womanish son-of-a-bitch," I says, an' all the fellers says, "You bet it ain't" an' "You're right, there."

"Get goin'," I says, an' starts to hit him again. Well, he made one jump that landed him outside the circle an' he run like a jack rabbit. We chased him at first but he run too fast for us an' we stopped. When he got out on the concrete headin' toward Canandaigua he was still hollerin' an' carryin' on. I thought we'd die laughin' to hear him cryin' way down the road. When we couldn't hear him no longer I went back an' picked up the watch. It was real gold an' I been carryin' it ever since.

11

The Sheep Killers

I DO NOT KNOW HOW LONG THE SOUND HAD BEEN coming to my ears before I wakened enough to realize that it was the distant baying of dogs. I lay in bed and listened, half-conscious, until like a sudden blow upon my brain a sentence of Maud's seemed to repeat itself: "We had a setter once, but Coley sent him away when some dogs around here began killing sheep." Then I was alert and straining. The baying had a fierce, excited note. I looked toward the window. Moonlight was streaming in and I knew I had not slept long. I jumped up, went to the sill and stuck my head outside. The air was cool and fresh. Down by the lake a patch of woods was an indistinct irregular mass. The voices of the dogs seemed to be echoing against it.

I was not sure that I should waken Coley. I thought about it a moment before I put my slippers on and walked to the Dugans' bedroom. "Coley," I said softly. In an instant he was standing beside me.

"What is it?" he said.

"I heard dogs by the lake, where your sheep are pastured. I didn't know——"

He ran to the kitchen. When I caught up with him he had a rifle in his hand and was opening the back door.

"Let's go," he said, and his voice sounded high and strained.

As we ran down the long slope toward the lake the barking grew louder for a time. But when our breath grew short and we began to walk we heard two sharp yelps and then no other sound. My feet were wet with the heavy dew that soaked my slippers. I looked at Coley and saw he was barefoot. Dark splotches were showing on the moonlit whiteness of the upper surface of his feet and I realized that the briers and rocks by the field had cut him. The cool air off the lake was a relief after my running, though I wore only pajamas.

Then we saw the sheep. They lay in a wide semicircle and their fleece looked almost silver in the strong bluish moonlight. The first one, a fat ewe, was still breathing when we reached her. She was making short moans as she struggled to get air into her lungs. From her mangled throat blood poured in a pulsing stream. Coley put the rifle to her head and fired. The sharp crack of the shot seemed to flatten out as the sound reached the steely surface of the lake and then suddenly it was hurled back at us from the hills on the far shore. The two other ewes were already dead. And the lamb lay on a slanting rock, her entrails coiled in a pool of blood beneath her ripped body.

"Well," said Coley with a little catch in his voice, "I guess that ends the great sheep-raising experiment."

We looked about for hair from the dogs but we found none, and we waited a half hour for them to return, but they did not come. Then we walked slowly back up to the house. Maud was waiting at the door with a lamp in her hand.

"We lost 'em all," said Coley briefly as we went inside. His feet were hurting him and I built a fire in the stove while Maud got water from the pump. We bathed the wounds and put bandages of torn handkerchiefs over them. Then Coley said there was still a chance the dogs might come back so he and I put on some clothes and we went about halfway down the slope and sat down under an apple tree to wait. We did not talk much. Coley sat stiffly with his back against the trunk of the tree and his hands clasped and unclasped the stock and barrel of the rifle nervously.

We had not been more than twenty minutes when we saw them coming—two large dark figures scurrying up the slope. The moon was behind the hills and it was hard to see what kind of dogs they were. Coley got up on one knee to take aim. The movement frightened them and they made off toward the foot of the lake at a dead run. Coley fired twice but missed and then they were out of range.

Dawn was coming rapidly as we again made our way back. When we neared the house we saw Let Washburn coming toward us.

"Dogs?" he said.

Coley nodded.

"Could you tell whose they were?"

"Think one of 'em is that big dog of Connolley's over the other side o' town. You know—half setter, half German shepherd."

Let grunted.

"I been thinkin' he might be one of 'em. Guess I'll go down and see what you can salvage out o' them sheep. See you later."

"We'll have breakfast for you when you come back," said Coley.

The Sheep Killers

I had taken a nap after lunch and was still dozing when I heard a rapping at the side door. I got up and went into the kitchen. Coley and Maud were standing side by side in front of a short man in overalls, gray flannel shirt, boots, and an old felt hat which he had not removed from his head. He held in leash a big nondescript-looking long-haired dog whose tail waved sociably.

"They tell me in town you said it was my dog that killed your sheep and I brought him over here for you to shoot."

Coley looked embarrassed.

"I didn't say definitely it was your dog. I said I *thought* it was."

"Well," said the man patiently, "nobody can say a dog o' mine kills sheep without gettin' a chance to shoot it."

Coley looked at him sternly.

"I'll shoot him all right," he said. "Just take him home and let him go. The first time he sets foot on this place he'll be a dead dog."

The man looked disappointed.

"Then you ain't goin' to shoot him now?" he said.

"You heard me," said Coley.

"I guess I'd better be goin' then," said the man. "Come on, Shep." He and his dog went out the door.

Coley sat down on the window seat.

"I'm glad Let warned me," he said. "That's the meanest old crank in the county. If I'd shot his dog he'd have had the sheriff up here in half an hour and I'd have had to pay plenty. He knows he doesn't dare keep the dog now. He just had it figured out I might as well pay for his loss. He's done it before, Let says. Besides, shooting his dog won't give me back my sheep."

Mary Julia Barkley was the daughter of the old general who built the house in which Coley and Maud live. Mary Julia lived to be ninety and is still the subject of many stories in the Bristol Hills.

As manager of the farm she was a slave driver, and never kept any hired men very long. The threshing gangs and sheep shearers used to say that she never went to bed, but hung herself up by her sunbonnet on a hook in the bedroom. When Mary Jule wanted to get the farm hands up in the morning she would call up the back stair: "Come on, boys, time to get up. You can see halfway 'cross the orchard."

She had a bunch of steers which were wild as mad bulls. Mary Jule, however, could walk into the lot where they were and they would never harm her. One time she sold a number of them to a dealer, telling him he would have to catch them himself. The hired help refused to assist him, so he chased the steers all over the lot. At dusk he returned to the house empty-handed. Next day he came back with a gun and took his cattle home dead.

Part Three

The World on
the Turtle's Back

View of Tonawanda Reservation

. . . and the turtle said, "I will lift my back above the water if you will dive for land to place upon it so that she may have a country in which to live."

12

The Faces

THE FIRST THICK SNOW OF THE WINTER WAS FALL-
ing on the morning when I finally set out from Geneseo to
visit Cornplanter on the Tonawanda Seneca Reserve. The
broad cement highway lying straightly westward was a gray
floor for scurrying white flakes blown by a steady wind and the
little segment cleared by my windshield wiper afforded my
only vision of them. The hills of the Genesee country fell
away as I reached Batavia after an hour's driving and it was
only a short run between the city and the narrow macadam
off to the right which was to lead me, through the little group
of stores and houses that is Basom, into the land of the Senecas.

I had been driving through the Lake Ontario coastal
plain, a level land with few slopes, but as I crossed the Reservation line, the surface of the earth suddenly seemed flatter
than I had ever seen it. It stretched before me unfolded and
unending—interrupted only by the frayed yellow sedge grass
showing above a thin coat of snow and by a few stunted and
gnarled trees.

I passed the first Indian dwelling and was startled by its
barren simplicity. Hewn logs that had weathered to a deep
gray were interspersed with light, almost white plaster giv-

ing the house a curious striped effect. The plaster had fallen away in some places and I shivered to think of the snow blowing through—but the chimney in the center of the roof was pouring out a steady stream of black smoke. I passed other homes—some like the first, others of unpainted boards, sturdy frame houses. I had driven perhaps two miles in the Reservation, bearing ever to the right according to the written directions of Cornplanter, when I recognized the Long House, a rectangular one-story boxlike structure with three windows in the visible long side and a brick chimney surmounting each narrow end-gable. About fifty yards behind it was a weathered frame house and I saw the tall figure of Cornplanter come out on the porch and beckon to me.

"I was afraid you'd got lost on the other side of the Reservation," he said as I rolled to a stop. "Come on in by the stove."

We walked across the porch into the house. In the center of the large room which we entered was an old iron stove. A woman stood beside it, lid-holder and lid in one hand, short log in the other.

"This is my wife, Yo-wes-on," he said. The woman smiled and dropped the log into the stove and replaced the lid. She was below medium height and her features were delicately though clearly defined—like those of an aristocratic Japanese lady. Her smile was infectious and it was evident that she considered it a sufficient greeting.

"Sit down," said Cornplanter. "You'd better keep your coat on because the wind is blowing hard."

I sat and looked about. On the wall beside me hung many kitchen utensils. Opposite these I saw a photograph of a man in uniform—obviously Cornplanter as a corporal in the

United States Army of World War I, and pasted on the wall beside it an official-looking document on which the one word Verdun stood out in large type.

"I wanted you to arrive this morning," said Cornplanter, "because I thought something might happen that would interest you. I can't guarantee it, you know, but you never can tell."

"What is it?" I said and saw the Indian's face turn suddenly expressionless, his eyes become like dark unluminous stone. I realized I should not have asked the question and hurried over it.

"It was a surprise to me to find that the Senecas still celebrate the rituals of their Indian Religion," I said. "I had supposed that the missionaries would have had you all Christians by now."

Cornplanter laughed shortly.

"A lot of Senecas are Christians," he said. "Some families have been ever since the first missionaries came to them before the Revolution. There's a Seneca hymn book—a translation of Protestant hymns into Seneca that was made over a hundred and fifty years ago—and across the creek where most of the Christian Senecas and the missionaries live they have a Hymn-Singing Society. They call us Pagan Indians but we call ourselves Long-House People and we live in this section called The Down Below."

"Why have you people held out against Christianity for so long?" I said.

"There are several reasons for that," said Cornplanter. "One of them is that we like our religion as it was taught by its last prophet, Handsome Lake, and his words are still in our ears for he died only a little more than a century ago. My father was a teacher of Handsome Lake's creed. Then, too, many of our old men speak no English and they have never learned of any other religion than their own. There's another reason—the strongest of all. After the American Revolution we were allowed to keep ten times as much land as we now occupy. More than a hundred years ago, just after the Senecas had fought for the United States in many battles of the War of 1812, the Ogden Land Company tried to get our land away from us and to persuade us to go to live in Kansas. We refused. Then they tried to get our chiefs drunk and make them sign the land away. The scheme didn't work. So they took a lot of Indians over to Buffalo, made them drunk, declared them chiefs, and persuaded them to sign papers. They added the forged signatures of the Tonawanda Seneca Chiefs and took possession of the land anyway, paying the Seneca Nation twenty cents an acre. Years later, when they found they would have trouble in dispossessing us of the land, they sold back a tenth of it to us—at twenty dollars an acre. So we said, 'If these are the ways of Christians we will live by the faith of our forefathers.' "

"Those are good reasons," I said. "And does that faith satisfy your people?"

"It is a good religion," said Cornplanter, "and I like the stories that are in it better than many that are in the Bible. Would you like to hear the Senecan story of the beginning of things—the one that parallels the Christian Genesis?"

"I'd like it very much," I said. " Does it tell of a Senecan Adam and Eve?"

"Not exactly. But there's a tree that causes all the mischief—only in a different way."

"Tell me," I said.

"A long time ago," said Cornplanter, stretching his feet out toward the warmth of the stove, "there was a beautiful island floating in the sky. A heavenly tree of enormous size grew at its center and spread its branches over the great white lodge of the old man, chief of the god-beings who lived on the island.

"One day the old man saw a young girl and he desired her so much that with one sigh he made her pregnant. Then the old man took her to live with him in the white lodge and soon he knew what most old men with young wives must find out—that a healthy curious girl is frequently a bore. He became more annoyed daily; the climax of his exasperation came when, out for a walk, he found that his mate had pulled up the celestial tree by the roots in order to find out what was beneath it. At that moment she was bending over the cavity she had made in a position inviting the very punishment he was about to inflict. The old man was so angry that he suddenly brought his foot into contact with her and she tumbled into the hole which extended right through the island and before she knew what had happened to her she was dropping through space.

"The earth did not exist then—all the land was covered with water and there were only the water birds and the water animals to realize what had happened. The ducks were the first to see the falling sky-woman. They pitied her and made a soft flying mattress of their interlaced wings upon which they received her and slowly wafted her downward. The muskrat and the turtle saw her and the turtle said, 'I will lift my back above the water if you will dive for land to place upon it so that she may have a country in which to live.'

"So the muskrat dove to the bottom of the waters and brought up soil to pile upon the turtle's back and the ducks placed her softly upon it. She lived there and gave birth to a beautiful daughter who in her youth was mated to an invisible lover while she was swinging on a grapevine. She gave birth to two boys, the first of whom grew up to be the Good Spirit of my people. It was he who brought them game to eat and furs to wear, fruits and vegetables and all the things that made life easier. But his younger brother was the Bad Spirit and he brought them poison ivy and rattlesnakes and nettles and gnats and all the wicked things of the world. His mother died at his birth and his good elder brother watched over her grave and poured water over it as she had told him to do. Then maize grew from her breasts with sweet milk in all its kernels, long leaves of tobacco grew from her head, the yellow squash came from her body, beans from her fingers, tubers from her toes. All Indians are grateful to their earth mother."

"It is a good story," I said, after a pause, "and do we all still live on the turtle's back?"

"He is very patient," said Cornplanter. "Only once in many years he gets restless and moves a little. That is what causes earthquakes."

I looked out the window. The Long House was a blurred rectangle almost obscured by blowing white flakes. The road that ran in front of it was no longer visible and the earth was a flat white surface broken by low dark underbrush. I heard a short plaintive cooing note—and suddenly realized that it was not part of the low whining of the wind. It stopped and the wind whined on—then it sounded again.

"Got any tobacco?" said Cornplanter.

As I passed him my cigarettes I saw that his eyes gleamed with excitement and his hand seemed unsteady as he took six of them from the package. Yo-wes-on, sitting on a chair near the stove, had the look of a child who anticipates something which is both frightening and delightful. She giggled nervously.

To my surprise Cornplanter rose, walked quickly to the stove and placed four of the cigarettes on the iron shelf that extended below the firebox. As he returned to his seat a movement at the window caught my eye and I gasped. A face, distorted, grotesque, inhuman, was peering into the room. At the same time I heard the cooing note again and a rasping rattling noise. Yo-wes-on had moved toward the door and stood with her hand on the latch looking at her husband.

"The Faces have come to beg tobacco," said Cornplanter. "It is their first ceremony of the winter. Open the door."

Yo-wes-on released the latch and as the door swung wide four human figures hurtled into the room. They moved so rapidly it was hard to believe that they were crawling along the floor. Like giant wriggling lizards they made for the stove and a chorus of complaining nasal coos sounded as with their left hands they seized on the cigarettes along the shelf. Each right hand carried a turtle-rattle, seemingly the hollowed body of a turtle filled with rattling particles, the neck extended far out to form a handle terminating in the turtle's gaping head. The tobacco stowed away in their pockets, they turned and made for Cornplanter. In a semicircle they arrived in front of him, rose on their knees, and, pointing to their horrid mouths, began a pitiful begging—still using the short yearning cooing sounds. Hastily I returned my pack of cigarettes to Cornplanter and while he doled out four more I got the opportunity of looking at the suppliants. Below the heads their costumes were various. One was in overalls; next to him was a figure in leather jacket and bathing trunks; one, wearing only shorts, had painted his brown skin in fantastic red and black patterns; and beside him knelt a sturdy body in a baseball uniform. Each visage, too, was different. I saw that the faces were wooden masks elaborately carved into grotesque features. Two were painted red and two black and all were made startling by long unkempt hair falling below the shoulders, by eyes encircled in bright metal, and by extravagant caricaturing of the noses and mouths. In one of the red masks no teeth showed and the lips were extremely thick—like an exaggerated Negro minstrel make-up. A thin forward-extending hawk nose hung above them. In the other the mouth itself was tiny, showing small white teeth, but the lips had been distorted into wide curving folds on either side. One of the black masks looked like the face of a ferociously smiling bull. Two black horns protruded from the forehead, the nose was flat, and the wide-spread mouth was filled with tremendous white teeth. The strangest mask, however, was the face of the crooked mouth. All the lines of this carving ran obliquely from the top toward a mouth set far to the side. It was a mask beautified by the grotesquerie of pathos—so appealing that in the midst of all this excitement I felt a strange sentimental stirring of sympathy.

Cornplanter tossed the cigarettes back to me and the four capered in my direction. "Ask them to dance for you," said Cornplanter. "Their dancing will frighten any disease or evil spirit in this house."

I handed out cigarettes.

"Will you please dance for me?" I said.

They jumped to their feet and the face with the crooked mouth led off, shaking his rattle in front of him. The others followed, leaping about but always hitting the floor on the beat of the rattles. Their feet made the floor sound like a muted drum in a long series of alternating strong and weak accents. Three times around the stove they danced, circling and waving their rattles as they advanced—then stopped before the chair of Yo-wes-on, who caught my cigarettes and distributed them, smiling trustfully and sympathetically at the weird, monstrous faces raised to hers. Then the bull-faced one caught up a handful of ashes from under the stove and blew them toward her and the gray flakes fell upon her hair and her blue sweater.

"That will cure her of any disease," said Cornplanter to me.

As suddenly as they had come The Faces were gone. Only Twisted Face, on his knees in the doorway, made a last gesture with his rattle before he slammed the door behind him. There was a sudden rush of feet outside and then silence—except for the incessant humming of the wind.

13

The Dark Dance

CEPHAS HILL AND I SEARCHED THE COUNTY'S butcher shops on the day before the Dark Dance and returned with a very large pig's head. Yo-wes-on and Jennie Blackchief built an outdoor fire and all the next day they prepared it according to the ritual directions. All day the messenger walked about the Reservation to tell people to come to Jesse Cornplanter's that night at eight o'clock for the Dark Dance. By nine they began to arrive and Cornplanter explained to me, "They come on Indian time—about an hour later than the time set. It is not dignified to be on time."

Three of the men brought their water drums and Cornplanter brought out two more. As they arrived the men sat down on a long bench along the side of the room; the women moved into a corner where they stood laughing and gossiping. The Dark Dance is a woman's dance. I sat on a chair in a corner near the stove and I was joined by Fenton, white Yale anthropologist, and an Onondaga Indian, Clinton Pierce, member of the United States Forestry Service.

I was surprised to find that the Senecas among themselves are a jolly, laughing people of mobile expression and a charming, imaginative sense of humor. There was a great deal of badinage carried on in Seneca with loud gusts of laughter. Then one of the old men, toothless and grinning, spoke to Fenton and me in broken English, teasing us because we had come to see a ceremony that was not to be visible. Everyone who came in looked curiously at Pierce whose clothes and manner distinguished him from themselves. At last a stocky middle-aged man spoke to him. Fenton said:

"That's Charlie Sundown. He's been pretty much everywhere in the world with a Wild West show though he's no more Western Indian than you or I. Pierce, he's speaking to you in Seneca."

"I can't speak any Seneca," said Pierce courteously.

Again Charlie Sundown spoke.

"That's Tuscarora," said Fenton.

"I don't know any Tuscarora," said Pierce.

"Try him in Onondaga," said Fenton. "That's his tribe."

Again a flow of glib syllables.

"I'm sorry but I don't know any Indian languages," said Pierce, smiling.

A scornful grunt from Charlie, a long pause, and then in tones of complete disgust:

"Sprechen Sie Deutsch?"

One of the old men began tapping on his water drum and tightening the head, and the other drummers followed his example. All the drums were small, about a foot in diameter. A piece of sheepskin had been stretched across the head of each and tied, the edges being left untrimmed. The rest of the drum, perhaps eight inches deep, was a wooden hollow, partially filled with water. Beaten with a wooden baton, the drum gives a sharp, liquid note that carries a long distance. If struck too hard the carrying quality lessens and the note itself is blurred. The Senecas are very critical of drumming technique.

Yo-wes-on made a slow circle about the room, putting out the lamps. When she had finished only the glowing cracks in the stove gave out light in an irregular reddish pattern. The men along the wall bench were silent. In the far corner the women giggled and whispered. There was a single sharp note from a drum—then a regular beating in fast time. The other drums joined in one by one. A strained high note from a man's voice—and every man began singing. The song was spirited and full of strong, staccato accents. It seemed pitched a little too high for the voices—but intentionally, so as to give a definite breath-labored effect. Then we heard the shuffle and beat of the women's feet. The women were dancing before us in the darkness and the sound of their feet on the floor was like that of a single deeper drum. The rhythm grew a little swifter and the dancers responded. We heard a woman laughing, a burst of laughter from three or four—then a single high cry from the leader of the drums—and silence. The first song of the Dark Dance sequence was over.

I was glad that my initial experience with the Seneca music for dance rituals was in the darkness where the sight of the dancing figures would not distract me. Fenton told me that while some of the songs had words with definite thought content many of them were simply syllable sequences without meaning. The music was not like any I had ever heard—certainly unlike the adaptations of Indian songs American composers have made. It had little of the haunting plangent minor quality associated with most folk songs. It was quick, fierce, gay.

The singing of the Dark Dance music takes an hour and a half. I could not realize that the period had passed when the last high staccato yelp sounded and Yo-wes-on began lighting the lamps. During that time I had stared into darkness listening to the rise and fall of men's voices, to the quick, steadily rhythmic thumping of the drums, to the feet of women striking metric patterns on the floor. Occasionally a spectator had lighted his pipe and the flame of his match had set gigantic shadows moving along the walls. Nothing else had been visible except the glowing lines drawn by the cracks in the stove.

The Dark Dance

Now that the dance was over everyone was very gay. The pig's great head was passed and passed again. A big pot of corn soup had been simmering on the back of the stove. Cornplanter lifted it off and Yo-wes-on invited everyone to "set down a pail." There was a good-natured rush and I discovered that each Indian had brought a pail with him for this very purpose. Cornplanter provided me with one and I was soon enjoying the soup and wondering at the big kernels, swollen until they had burst, which characterize this most popular of all Seneca dishes.

Soon after the feasting, Cornplanter's guests began to leave—drifting off in scattered groups across the snowy waste toward their homes. At their host's request, however, some of the older men stayed a while to tell over the origin-legends of the Dark Dance and some of the other rituals of the Senecas. It was a late hour when I went to bed but I had heard many things that filled me with wonder. And I felt ashamed that the people of my native state had not long ago realized the wealth that lies in the literature of the tribes of the Iroquois Union. While the tribes of the West—the Hopis and the Navajos—have been praised for their craftsmanship with beads and woolen strands and silver, these people have been neglected. The contributions of the Iroquois to a forgetful posterity are two: a record of a wise and successful form of communistic government—the Constitution of the Five Nations—and a mass of folklore of such simple beauty and varied fancy that it deserves the attention of all lovers of those strange inventions with which poets choose to explain life and the universe.

I am telling here a few of the stories I heard that night. All of them were beautiful but I liked these best:

LONG AGO, EVEN BEFORE THE EXISTENCE OF MAN, THE Creator of all good things decided to take a walk about the earth in order to observe all the beauty he had made. He looked on the swelling green hills and blossoming trees, on clear brooks and colored flowers, and he was glad that he had designed them as they were.

But as he walked he saw another walker very like himself striding happily about and seeming to enjoy all the loveliness of earth. The Creator knew that he had not made such a being and in great surprise he approached the stranger and asked him who he was.

"I am the Creator," said the being.

"That is untrue and quite impossible," said the Good Spirit. "It is I who have made this splendid world and all the fine things in it."

"What you are saying is ridiculously false," said the other. "I created all things on the earth and I am walking about to enjoy them."

"This argument is barren," said the Creator, "but I know of a way by which the truth of my claims may be proved if you dare submit to a test."

"If it is a good test, it will prove me right," said the stranger.

The Dark Dance

"We will both turn our backs to yonder mountain," said the Creator, "and we will stand with our toes to this line which I draw upon the earth. First you will order the mountain to move toward us, then I. The one for whom the mountain moves farthest will have proved his claim. I warn you, however, that neither of us may turn about to look before the mountain has moved."

"It is a good test," said the stranger.

Then they both toed the line and the stranger ordered the mountain to move toward them. They waited with their backs turned until it had had enough time to move and then they turned to look. They could see that the mountain was nearer to them than before and the stranger rejoiced and claimed the victory.

"Wait," said the Creator. "Now it is my turn. And remember that we are not to turn around until the mountain has moved."

They toed the line again and this time the Creator gave the command. He had hardly given it when the stranger turned to see its result and as he did so the steep wall of the mountain descending at their heels scraped the side of his face, drawing it out of all proportion and giving it the pitiful twisted look it has worn ever since.

The owner of the face admitted the power of his adversary and asked only to be allowed to serve him. The request was graciously granted and now He-of-the-Twisted-Face lives in the world beneath the earth and at appointed times comes out to frighten evil spirits from the bodies of those who worship the Creator.

A LITTLE BOY SET OUT ONE MORNING WITH HIS BOW AND arrows to hunt squirrels. He had killed two gray squirrels when he came suddenly on a clearing in the woods, and found himself on a cliff so high that the top of a tall tree below it was level with its surface. On the highest branch of the tree sat a black squirrel.

As the boy was aiming at it he heard high thin voices below him, and looking down, he saw two little people vainly shooting tiny arrows from tiny bows at the same animal. They shouted encouragement to each other and their arrows went higher and higher but they fell far short.

Then the little boy shot the black squirrel and it fell at the feet of the little men. They thought they had killed it until they saw that the arrow with which it had been slain was so large they could not even extract it. Then they looked upward and saw the boy and called to him to come down and remove the arrow. So the boy climbed down the cliff and obtained his arrow but he gave the squirrel and the other two he had killed to the little men. They were delighted but they explained that the black squirrel alone was a heavy burden for them and begged him to come with them and carry the gray squirrels.

The boy agreed and before long his companions came to their house where their little parents greeted them affectionately. Their mother gave the boy a tiny bowl of corn soup and he was disappointed because he was hungry and he thought it held hardly enough for one mouthful. But no matter how much he ate the bowl stayed full and soon he had had more than enough.

After he had eaten, the father of the household said they must all celebrate their new bonds of friendship with a ceremony. So he sang many songs and the boy repeated them after him until he had learned them and could sing the whole ritual from beginning to end. Then the old man told the boy the order of the ritual from the tobacco-burning invocation to the feasting on pig's head and corn soup at the end.

The little people took the boy back to the cliff where they had found him and from there he went home, where his mother greeted him joyfully, for he had been away from her much longer than he knew. When he told her of his adventure with the hunters she at once identified them as members of the *djogao*, a race possessing supernatural powers.

Four days later, keeping a promise he had made to his new friends, the boy attended a ceremony given in their honor and sought to teach the members of his tribe the ritual he had learned. During the total darkness while the songs were being sung he saw the little people enter, though they were invisible to everyone else. They sat beside him and prompted him while he taught and soon the whole tribe had learned the songs and ritual.

Even to this day the little people are known to be near the spot where the boy first found them. It is in the valley of Zoar not far from the town of Salamanca. And hunters who have climbed down the cliff that overhangs the stream there say that they have seen tiny footprints in the clay banks that edge the water. Often in the silent woods beside Cattaraugus Creek the beat of little drums may be heard and then the Senecas know it is time to sing the songs and hold the ceremonial.

A SENECA YOUNG MAN DISTRESSED HIS PARENTS GREATLY BY failing to marry. None of the girls in their village seemed lovely enough to him. His father and mother often argued with him about this, for they wished him to wed and have children.

Then one day at a dance in the village he saw a strange girl of such beauty and grace that he loved her at once. She returned his love and came to his home to live with him and he and his parents were very glad.

As time passed only one thing disturbed the bliss of the young couple—the girl longed to see her own people again. She begged her husband to go with her to visit them and he consented. After many days' journeying they entered a country of flowering fields and blossoming forests. And toward sunset of the last day of their travel they came to a wide-spreading low house. In the dusk they could see people assembling there and already the sound of feasting and revelry had begun within. "This is the end of our journey, it is my home," said the girl.

Then they entered and were heartily welcomed within and they joined in the festival and dancing. They stayed in the house for many months and were very happy though the Seneca could not approve all the erotic rites of his wife's strange people. One day after the hunters of the sky had wounded the heavenly bear and his blood had stained the falling leaves, the Seneca's wife came to him and said, "I must go away for a little while. Do not be sorry. I will see you again in the spring."

In vain he protested. She would not explain. Finally he said:

"You have promised to come back to me in the spring. You will not forget."

"No, I shall come back."

As she said this she vanished and with her the house and all her people. He stood alone in the midst of a desolate marsh while all about him countless frogs set up a dismal crying. He realized at last that he had married a lovely frog-woman and he went home in heartbroken despair.

But he remembered the series of songs the frog-people had sung in the big low house and he taught them to his people. They call them the *Yei o da ta* and when the frogs have gone beneath the red-stained leaves for the winter the Seneca singers gather to sing them and to tell again this tragic story.

14

Tonawanda Morning

SUNLIGHT WARMED THE STEPS OF THE SCHOOL-house. Inside, Seneca craftsmen were carving masks and war clubs modeled after ancient patterns. Cephas, college-bred foreman, wearing a beret, symbol of his artistic talent and an education far superior to that of most of his co-workers, joined Cornplanter and me for a cigarette in the mellowing air.

"You can tell an Indian witch at night," Cornplanter was saying, "because when he breathes out a light comes from his mouth and nostrils."

"When you see one coming down the road," said Cephas, settling his young body down on the porch step, "you get the effect of a flashlight being turned on and off continuously."

"Of course," said Cornplanter, smiling, "we don't believe these Indian superstitions—still some awful funny things happen sometimes."

"Did any ever happen to you?" I said.

"Well, when I came back from the war there was a family on another Reservation that had hard feelings toward me. I didn't think much about it until I got sick and began to

· 118 ·

lose weight and couldn't eat. I went to a doctor but he didn't seem to be able to help. I nearly died. I could almost taste strawberries. And——"

"What does that mean," I said quickly, "that about tasting strawberries?"

Cornplanter laughed.

"Strawberries grow beside the heaven road," he said. "Mortals would not have them if the sky-woman in falling through the hole in the celestial island had not grasped at the edges and brought a vine with her. When a Seneca dies, his friends hear a flute song floating through the air and they know it is he. They say, 'He is on his way to eat strawberries.'"

"Go on," I said.

"So I went to one of the old men here and he said I'd been witched. Every day for four days I went to him and he gave me an emetic, a powder made out of touchwood fungus in a cup of water. I lay down for an hour after taking it and then I would drink twelve quarts of water and then vomit three times, four quarts each time. The old man dug a hole in the ground and I always vomited into that. On the fourth day he told me to stay out of sight of everybody until I came to him. And on that day I retched up a little sliver-like piece of wood. We built a fire then, and burned some tobacco over it and then we burned that piece of wood in order to turn back the spell on the one who made it. Just a short time later the person I suspected of having witched me died. I was sorry—but it was her life or mine."

"What about you?" I said to Cephas. "Have you ever had any personal experience with witches?"

"Only one, I guess," said Cephas. "When Willy Abrams died I was in his house and everybody there heard pigs running about and squealing behind the woodshed. An old lady suggested they might be witches, so I took a shot at one of them from a window. The next day some school children, playing near an abandoned log house, peeped in and saw a man with his pants down picking buckshot out of his backside. They shouted 'Witch!' at him and he pulled up his pants and ran away."

"There are a good many witch stories about humans changing themselves into animals," said Cornplanter. "I could tell you the names of two or three who actually do it if reports around here can be believed. There's an old man who lives down the road who went to the Lockport Fair on the same hay wagon with a lot of us from the Reservation. He wasn't ready to leave when the rest were, so they left him. On the way back a pig came trotting along behind the wagon at a swift pace. As he passed the driver took a crack at him with the whip but missed. He said the pig stopped and looked at him with such an evil eye it gave him the shudders. When they passed the old man's cabin about an hour later his lamp was lighted and there on the porch sat the old man. He never would tell how he got back ahead of 'em."

"I knew an Indian fellow who took a girl to a dance who was not his regular girl," said Cephas. "On the way home he and the girl were following a path along the top of a ridge when they heard the sound of a galloping horse. They just had time to jump aside to avoid being run down. As the horse went by the Indian shot it in the shoulder and it screamed and ran off in the woods. Not long after that the mother of his regular girl died. When they prepared her for burial they found a gunshot wound in her shoulder that no one had ever known about before."

"But how does an Indian get to be a witch?" I said.

"Usually through the help of another witch," said Cephas. "Witches make a brew that will make others into witches if they drink it. An Indian friend of mine who lives here on the Reservation tells how he and a friend of his had had their supper and gone for a walk when they suddenly remembered that there was a dance at the Long House over ten miles away that very evening. He says his friend gave him a bottle of something and said, 'Drink some of this.' He drank some and they started running to the Long House. He says every step they took was over ten yards long and when they came to a stream or a fence or a patch of woods they just leaped up and over with no effort at all. In five minutes they were at the Long House. But just as they were about to enter my friend coughed and as he did so he saw light shoot from his mouth and nostrils. His companion saw it, too, and said, 'I wouldn't do that inside if I were you.' Then they both went in and had a good time at the dance. When they came out at the end of it the Indian who had had the drink was scared for fear he had been made into a witch because he could still cover great distances in a few moments and leap over rivers and houses—but gradually the effect wore off and he was himself again. But he's always stayed far away from the witch Indian who gave him the drink."

"Don't witches ever try to help other people with their spells and mixtures?" I said.

"Sure," said Cornplanter. "You should hear Peter Doctor tell about how his uncle fell in love and a witch told him she would make a love potion for him if he would get her a whippoorwill's brain to put in it. Peter and his uncle went out and hunted all day and just at dusk they got close enough to a whippoorwill to aim at it. It fell when Peter shot and they both whooped and ran up to get it—and found that Peter had hit it in the head with enough buckshot to scatter the brains all over the Reservation!"

"There are many supernatural things that just aren't understandable," said Cephas. "We don't know whether to attribute them to witches or not. There's the worm called the onjah that has a head and neck like a pig and no body. The head is yellow and there are two rows of red spots on the neck. Seeing an onjah is a sign of death in the family unless you kill it and bury it. Then there's the strange animal called 'the legs.' It is just a pair of slim black legs that run about very swiftly. They are most often seen along woodland paths and they bring bad luck to the family of the one who sees them. And not long ago an Indian was bringing in his last load of hay from the field at twilight. As he stopped to open his pole-gate the horses snorted and reared in terror. He had a very difficult time getting them to approach the gate. Finally they bolted through it at top speed. As they reached the road he looked behind and saw hundreds of pairs of clutching hands reaching for him."

"I wouldn't like you to think," said Cornplanter, "that many of us believe all these things. They are just folk superstitions that a few of our older people have faith in. The younger people don't really believe in them. It's just that queer things you can't explain happen sometimes."

"Something queer is going to happen to me if I don't get back on the job," said Cephas, stretching. He rose and vanished into the schoolhouse, leaving Cornplanter and me sitting in the sunlight of the first spring day, too filled with lassitude to talk about witches any more.

Tonawanda Morning

WHILE I LIVED ON THE TONAWANDA RESERVATION I PER-
suaded a number of the Senecas to tell me some of the
superstitions held by various members of the tribe. Cephas
Hill was helpful in gathering others. I found many of these
strange ideas poetically beautiful. Many, too, were surprisingly like those I had gathered among the Negroes of the
deep South. The following folk beliefs are part of the harvest
from Cephas' notebook and from my own:

To make an effective love potion, you must always use
the brains of a whippoorwill.

To make your girl love you, you must first take hair from
her head; tie it with Indian tobacco and rouge or powdered
pokeberry. Sprinkle the tobacco on the fire and pray to the
Creator, asking him to help you; tie the charm in a poplar
tree where none will see it; later, move the bag and put it in
the roots of the tree.

To bring back your girl: Put jack-in-the-pulpit in hot
water. Stand it in the hot sun and leave it for a day. Then
sprinkle your body and wash your face with it. Do not dry
yourself but allow the potion to evaporate. Afterward, make
a fire and throw on it sacred tobacco, at the same time ask-

ing that your girl be brought back. Bad-looking people will always have to use this potion.

To bring your lady friend to you, chew Indian tobacco.

To prevent yourself becoming pregnant again, drink no water for a whole month after your baby is born. Instead, drink only the medicine which is given you.

To prevent your baby from having a hard delivery, do not stand in open doorways while you are pregnant.

To prevent your baby from having harelip, eat no meat of wild animals while you are pregnant and under no condition eat rabbit meat.

To prevent your baby having a bunch on his head, do not knot your own hair while you are pregnant.

To prevent your child being homely, do not look at an ugly person while you are pregnant, else your baby will be ugly too.

To give your baby high ideals, carry him onto a roof.

Your baby should always be named after the first thing the midwife sees following his birth.

To keep your baby being spirited away to the world beyond, burn the root end of a pond lily and mark his face with it.

A child born with holes in its ears is a person who has been born again.

Twins are clairvoyant and prophetic, and they have other supernatural qualities including the power to dip water from a well with a sieve.

When whipping children, use only red dogwood shoots.

Tonawanda Morning

To cause a child to turn over in the womb, rest a medicine bundle by the fire and say: "Let her child turn over; let it come true; let it happen soon."

To see three crows is a sign of bad luck, but to see two crows is a sign of good luck.

To hear the song of a whippoorwill or the cackle of a hen is a sign of bad luck.

To find a mouse in a truck or in a drawer is a sign of bad luck.

To sing while eating is to come to sorrow.

To hear a screech owl singing near the house at night is an ill omen for a friend or a relative. When an owl sings as a sign of bad news it is called a poison bird.

To see a pheasant near the house is a sign of death in the family.

A person dying of violence has not lived out his span and so will be earthbound until judgment day.

If a door flies open of itself it is the Spirit of Death and you must say: "Have pity on us. Go somewhere else where they can spare more people."

To dream of a dead Indian is a sign that he lies uneasy in his grave.

To make an Indian lie easy in his grave, remove his shoes, his store-bought clothes and his gold teeth, for these are a white man's things.

To sweep dirt from the inside of the house to the outside is to invade the realm of the dead.

A person must not clip nor comb his hair nor clip his nails at night lest he invade the realm of the dead.

A doll made of cornhusks brings good luck.

Never point at shooting stars. If you do they will reveal you when you are in hiding.

Windows should be covered after dark for fear a skulking or a shriveled face might look in.

If you find a milk snake sunning itself on a stump it is a sign of rain the next day.

The ringing clash often heard in the spring is caused by the struggle between the spirit of cold and the strawberry spirit.

Baskets will sell well if four-leaf clover is boiled down and sprinkled over them.

To find out whether a woman has gonorrhea, chew the roots of cattails. If, when she smells the roots being chewed, she groans, it is because it hurts her and you will know she has the disease.

Manroot, which is sometimes called man-of-the-earth or wild potato vine, is good medicine for all kinds of diseases. Do not use it if you find it lying down, for then it will have lost its potency.

To mend a broken limb, use boneset. Place an offering of tobacco before the first plant you see; take the second plant. If the medicine is to be brewed, take water from a running stream. Be sure to dip downstream.

To dip water for medicine always turn the dipper downstream; you will wash away the sickness and not antagonize the Water Spirit, but ask his help.

Cut all herbs and other medicinal plants from the top down. In cutting elm, be sure to cut below the ground.

The yellow birch is a valuable medicine because it sustains the deer which is the mainstay of life.

Use the inside of basswood bark as an astringent for cuts. An emergency poultice may be made of leatherwood bark if you cut your foot with an ax.

To cure whooping cough, take a black frog—the kind that sound like wagon wheels—and whip it while it is still under the water; then string it up until dry and store it until required. Sufficient medicine may be brewed from the powder of one leg.

Herbs should be dug only after the first snowfall as insects will be gone then and the medicine will be pure.

To cure diarrhea, use common elm cut next to the ground on the side to the east.

To cure eye troubles, cut the thorns from jimson weed and peel it; place it in warm water and use it as a poultice.

If you do not feel like working in your garden, someone has passed a spell on you. To counteract it, burn tobacco and tell the spell to go back where it originated. "Go there to whoever hired you and get in their way. Do not interfere with my behavior. Let me have good luck. Now go there forever."

To protect yourself against rattlesnakes, wear eelskin wrapped around your knee.

To get rid of an enemy, make a doll out of a root. Then place the doll in a coffin and put a corn grub in with it. Stick a pin through both the grub and the doll into the wood and bury the whole thing. As you bury it, name your enemy and you will soon be rid of him.

To witch a person, take a long garden snake or a garter snake and cut off its tail. Force a crotched stick into the ground about two feet from a small tree and suspend another stick between them about three feet from the ground. Then hang the snake over the stick so that its tail is about ten inches from the ground and its blood will drip into a small fireplace which you will have made.

To make a person crazy, get some hair from his head; then take a little phlegm in a red cloth and wrap the hair in it. Place the bundle between the prongs of a split basswood stick. Sharpen the stick and shove the whole thing as far as possible down into an anthill. Sprinkle sacred tobacco on the fire and say your victim's name, but do not pray to Hawenyn as he dislikes this. An ant will then eat your basswood stick and its bundle and the person will go crazy. Antidote: Burn wild ogite (fresh-water clam) shell. Then put a pinch of the powder in a teacup and drink it and you will no longer be crazy.

To keep the dried heart of a dog strangled at midnight is to have protection against all dogs.

To lure a dog from its owner, feed it the scrapings from your head and food which has been held in your armpit.

To make an antidote for any kind of poison—use a little bloodroot. Gather in during the last quarter of the moon and if you are a man you must take a girl with you. Leave home at four in the afternoon but do not collect it until dark. Where the plant grows you will see lights which will all go to one spot. Put a stick in the ground there and go away. Return the next day and gather the roots of the plant where the stick is. Mash the roots and put in a wooden cup covered with a black cloth. Let it stand a half hour and you will see the face of the one who has bewitched you. When you see this face by lamplight, stick a needle in its eye to make the witch's eye sore.

To make a poison, cut a thousand-legs in two. Put the juice on tobacco or on food and give it to your victim. Antidote: Burn a turkey feather; put the ashes in water and drink it.

To become an owl, you must sit ten nights in a swamp wishing to become an owl. Then when on the tenth night an owl approaches, gather it in your arms, and while you carry it home, tell it your wish. Kill the owl and skin it, and make its head and feathers into a mask and cloak. Then, whenever you wish to become an owl, put on the mask and the cloak and you will be able to fly away.

15

The Maple Thanksgiving

FOR TWO WEEKS NOW CANS, JARS, MILK BOTTLES, and oil tins had been hanging from wooden spigots driven into the maples. Charlie Blackchief, who had left the Long-House People for the Christians long ago, had proved that he still remembered the joys of his youth by donating fifteen quarts of white corn for the mush. From the early morning of a March day the women had been working up at Julie

Black's, pounding the corn to flour and sifting out the chaff in winnowing baskets. By four o'clock the fires were burning under the kettles of water hanging from trammel irons in the fireplace of the cookhouse and the newly-made white flour soon to be stirred into mush was in a sack nearby. All the Long-House People had received a message in the words of old Chief Twenty Kettles—"The Faithkeepers, all the people, and the little children have agreed on the meeting for the Maple Thanksgiving"—and they awaited the evening.

Cornplanter, Yo-wes-on and I wandered over to the Long House at seven-thirty, the time appointed, but it was an hour later before the company had straggled to its seats. The interior of the house was quite as simple as its exterior. It was a rectangular undecorated hall, its long sides lined with three rows of simple wooden benches, the short end-sides by one row. Cornplanter pointed with pride to three new gasoline lamps hung at regular intervals from the ceiling. A stove at each end sent out a steady radiance soon lost in the drafts from the two end doors and in the inverted V of the high ceiling.

As they came into the Long House the women sat together on one side, the men on the other. The chiefs and Faithkeepers sat on the bench at the south end of the hall. It was about nine o'clock when Chief Lyman Johnson (The All-Breaker) rose and removed his hat. At once there was silence. For ten minutes he spoke in Seneca. He was an old man but he stood very straight and his voice rose and fell in sure and vigorous cadences. Sometimes, during his pauses, Cornplanter leaned to me to whisper a hasty translation. They had gathered, the chief said, to thank the Creator for the maple tree and for the fact that once more the sap had risen and flowed to sweeten the food that sustains men. This led him to think of all the other earth-forces that made the life of man easier and pleasanter and he wished at the same time to thank them as well. Now they would all go outside the Long House and there beside a maple tree Chief Twenty Kettles would burn tobacco and make invocation to the Creator. The All-Breaker walked out into the night, followed by Twenty Kettles. A Faithkeeper moved toward the nearer stove carrying a shovel and a brass kettle. He opened the fire door and shoveled bright embers into the kettle. Then he took it outside. A moment later he reappeared in the doorway and bade everybody follow him.

Just a few yards from the doorway Twenty Kettles knelt beside the brass kettle, the live coals throwing a red gleam on his lined old face. The Long-House People gathered in a circle around him and, though the night blurred their features, I could see a great seriousness in their upturned faces. Twenty Kettles began to speak and as he did so he scattered tobacco from a sack that lay at his feet on the yellow embers. The pungent sweet smell of burning Indian tobacco spread among us. All ceremonies to please Seneca deities begin with the offering of tobacco, for it is the one possession which their gods envy mortals. The words of the Seneca ritual were strange in my ears. I looked away from the glow of the coals in the brass kettle toward another glow to the westward, the light on the sky that flows from the countless lamps of the city of Buffalo, and thought how the distances between peoples are greater than the geographic distances between places. I did not know then what Twenty Kettles was saying, but I have found out its meaning since, through the kind help of Arthur Parker who has translated it:

Tonawanda Indian Reservation

O partake of this incense,
You the forests!
We implore you
To continue as before
The flowing waters of the maple.

It is the will of the Creator
That a certain tree
Should flow such water.
Now may no accidents occur
To children roaming in the forests.
No, this day is yours,
May you enjoy it—this day.

We give thanks, O God, to you,
You who dwell in heaven.
We have done our duty
You have seen us do it
So it is done.

When Twenty Kettles had finished we all filed back into the Long House and sat where we had sat before. The All-Breaker rose and spoke a few words. Four men carrying rattles and drums moved two empty benches to the center of the floor and sat on them.

"He says this will be the Trotting Dance," said Cornplanter.

The drums and the rattles began a swift alternating beat. Suddenly the All-Breaker bounded forward and began to dance in short running steps with frequent pauses for the elision of a beat. A moment later Jumbo Ground, the Faithkeeper who had carried the coals outside, followed him. He stood so close to the All-Breaker that the two seemed to move as a single being. A slight variation in the steps would have caused collision and spoiled the rhythm—but there was no variation. Jumbo danced as if he were the old man's shadow. Slowly other men emerged onto the floor and fell into line. The path of the dance became a circle around the benches on which the drummers sat. Two old women walked up to the end of the line and began the quick stepping trot, hardly lifting their feet from the floor. Then a young woman carrying a baby wrapped in a shawl joined them. The All-Breaker began to sing as he danced. The drummers joined in strongly. The old wooden hall resounded to the beat of the drums, the harsh grating of the rattles, the wild staccato vowel sounds of the songs, the quick stamp of feet. Then a high ending note from the All-Breaker—and the dance was over.

As the dancers took their seats a group of young men, dressed in blue suits and white shirts and looking very clean and neat, entered by the south door.

"Lacrosse players," said Cornplanter. "Just back by bus from Buffalo."

"Did they win?" I said.

Cornplanter laughed.

"Some of them must have. There are only one or two white professionals. White managers have organized a lacrosse league in New York State. As I remember it there are two Negroes and one white man on the half dozen or so teams that play for upstate cities. The rest are Indians from the seven reservations in the state."

"Are the players well paid?" I said.

He laughed again—shortly.

"What do *you* think?" he said. "But lacrosse wages are the only income many Indians have."

"I thought the Federal Government helped out somehow," I said lamely.

"Aside from pensions for war service and wages paid to Government employees," said Cornplanter, "I don't know of any Seneca who gets more than three dollars a year from Washington. But a good many white people think we get our living from the Government as well as this tax-free land."

"But how *do* Indians make a living?" I said.

"Some of them farm this land. It isn't very good but they can grow food on it. Some of them get jobs as carpenters, watchmen, gardeners in Buffalo and the nearby towns. A good many have to depend on charitable agencies, social welfare people and so on."

The All-Breaker was speaking again.

"Fish Dance," said Cornplanter.

The accompaniment of this dance was simple. The drums took the accented beats, the rattles the interims between them. Again the All-Breaker and Jumbo Ground led off and others straggled into line. The steps of the Fish Dance were amazingly like those of the Charleston, whose Negroid antics captured white dancing in the twenties. Last in line this time were the lacrosse players, circling solemnly as their feet flashed in quick circles under them. The woman with the wrapped-up baby held to her shoulder turned slowly about, keeping perfect time. A group of three girls and a woman of middle age were dancing a different step which I later found characteristic of most of the woman-dances. They stood close to each other, side by side, instead of facing straight ahead like the rest. Their feet never left the floor—only their toes reached out to the right and their heels were brought over behind them. The resultant effect was strangely like that produced by the movement of a many-legged caterpillar. This dance was gayer and brighter than the preceding one—the men whooped and put in amusing variations, the women giggled.

When it was over the All-Breaker said a few solemn words in Seneca and a woman at the north stove spoke the familiar "Come put down your pails." Cornplanter had brought a pail for me and soon I was enjoying my corn mush and maple syrup as heartily even as the lacrosse players.

"Let's take the rest over to my house," said Cornplanter. "A few of us want to ask you a question."

So we walked over to his house and sat on the porch where we could see the stars and the lights of the Long House still burning. We were four men and there was a certain solemnity in the pause that preceded the talk.

Finally Cornplanter said, "You have heard of the Wheeler-Howard Bill, haven't you? It has passed the United States Congress but it must be voted on by each reservation separately."

"I know something about it," I said. "The Government offers to lend you money to buy equipment, a plow or a team of horses, say, and it will wait for repayment until by means of the equipment you have earned the money you owe."

A low growling came from my left and a middle-aged Indian began to speak. Even in the dim light I could see the shine of his eyes and their intentness.

"What security does the Government ask?" he said.

"Why, none," I said.

"You can't make me believe," said the Indian, "that the Government offers loans to us without asking security. Suppose we don't make money with our plows. Suppose our horses die before we can pay back. What then?"

"Why, nothing, I guess," I said.

"I'll tell you what then," said the Indian, pointing a fore-finger at me. "We have nothing to offer as security. All that we own in the world is this land. And when we owe the Government money and can't pay, what will the Government do? It will take away the last thing, the one thing it hasn't taken before, our homes."

"But I'm sure that is not the intention," I said. "I'm sure the Government passed this bill to help you—and that's the reason it doesn't ask security."

"That's what the Government says, all right," said the Indian, "and when have we believed in the Government and not been fooled? Maybe Commissioner Collier means what he says now. Wait until we owe the money—then see if politicians don't vote to take our land in payment."

"I shall vote against accepting the bill," said a quiet voice on my right, and I turned to look at a bespectacled, earnest-looking, white-haired old man. "We are a nation, living on land of our own. We are not citizens of the United States and I hope we never will be. We must insist on our rights as a separate territory not responsible to any other government. We must rule ourselves. We must not pay taxes to the United States or we will lose our status as a separate nation. Over near Oneida a little while ago some white farmers tricked an Indian into paying taxes on his tax-free land. Now the whites own the land and the Indian is penni-less. We must not let that happen to us all."

"You didn't get me over here to ask me questions," I said. "You got me here to tell me answers."

They all laughed at that and stood up to go.

The Maple Thanksgiving

"The bill will be defeated on the reservations of the Iroquois," said the old man and I knew he was speaking the truth.

Cornplanter and I went inside when they had left. Yo-wes-on was lighting a lamp as we entered. She had passed us so silently during our talk that I had not heard her.

"I'm very tired," I said. "I think I'll go right up to bed. Good night."

"Good night," said Cornplanter.

"Good night, Carmer," said Yo-wes-on. It was the first time she had called me by name. I had been feeling very much alone and I was comforted. Upstairs, when I had blown out my lamp, I went to the window and raised it. The moon had just risen and its rays seemed almost to parallel, at the same height as my eyes, the flat line of the earth. An old white horse wandered aimlessly about the Long House. A dog howled far off to the south and many others barked querulous replies. The moonlight whitened the plastered crevices in a log house a quarter-mile away. The glow from Buffalo was still in the western sky. And from some distant cabin far across the level land came the soft, liquid, beating of a water drum.

THE TEACHINGS OF HANDSOME LAKE ARE AN INTEREST-
ing mixture of old Seneca creeds, Quaker teachings to
which the prophet had plentiful opportunity to listen, and
his own personal common sense. Occasional passages are
imaginative and poetic—as, for example, the following translated into beautiful rhythmic English prose by Arthur
Parker, Curator of the Rochester City Museum, whose father was a full-blooded Seneca.

The day was bright when I went into the planted
field and alone I wandered in the planted field and it
was the time of the second hoeing. Suddenly a damsel
appeared and threw her arms about my neck and as
she clasped me she spoke, saying, "When you leave
this earth for the new world above, it is our wish to
follow you." I looked for the damsel but saw only the
long leaves of corn twining round my shoulders. And
then I understood that it was the spirit of corn who
had spoken, she the sustainer of life. So I replied, "O
spirit of the corn, follow not me but abide still upon
the earth and be strong and be faithful to your purpose. Ever endure and do not fail the children of
women. It is not time for you to follow for the good
message is only in its beginning."

And here is a bit of advice from the prophet's store of worldly wisdom:

Now it may happen that a man and wife live together happily. At length the man thinks that he will go to another settlement to visit relatives there. His wife agrees and he goes. Now when he gets to the village he induces some agreeable woman to live with him, saying he is single. Then after some time the man goes back to his own family. His wife treats him cordially as if no trouble had occurred. Now we, the messengers, say that the woman is good in the eyes of her Creator and has a place reserved for her in the heaven-world. Now the woman knew all that had been done in the other settlement but she thought it best to be peaceful and remain silent. And the Creator says that she is right and has her path toward the heaven-world, but he, the man, is on his way to the house of the Wicked One.

Some of the lines of the ceremonies for the Little People are here quoted in the translation of Arthur Parker:

Now again you receive tobacco—you, the Pygmies. (Throws tobacco)
You are the wanderers of the mountains;
You have promised to hear us whenever the drum sounds,
Even as far away as a seven days' journey.
Now all of you receive tobacco . . . (Throws tobacco)
Henceforth give good fortune for we have fulfilled our duty and given you tobacco.
You love tobacco and we remember it;

So also you should remember us.
Now the drum receives tobacco,
And the rattle also.
It is our belief that we have said all,
So now we hope that you will help us.
Now these are the words spoken before you all,
You who are gathered here tonight.
So now it is done.

Part Four

"Truth Shall Spring out of the Earth"

Meeting House at Mt. Lebanon Shaker Settlement

When you are actually in America, America hurts, because it has a powerful disintegrative influence upon the white psyche. It is full of grinning, unappeased aboriginal demons, too, ghosts. . . . One day the demons of America must be placated, the ghosts must be appeased, the Spirit of Place atoned for. . . .

There are terrible spirits, ghosts, in the air of America.

From *Studies in American Classical Literature,* by D. H. Lawrence

16

Spirit Way

ACROSS THE ENTIRE BREADTH OF YORK STATE, UN-deviating, a hilly strip scarcely twenty-five miles wide invites the world's wonder. It is a broad psychic highway, a thoroughfare of the occult whose great stations number the mystic seven. For where, in its rolling course from east of Albany to west of Buffalo, it has reached one of seven isolated and lonely heights, voices out of other worlds have spoken with spiritual authority to men and women, and the invisible mantles of the prophets have been laid on consecrated shoulders. In no other area in the Western Hemisphere have so many evidences of an existence transcending mortal living been manifest. It is impossible to reckon the number of listeners who on the plateaus of this strange midstate avenue have knelt before seen or unseen supernatural visitants to hear counsel. And the sum of those whose lives have been affected by that counsel, save for the fact that it is in the millions, is incalculable.

The years have lessened the power of a few of these teachings. Mother Ann's sayings are remembered by less than a dozen Shakers who will soon be dust. The Millerites and the Harrisites are few. The Jemimakins live only in the bone and sinew and brains they gave to their descendants, not in the heeded admonitions of the Universal Friend. But those who believe in the revelations which the two little Fox sisters gave to American spiritualists still flourish and increase their number. The children of the Oneida Community propagate and, though they have discarded much, they have kept much of the spirit and vigor of John Humphrey Noyes. And the followers of Joseph Smith are a legion of a million throughout the world.

I cannot pretend to offer reasons why this magic road stretches across the York State hill country. It may be pointed out that the great evangelistic awakening which came to New England in the last century brought with it theological interpretations which were not always conventional and that York State was a kind of idea-frontier, a tolerant refuge from the grim orthodoxy of Puritan sections. But this is not a comprehensive explanation nor is it wholly sound. Until its evidences of enchantment have been academically explained away I shall prefer to believe that a special quality of this strip of land has made it the track that leads to things seldom in men's knowing.

During my sojourns with my sister and with the Dugans I visited each of the seven stations on that track. Here are the stories of their beginnings and of their present estate.

17

Hands to Work
and Hearts to God

THE BLUE EYES OF AN ENGLISH BLACKSMITH'S
daughter looking into a world that other eyes could not per-
ceive inspired the events that begin this story. Slight of body
and sensitive of mind, Ann Lee worked in a Manchester
cotton factory during the middle years of the eighteenth
century. She had not learned to read but her hours away
from the spindles were filled with awe at the mysteries her
eyes beheld. Behind the veil that separates the mortal from
the spiritual she had seen visions which told her of man's
sinfulness and its greatest cause—the lusts of the flesh.

Though her supernatural experiences had forewarned her
Ann Lee could not save herself. Her yellow hair and fair
skin brought a man to her side, Abraham Stanley, a blacksmith like her father. She begged to be allowed to forego
the sins of matrimony but to no avail—her father and her
lover were too strong.

In the next nine years she bore four children and they all
died in infancy—a fitting punishment, she said, for her sin
in submitting to her husband's desires. And during that

time, according to testimony later given, "she labored day and night for deliverance from the very nature of sin. . . . She was often in such extreme agony of soul as caused the blood to perspire through the pores of her skin. Sometimes for whole nights together, her cries, screeches and groans were such as to fill every soul around her with fear and trembling." She found some release from the suffering occasioned by Abraham Stanley's insistence through uniting herself with the Shaking Quakers. This group of evangelistic Christians, generally known as Shakers, and so called from their manner of worship, had found their inspiration in the martyrdoms, on the wheel and in the fire, of the French Protestant Camisards. Soon the penetrating blue eyes and the sure manner of the new convert made her recognized by this cult first as a leader and then as the expected feminine messiah returning the spirit of Christ to the earth and fulfilling the complete masculine-and-feminine god-head as their teachers had foretold. Their claim to her divinity and their practice of worship by ecstatic physical manifestations of the power of God within them immediately aroused antagonisms in other sects. On one occasion the intervention of an English nobleman, roused from his bed by some mysterious compulsion to gallop through the night to her rescue, saved Ann Lee from death at the hands of a mob of persecutors. And once she was thrown into "Bedlam," a madhouse prison, and made to occupy a dark stone cell where she could not recline at full length. There in the utter blackness a supernatural light blinded her for a moment before she was able to see a vision of such transcendent beauty and purity that at last she knew the celibate path which she must go, preaching the open confession of sin and the taking up of a daily cross against all worldly desires.

Another vision came to her soon after she had left the prison. She saw a little town in a distant country and in it many people whom she did not know—but all their faces were turned toward her as if awaiting her. It was not long after this that Ann Lee, now known to the Shakers as Mother Ann, set sail for America on the ship *Mariah* with a little band of eight followers including her converted husband and her brother, William Lee. On the voyage a great storm frightened the captain and the crew, but the blue eyes seeking for a sign of God's care saw two angels standing at the helm and all was well.

Then came a period of poverty and uncertainty. While Mother Ann applied herself to menial tasks in order to make a living in New York City, her husband tired of the asceticism of her teachings and demanded that she again become his wife in more than name. She refused and he abandoned her. In the meantime a few of her disciples had acquired land in the forest northwest of Albany at Niskayuna, now Watervliet. Here they raised log dwellings and began the thrifty husbandry which was to bring material prosperity to their communal undertakings.

On Christmas Day, 1775, the Niskayuna Shakers found Mother Ann in domestic service in a house on the New York street now known as Pearl. They took her north and established her in their wilderness home as the Divine Mother in whom the Christ spirit had made a second appearing. And in the lonely woods they continued the rites of dancing and shaking which had given their sect its name.

Soon the opportune moment was to arrive when they might communicate their beliefs to others and find them well received. In New Lebanon, east of Albany near the Massachusetts line, a great evangelistic revival was getting under way. People who had felt its power had lost control of their movements and had been seized with inexplicable shakings and twitchings. Some of them made the journey to Niskayuna and, having seen the worship practices of the Shakers, found them good. Soon there was a large communist Shaker group or "Family" at New Lebanon—and another just over the Massachusetts border at Hancock. In the country about Albany, wayfarers might often see grown men dancing down the dusty turnpike or grave young whirlers gyrating underneath the moon, lost in rhythmic physical expression of the religious ecstasies that possessed them.

Mother Ann saw that the fields of her families were as full of harvest as their hearts were full of the love of God and determined to spread her gospel throughout the land. From the early summer of 1781 for a little more than two years she and some of her elders visited no less than thirty-six towns in Massachusetts and Connecticut as missionaries of their faith. The Christians of other denominations met her visits not only with unchristian scorn and ridicule, but with mob violence. Time and again her elders were beaten until their backs were jellied by the lash.

In these disorders Mother Ann miraculously escaped physical injury until her party, on its way back to Niskayuna in the early autumn, stopped at New Lebanon to rest among her followers there. There was little rest, however, for the New Lebanon Shakers were so inspired by the visit of the Divine Mother that their religious "labors"—their zealous dancing—and their "operations"—the physical evidences of the power of God working within them—lasted throughout the night. Just before the end of darkness Mother Ann left Isaac Harlow's house where these exercises had taken place and went to the home of George Darrow, where the Shaker Meetinghouse now stands. Hardly had she arrived when a mob began to gather about the house. Immediately the believers in the neighborhood swarmed into the house to protect their leader.

The mob attacked suddenly and with extreme ferocity. The three doors of the house, valiantly defended by Shaker men, were forced and the rioters dragged some of the defenders into the open by the hair. Many of the women who had gathered in the kitchen were brutally beaten and hurled outside. One man was three times thrown from a doorway high above the ground. In the yard the ruthless persecutors seized on those who had been ejected, grasping them by their arms and legs and, swinging them to gain momentum, cast them with stunning force into a mud puddle near the door.

Meanwhile a vicious struggle was going on in a little back room where the Shakers fought desperately to save Mother Ann, who had been hidden in a ceiled closet. The mob finally tore down the walls and dragged Mother Ann by the heels to her carriage which had been made ready outside. Throwing her headlong into it they cut the reins of the harness and began to lead her horse to the home of a local justice, Eleazar Grant, bitter enemy of the Shakers. Another sharp struggle occurred at a narrow bridge over a ravine into which the mob tried to upset the carriage but Shaker Medad Curtis proved himself another Horatius and the procession moved on.

Though fearfully whipped and beaten, Mother Ann's courage did not desert her. Driven out of her usual Christ-like patience as she stood before the sneering tribunal, Justice Grant, she said, "It is your day now, but it will be mine by and by, Eleazar Grant. I'll put you in a cockleshell yet."

Harassed by the mob all the way to the ferry opposite Albany, Mother Ann and her exhausted group of followers crossed the river and made their way to Niskayuna where they arrived at eleven o'clock at night. Their long missionary expedition was over.

But twenty-six months of evangelism and suffering from persecutions had taken their toll. Less than a year after the return, Mother Ann's stalwart brother William, former officer of the horse in the Oxford Blues, volunteer regiment of the British king's royal guard, died at the age of forty-four. Mother Ann knew that she would soon follow him. Though her body was wasted and her cheeks sunken, the great blue eyes blazed out of their hollows with unquenched spirit. "Her words were like flames of fire and her voice like peals of thunder." Earnestly she urged on her people the teaching she had given them: "Hand to work and hearts to God." And when there was little time left to her she prophesied, saying, "You will see peaceable times; then you may worship God under your own vines and fig trees, and none of the wicked will make you afraid."

Mother Ann died just a year and four days after her return to Niskayuna. She was over forty-eight years old but she had seen only twelve birthdays, for she had been born on the twenty-ninth of February in 1736. Many of her followers, on hearing of her death, were so distressed that they found it difficult to think of continued earthly existence. Then a sister reported that while she lay prostrate upon the floor in secret retirement expecting to breathe out her soul in sorrow, she saw the appearance of Mother Ann about the size of a child three years old. The appearance held in each hand something that looked like a wing which she waved inward as she said, "Hush! Hush!" And after they had heard this the Shakers were comforted.

There was no faltering among the Believers after the loss of their leader. They sang:

> Well done, good and faithful Mother.
> Now receive thy just reward
> In the kingdom with thy Savior
> Reap the glory with thy Lord . . .

and they devoted their hands more eagerly to work, their hearts more ardently to God. With each religious revival their numbers grew. Under wise leadership their lands and holdings increased. In New Lebanon the number of Families increased to seven, each under the leadership of an elder and two eldresses, and there began an era of prosperity which reached its highest peak around the middle of the nineteenth century. New converts gave their belongings into the general property. If married, they gave up conjugal relationships and entered a Family house to climb the separate stairways to the dormitories assigned to their respective sexes. Each member of the commune was given work thought suited to his abilities, and the women took an equal share with the men.

The Shakers were a people not only of the highest integrity but of imagination and business acumen. To their fundamental occupation of farming they added many others. Their garden seeds were purchased throughout America. They built up a large business in medicinal herbs, some of which they gathered, others they purchased as the business grew. Jerusalem oak, goldthread, skunk cabbage, bugle, scurvy grass, cohosh, life everlasting, skullcap and scores of other plants were among their remedies. They made shoes and brooms, dippers and pens, whips and churns, buttons and straw bonnets, "Turkey Crop" court plaster, and napkin rings, rose water and shingles. Their chairs, admirable in their simplicity of design, lightness and strength, and still obtainable from Shaker workers at New Lebanon (now Mount Lebanon), found ready sale in great quantities at Marshall Field's in Chicago, at Lewis & Conger's in New York. P. T. Barnum for years bought from them the gray woolen horse blankets for the "Greatest Show on Earth." Shaker communists invented about forty labor-saving devices, including the first American one-horse wagon, a pea sheller, an apple corer, a metal pen, a machine for filling herb packages, a circular saw and cut nails (invented by a woman), a stove-cover lifter, a revolving oven, a threshing machine, a fertilizing machine.

Mother Ann's prophecy had come true. The days of persecution were over. Unafraid beneath their fruit trees the Shakers worked and worshiped at peace with friendly neighbors. Hepworth Dixon, in the late sixties, wrote of Lebanon in his *The New America:*

> No Dutch town has a neater aspect, no Moravian hamlet a softer hush. The streets are quiet; for here you have no grog-shop, no beer-house, no lock-up, no pound; of the dozen edifices rising about you—workrooms, barns, tabernacle, stables, kitchens, schools, and dormitories—not one is either foul or noisy; and every building, whatever may be its use, has something of the air of a chapel. The paint is all fresh; the planks

are all bright; the windows are all clean. A white sheen
is on everything; a happy quiet reigns around. Even in
what is seen of the eye and heard of the ear, Mount
Lebanon strikes you as a place where it is always Sunday. The walls appear as though they had been built
only yesterday; a perfume, as from many unguents,
floats down the lane; and the curtains and window
blinds are of spotless white. Everything in the hamlet
looks and smells like household things which have
been long laid up in lavender and roseleaves.

In these streets the Shakers walked sedately, the women
in their big bonnets and unadorned gray dresses with ker-
chiefs around their shoulders, the men in simple work-suits
and unstyled, broad-brimmed hats. Usefulness was the sole
test of Shaker manufacture. Decoration was sinful. But
whether they wished to achieve it or not the simplicity of
their designs frequently wrought beauty in an age of increasingly tasteless ornamental fantasy.

There was good food and plenty of it at the two long
tables, one for the brothers, one for the sisters, in the big
dining halls of each Family house. But visitors to the board
were handed printed slips on which they were requested in

verse to comply with the practice of taking no more upon their plates than they could eat—and to this day in portions of York State and New England children are urged to "Shaker" their plates (eat them clean). Sister Amelia Simmons, who signed herself "An American Orphan," wrote at New Lebanon a book entitled *American Cookery: Or the Art of Dressing Viands, Fish, Poultry and Vegetables and the Best Way of Making Puff-Pastry, Pies, Tarts, Puddings, Custards and Preserves and All Kinds of Cakes; Adapted to This Country and All Grades of Life.* In her preface to this Shaker contribution to the national cookery, Sister Simmons says her treatise is "calculated for the improvement of the rising generation of Females in America," and in her second edition expresses her gratitude for the "kind patronage of so many respectable characters in her attempts to improve the minds of her own sex." Among her Shaker recipes are "To dress Beef-Stake sufficient for two Gentlemen, with a fire made of two newspapers; To make a fine Syllabub from the Cow; Independence Cake; Election Cake," and six ways for preparing Rice Pudding, including "a cheap one."

And in *A Manual of Good Manners*, printed at New Lebanon in 1844, the Shakers added their bit to national social usage with many sage counsels, including, "Never be squinting and scowling and examining the victuals to see if you can discover a coal, a spec, or a hair; and if you do find one take it out decently and not make a great ado about it. For your honor's sake never make a mountain of a molehill."

Since honest, thorough work was a part of their religion, the products of the Shakers received preference in many markets and their profits grew. With the security this afforded them they happily extended their communes to include another New York State group at Sonyea in the Genesee Valley, and over twenty-five others mostly in New England, Ohio and Kentucky. They were, of course, handicapped in their expansion by the fact that as a natural result of following their religious beliefs no children were born to them. They remedied this somewhat, however, by securing new converts and by accepting orphan children for adoption. As their conscientious care for these children became known, the number of children offered them increased greatly.

With their material success the Shakers found more reason than ever to worship God with song and dance. At New Lebanon they built a huge white meetinghouse with a roof curved in a wide arc over it. Hundreds of nonbelieving visitors, "Adam's kind" the Shakers called them, attended the services here, watching from bleacher-like benches that lined the two long sides of the big auditorium. Here, when the elders anounced "Travel" or "Labor" rites, the men Shakers stood on the east side of the hall, the women on the west. As the singing of the Travel hymn began each sex formed in a column of twos and began marching, holding their hands out from the elbows, palms upward as if receiving blessings into them. The step, at first a short trot, changed at a measure in the music to a peculiar shuffle, the foot being slid along the floor a little, then raised about four inches and brought down toe first. As they marched they performed evolutions which brought each group into columns of threes or fours, and the music became faster, the singing louder. Frequently they sang *The Gospel Trumpet:*

> Mother taught the gospel plain
> And showed what God through Christ is doing
> To redeem poor fallen man
> And save his soul from endless ruin
> By her sufferings overcame
> And taught the way of self denying
> Put the nasty flesh to shame
> In which old Adam's race were lying.

Soon the slip and beat of the feet and the accent of the song had its effect on the marchers' aroused senses. They would clap their hands at regular intervals, then turn their palms downward to let sin run out at the finger tips as the violence of the dancing shook their bodies. One of the younger women would leave the "Square Order" to whirl in "Quick Manner" in the center of the room until she dropped to the floor in an ecstasy of emotional exhaustion. Then as the music ended, suddenly rising from the floor in a hypnotic state she would begin swaying from side to side, at first slowly, then more and more rapidly. Suddenly the "gift of unknown tongues" would descend upon her and she would speak out clearly in a language unknown to this world:

> I lo le vitica vum vole os ca nere von
> I lo le viteca vum se ra osca nera von
> I le vitica vole vum se ra os ca nere von
> I le viteca vole vum se ra os ca nana.

In some cases the inspired one would speak in a combination of the unknown language and English—as in this popular example which is not without its similarities to certain methods in modern radical verse:

Selera vane van vo canara van se lava
Dilera van se lane cinara van se vo
'Tis Mother's holy love, love, she sent it by her dove, dove
'Twas van van se vane, 'twill evermore endure.

As the services progressed, more and more of the marchers in the Square Order Manner would begin leaping, whirling, shaking and shouting until the watchers on the side benches were sometimes frightened by the intensity and fury of their exaltations. One of these spectators has told that toward the end of a Travel service he saw Shakers pass among the very old who were physically incapable of strenuous exertion and shake them heartily while others shook the babies in their cradles—so that all might be blessed by having their sins cast from them.

At some of these meetings in New Lebanon, several years before the two little Fox sisters of Hydesville gave great impetus to the spiritualistic cult in America, Shakers went into mediumistic trances and spoke with beings who existed in the unseen world. Sometimes they talked with departed Shakers, sometimes with whole groups of Spirit Indians, Persians, Japanese, Arabs, Hindus who had come to be instructed both in the faith and in the practical industries of Shaker life. A particularly pathetic account has been preserved of how Mother Ann appeared to the New Lebanon Shakers and of how, clad in their dull, drab costumes, they listened eagerly while she told them of what they should wear in heaven. The men should have "beautiful fine Trowsers, as white as snow . . . with many shining stars thereon" and with sky-blue glass buttons. The jackets were also to be sky-blue and have gold buttons on which "many elegant and pretty flowers of different colors" had been

wrought in fine needlework. About their necks were to be
white silk handkerchiefs bordered with gold. Their feet
were to be cased in shoes perfectly white and their heads
were to be covered by fine fur hats "of a silver color." The
sisters should wear gowns that blended twelve different
colors, colored handkerchiefs about their necks, blue silk
gloves, silver shoes, and bonnets "of silver color trimmed
with white ribbon."

There were, of course, occasional defections among the
members of the Shaker communes throughout the course
of their existence, but so few as to make them extraordinary
exceptions to the general rule. Usually such suggestion as
the following hymn stanzas offer served to keep everyone in
a tractable frame of mind:

> I love a good believer
> Whose faith is firm and strong,
> I hate a halting Shaker
> Who must be dragged along.
>
> I hate my carnal nature
> With all its vile contents,
> I hate to see vile passions
> Rise up among the saints.

When sins were committed, however, one method of
discipline reported from New Lebanon by Elder Philemon
Stewart must have been singularly efficacious: "When anyone is lacking in obedience or does not willingly co-operate
with the spirit of a meeting, they are subjected to a warning
gift. One sister commences crying, 'Woe! Woe! Woe!
Woe!' and is soon joined by several others—'woe! woe! to

them that should leave the ways of God, or oppose it.' And they accompany these imprecations with a general concert of groaning, shouting, shaking, stamping, and altogether create a tumult which is indeed a caution to the unfaithful."

So earnest and upright were the Shaker people, so fairly and so wisely were they governed, that there was little to criticize in their administration of either their worldly or their spiritual affairs. Theirs was a peaceful, diligent and not uninteresting way of life. In ascetic religious communion they felt that they had discovered an escape from many of the torments and bitternesses of competitive life. And it would seem that only the advent of the machine age, with its emphasis on quantity of production rather than quality of craftsmanship, and their own failure in their plans for extension of the cult could have accomplished what the last half-century has witnessed—their gradual passing.

The late-winter sun was promising the spring when I turned off the Pittsfield road east of Albany and saw before me, along the upward slope of a mountain, a confusion of white patches of snow and patches of a more dazzling whiteness which were Shaker houses. I drove onward and upward—past the meetinghouse with its famous curved roof—and stopped at a tall three-story frame residence.

I must have waited several minutes after I had rung the bell before the door slowly opened. I remember my surprise at seeing that the old lady with her hand on the knob was wearing the gray dress and shawl-like kerchief that have long been the Shaker sisters' costume; and my impatience with myself for being surprised.

"I hope you'll forgive a stranger's coming to call on Sunday afternoon," I said, "but I have been wanting to see you and talk to you about the Shakers for a long time."

She smiled and I saw the kind of loveliness in her face that sometimes a life of service and asceticism seems to create.

"Sunday afternoon," she said in a clear voice, "is a good time to talk. Won't you come in and climb the stairs? My sister and I are sitting in the sunlight that comes through the windows of our room on the top floor. You go first, for it will take me longer to get there than you."

I walked up the two long flights slowly. At the top stood an erect, white-haired, pink-cheeked little figure. The kerchief about her shoulders met in a fold just above her tiny waist and her gray skirt spread out voluminously below it.

"He has come to talk with us about the Shakers, Sister Emma," said the woman behind me. "I think he wants to write about us."

"Will you come in and sit down?" said the little lady. "There aren't very many Shakers left to write about."

I entered a room flooded with sunshine, a big room so clean that it smelled clean. It was simply furnished with a few slat-backed Shaker chairs, a simple desk, a straight-lined table. We all sat down and I looked at my most recent acquaintance closely. She was undoubtedly the older of the two and yet when she spoke there was a humor about the mouth, a sparkle in the eye that made her seem younger.

"There are just a few left at Watervliet," she continued, "and here we keep only a few houses open. This one is for the Church Family. They took in the members of the old Center Family years ago. And the house beyond us is where the South Family lives. They took in the Second Family.

There were four others here—the Upper and Lower Canaan Families, the North and the East. They have all died out just as we are dying out now."

"You see," said the younger sister, "we used to add to our members by adopting orphan children. But when state and denominational orphan asylums became more numerous, the children who were offered to us frequently turned out to be more suited to reform schools than to our way of life."

"And now," said Sister Emma, "we take no more children and I am ninety-two and my sister is in her late eighties. But you came here to ask us questions. I suppose you want us to tell you about Shakerism."

"Very much," I said.

She paused for a moment and a reminiscent smile came to her face.

"It was a noisy religion," she said. "We used to dance in the Square Order Manner—and then there was the Quick Manner. I'm sorry that I am too old to illustrate that for you."

"Perhaps I——" began the younger sister.

"Nay," said Sister Emma with gentle emphasis and a sharp glance. "You are too old to try it again." Then she turned to me. 'But if you will excuse my moving slowly I will show you how our Square Order Manner went. It was not different from your waltz in some ways." She rose and lifted the many folds of her wide-spreading gray skirt until I could see the little black-clad feet beneath them. I shall not forget how straight she was nor with what grace her tiny figure advanced and turned.

"You see," she said, smiling, "toe to heel and the other heel raised—like this."

"Yes, I see," I said.

Then we talked about Mother Ann for a while and went over all the familiar anecdotes that are a part of the story I have already told about her. And just as I thought it best to be leaving, Sister Emma said:

"If you are going to write about us, you must surely mention Norwood's Tincture of Veratrum Viride. As you know, it is made from American hellebore and it is still one of the very best of heart remedies. We should sell much more of it than we do."

"I will surely mention it," I said. "And now I'd like to take a picture of you two with my Kodak if I may."

"I am sorry to have to refuse you," said Sister Emma. "I suppose it's all right but our religion never approved of the singling out of any members. What work we did, we did for the whole Family and no one ever claimed individual credit. I feel that a picture might be considered vanity."

"There is a little shop across the hall," said her sister. "Perhaps you would be interested in seeing some of the things the Shakers still make?"

"I would, indeed," I said.

"Then we will say good-bye to each other now," said Sister Emma, taking my hand. "I suppose it's really all right but I never enter the shop on Sunday."

From the collection of dolls in Shaker costume, brooms, needlework and furniture I finally purchased a sturdy, rush-bottomed stool. And after I had paid for it I saw Sister Emma standing on the threshold but not entering. Once more she held out her hand and I went quickly outside the shop to take it.

"I hope you did not consider me rude," she said.

Hands to Work and Hearts to God

I assured her I had not thought so and asked if I might return to see them both. They said I might and then I left them standing at the top of the stairs.

Time had passed more swiftly than I realized and the sun was already behind the hills when I reached the main road again. A deep violet shadow had invaded Mount Lebanon and in it the white Shaker houses seemed to be growing luminous.

FROM A NUMBER OF SHAKER HYMNALS, EACH COPIED IN perfect handwriting by a believer, I list several titles:

Mother Ann's Words	The Foundation Pillars
Seventh Trumpet	Revealed
Pretty Garment	Typical Trumpets
Sinai Cherub	Typical Dancing
Pleasant Road	Battle Axe
Mother's Garden	Babylon Is Fallen
Windows of Heaven	Old Adam Disturbed
Union Plant	Resolution against a
Ardent Desires	Carnal Nature
Beautiful Tree	Dragon's Rage
Anchors of Safety	Earthquake
The Cordial	Noah's Ark a Figure

RECITES FROM THE SHAKER COOKBOOK

To Make a Fine Syllabub from the Cow

Sweeten a quart of cyder with double refined sugar, grate nutmeg into it, then milk your cow into your liquor, when you have thus added what quantity of milk you think proper, pour half a pint or more, in proportion to the quantity of syllabub you make, of the sweetest cream you can get all over it.

Loaf Cakes

Rub 6 pound of sugar, 2 pound of lard, 3 pound of butter into 12 pound of flour, add 18 eggs, 1 quart of milk, 2 ounces of cinnamon, 2 small nutmegs, a teacup of coriander seed, each pounded fine and sifted, add one pint of brandy, half a pint of wine, 6 pound of stoned raisins, 1 pint of emptins, first having dried your flour in the oven, dry and roll the sugar fine, rub your shortening and sugar half an hour, it will render the cake much whiter and lighter, heat the oven with dry wood, for 1 and a half hours, if large pans be used, it will then require 2 hours baking, and in proportion for smaller loaves. To frost it. Whip 6 whites, during the baking, add 3 pound of sifted loaf sugar and put on thick, as it comes hot from the oven. Some return the frosted loaf into the oven, it injures and yellows it, if the frosting be put on immediately it does best without being returned into the oven.

18

The End
of the World

WHEN WILLIAM MILLER WAS A YOUNG MAN HE
had acquitted himself creditably against the British in the
battle of Lake Champlain. After he returned from the war
he became a hard-working York State farmer and a constant
reader of the Bible. In that prophetic book he found the
basis for mathematical calculations such as few had
dreamed. For fourteen years he studied, drew charts, added,
subtracted, divided. At the end of that time, in the summer
of 1832, he was fifty years old and he had come to a conclusion that was to change the lives of many thousands of
people.

"The end of the world is at hand," he said. "The evidence
flows in from every quarter. The earth is reeling to and fro
like a drunkard. . . . See the carnivorous fowls fly screaming through the air! See—see these signs! Behold the heavens
grow black with clouds; the sun has veiled himself; the
moon, pale and forsaken, hangs in the middle air; the hail
descends; the seven thunders utter loud their voices; the
lightnings send their vivid gleams of sulphurous flames
abroad; and the great city of the nations falls to rise no more

· 167 ·

forever and forever. At this dread moment, look! The clouds have burst asunder; the heavens appear; the great white throne is in sight! . . . He comes! He comes! Behold the Savior comes!"

Like many another prophet, William Miller got slight attention at first. Then something happened so portentous, so ominously linked to his teaching that even the scoffers were shocked. A little over a year after his first pronouncement, just before the dawn of a November day, the stars of the heavens fell toward the earth. For over an hour like shining snowflakes countless meteors shot downward over the awe-struck populace. In the South the slaves threw themselves on their black faces in an agony of terror. "It's Massa Jesus on his way," they cried. In the North over the great falls of Niagara appeared a greater cataract of flame, and watchers said, "It is a sign of the last days."

"Ten years from now," said William Miller, "the Christ will appear a second time in the clouds of heaven, He will raise up the righteous dead and judge them with the righteous living who will be caught up to meet Him in the air. The earth will be sacrificed by fire and the wicked and all their works shall be consumed."

The warning caught the imagination of the people. In ever-increasing numbers they thronged the camp meetings and the great city tabernacles to listen with mingled religious ecstasy and dread while Miller and the ministers who believed in him preached the end of the world. As the decade waned the hysteria grew—the sneering of the cynical went strangely weak.

The year of foretold destruction came and with it another amazing and convincing phenomenon. At the noon of a clear day in early spring a great light appeared in the heavens and it was not that of the sun. It made a trail of flame against the blue and as twilight came it grew brighter and blazed more fiercely. It was a comet, wandering star passing the earth and filling the hearts of the people with grave misgivings.

> We, while the stars from heaven shall fall
> And mountains are on mountains hurled,
> Shall stand unmoved amidst them all
> And smile to see a burning world . . .

sang the Millerites, more confident than ever that the end was very near. One said he had beheld a jeweled crown in the night sky; another had seen the moon drip blood. Miller's calculations had fixed upon March twenty-first as doomsday. It came and went while anxious crowds of those who had been preparing themselves for ten years searched the heavens for the coming of the Lord. Then Miller's associates announced that an error had been made in the calculations and the true date was the twenty-second of October. Immediately preparations began again and with doubled fervor. Many an upstate farmer left his crops unharvested that summer—since they would inevitably be destroyed by the October flame. Many a merchant sold his shop for less than it was worth—hoping in his thrifty soul that he might take the money along when he was "caught up into the air." Throughout the mid-year heat housewives toiled to make white ascension robes for their families and themselves. Honest men published notices asking that they be informed of all debts they owed in order that they might pay them before it was too late. "Time is almost gone," they said.

On the evening of October twenty-second the Millerite

families ate a solemn supper—the children wide-eyed and fearful, their parents silent and devout. It was to be their last meal before the burning of the world and the coming of the Lord. After they had eaten they all put on the spotless raiment in which they expected to make their long journey through the air. As the hours wore on toward midnight, fateful moment when most assumed the end would come, the robed figures sought high unencumbered places whence they might easily be caught up. In Rochester the summit of Cobb's Hill was white with the expectant assembly. In the towns of the level lowlands many crouched miserably in the eaves that lined the steep slanting roofs, others climbed trees and all night gazed hopefully into the sky.

At last sunrise reddened the horizon. As the leaves of late autumn tumbled in the morning wind, white-faced, white-robed, the Millerites climbed down from the high places and walked slowly back over the paths which they had taken with hope and exaltation only a few hours before.

Considering each day mentioned in Biblical prophecy as a year, William Miller's preliminary figuring brought him to the number 2300 from which he was able to make other significant calculations. Here is his first calculation:

From the date of the commandment to rebuild
    Jerusalem, B.C. 457 to the crucifixion of
    Christ, 70 weeks, or 490 years   490
From the crucifixion of Christ to taking away
    the daily abomination which is supposed to
    signify Paganism   475
From taking away of Pagan rites to setting up
    the abomination of desolation, or Papal Civil
    Rule   30
From setting up of the Papal abomination to
    the end thereof   1260
From taking away of Papal Civil Rule to the
    first resurrection and the End of the World
    in 1843   45
                            ————

These being added present the sum of the years   2300

Subtracting from 2300 the seventy weeks of years, 490,
up to the crucifixion of Christ and adding to the resultant
figure the years of the Savior's life, 33, gives the date of the
end of the world as A.D. 1843.

Or merely subtracting from the 2300 previously arrived at
the date of the commandment to rebuild Jerusalem, B.C.
457, at once gives the date of the end of the world—1843.

Or simply add to the second item of the first calculation
above, 475, the number of years in the Savior's life plus
Daniel's number, 1335, and the date of the end of the world
is obviously 1843.

19

Children
of the Kingdom

THIS IS A TALE NOT ONLY OF CONSCIENTIOUS
Yankee craftsmanship and business acumen but also of such
courageous social experiment as the world has witnessed but
once. The American businessman may know that the firm
now incorporated as Oneida, Ltd., and devoted to the manufacture of silverware, began as a stock company in 1881.
He may know that it started with a capital of 600,000 dollars, which has grown, despite strenuous competition, to
several millions. But he probably does not know that the
business began some years before its incorporation and
served to swell the coffers of the Oneida Community, which
for thirty-eight years carried on a materially successful communistic experiment in America.

Community Plate is still made by the descendants of
those who began its manufacture in 1877. In its expansion,
however, the company has come to be associated with three
place names—Oneida, the nearest city; Sherrill, home of the
factory workers who make Community Plate; and Kenwood.

People who have visited Kenwood do not think of it as
a town but as a house. They have learned to call the house

"The Mansion," and while they know that other residences are grouped about it, they never hear the name Kenwood but that the low-spreading, balanced red-brick structure enters their memories. About a hundred yards wide and almost as deep, it stands on a knoll, surrounded by a wide expanse of grass, and framed unevenly by old elms, maples and hemlocks. Under its central gable, crowned by a cupola, is a one-story pillared entry. Wings are set back from this middle structure, each of them supporting a square side tower a story higher than the rest of the building. The wing on the right, built around 1870, is simple, undecorated, of a classic New England severity, but the left wing, built a few years later, is decorated with dormers and with carved wooden lintels above each window.

The interior holds a central hall, at the end of which lie a big communal living room and a larger dining hall. All the residents of The Mansion and many who live in the houses nearby come here for meals. On the second floor are the large library and the old community meeting room, the latter preserved almost exactly as it was in the seventies. The other rooms, small but with high ceilings, each once the dwelling of a member of the Community, have been grouped into family apartments save for a few single guest rooms. Many of them look out on a grassy court such as one seldom sees outside of England.

The Mansion was built about eighty years ago by American communists as a communal dwelling. It is now occupied by a few of its original residents and by many of their progeny, and is run by Oneida, Ltd., as a community clubhouse, apartment hotel, and guesthouse. In it and in the houses near it live most of the descendants of the Oneida Community, all but a dozen or so of them employed by

Kenwood Mansion near Oneida

Oneida, Ltd., in the executive and white-collar positions afforded by the plated-silver business. It was as their guest that I lived in The Mansion several years ago, observed their ways of life and heard the story that is their background.

When Pierrepont B. Noyes walked into my room in The Mansion on my first evening there, I felt, by those channels through which the forces of personality move, the impact of an extraordinary man. He is tall and walks with the sure movement of an athletic body. In spite of his white hair and rugged, strong-lined face, he has an engaging openness that is both eager and youthful. He told me that the rest of the children of The Family, the old community's name for itself, would be along shortly, and soon they began to arrive.

The "children" were all past middle age. I had been warned that I was to meet so many people named Noyes that my head would swim. I was bewildered after the first few introductions—"Mr. Noyes, Mrs. Noyes, Mr. Noyes, Mr. Noyes, Mr. Noyes, Mrs. Noyes."

A white-haired lady laughed at me. "My father" [he was John Humphrey Noyes, the founder] "had ten children, each by a different mother," she said. "Most of them are here tonight. Other men of the community were almost as prolific. If you'd like to be more confused, I'll tell you that my husband and I, who are unrelated to each other, have a common half-brother."

"I couldn't be more confused," I said. "Do all the children of—of—"

"The stirpicultural experiment," she said, her eyes dancing. "That's what they called it."

"Do they all live here?"

"No, indeed. Only if they want to. There's Kenneth

Hayes Miller, the painter, whom you must have known in New York. He's taught most of our good American painters, I think. And lots of others. But there's always a job at Oneida, Ltd., for us or our children. That's brought a good many back to the fold."

"How many children were there in all?" I asked.

"Fifty-eight," she said, "and fifty-four of them were 'planned.' You'll find out what that means. But you can see that with our children and grandchildren we make up quite a group."

I cannot, of course, report in full the conversation that went on that night at dinner at The Mansion. There were too many stories, too many opinions. But gradually I began to get general impressions. The Family loved to talk about themselves. Perhaps their common origin outside of the wedlock recognized by society served to help them to an honest perspective, possibly their heritage of eager minds in strong bodies gave them their impersonal, humorous attitude toward themselves and their immediate ancestors. Whatever the cause, I was enchanted by these people. Most of them were big—I sensed the physical vitality in them; all of them were intelligent; and many of them were blessed with understanding sensitivity. Living in Kenwood, off the main lines of communication, traveling little, they yet succeeded in being sophisticated in the best sense of the word. They were people of taste, poised and articulate. All this they would seriously deny, satirically pointing out their own faults, belittling their virtues. They love to apply the psychoanalytical yardstick to themselves and to their parents.

Strong in their amused admiration for the combination of religious fanaticism and Yankee initiative which brought them into the world, they pointed out that they themselves had only a certain New England shrewdness left. Few of them belonged to churches. Most of them relaxed in a comfortable agnosticism. None of them possessed the religious power and drive which made the Oneida Community.

I found that they were not telling the whole truth when they spoke of their heritage being chiefly competence in running the silver-plate business. This they undoubtedly inherited, and the fact that they fitted a doctor into the job of head of the advertising department, a man without artistic education into the job of head designer, a scholar trained in the classics into an efficiency expert, is an interesting and iconoclastic comment on modern business methods. A member of The Family would be shifted around in the business until his superiors believed he suited his job, then promoted as he showed ability. But there could be no selection of the "best-trained man for the job" here. The man had to adapt himself to his work after he got it. Meanwhile, the business went on being thoroughly successful.

The Family turned the evangelist fervor of their parents into other channels. The Yankee penchant for dreaming found varied outlets among them. There was not one of them in whom the creative urge lay dormant. For example, P. B. Noyes himself, successful executive and president of the silver company, was a novelist. His daughter was a novelist. A shy little woman who sat near me wrote verse that appeared chiefly in the *Atlantic Monthly*. Edith Kinsley was a painter. Her mother, at the age of seventy-six, had taken up painting and, being dissatisfied with it as a medium of artistic expression for herself, had invented the braiding of picture-tapestries. With the mystic verses of Spenser, Coleridge, de la Mare as her inspiration, she braided such loveliness of color and form into her work that collectors begged her for it. The advertising man, who reminded me of the days when Community Plate was advertised by Coles Phillips' posters and asked me if I thought a similar campaign advisable in the present day, was a gifted sculptor in his spare time. And a sweet, white-haired lady who joked them all with charming aplomb said "we creative artists of Kenwood" with just enough amused edge to get me to ask her the inevitable "And what do *you* do?" so that she might reply, "I write for *True Confessions.*"

"One of the chief ways in which we differ from other middle-class groups of people of our circumstances," said a tall blond woman, "is that there is no gallantry in Kenwood. After the Break-Up, when the eugenic and communist experiment was at an end, the value of extreme respectability was high. Even today an occasional idiot leers at one of us and says, 'And what goes on at the Community *now*?' The result of our desire to conform was that the pendulum swung as far as it could away from sex. There's no flirting at Kenwood. At our parties the men go off in a corner and talk shop or sport—the women amuse themselves as best they can. We have comradeship, intellectual companionship from our men, but not an admiring glance. No one even bows us through doors. Once the people of Kenwood acted that way because they were afraid of public opinion. Now it's a habit."

P. B. Noyes laughed. "We don't see as many new faces as we should, I guess. Kenwood wakes up only once a year—for agents' week."

"Even then," protested the woman, "you've always got the agents in conference telling them how to sell silver on the road or you've got them playing golf."

"Don't let her fool you," said one of the men. "Agents'

week is a gay time here. And you should see how the agents (our name for our traveling salesmen since the old Community days) enjoy it. They look forward all year to living at The Mansion, associating with The Family, playing golf and drinking highballs."

"Look here," I said. "I'll never understand you people unless I understand what produced you. Your parents are not to be known through the few words printed about them. You knew them—you tell me about them."

"I've told him we'll give him everything except the diaries," said P. B. "You know there are still a few of the grandchildren who look on their parents' origins as not quite respectable. So we're delaying the publication of the diaries until the great-grandchildren are adults. By that time they'll be proud of their ancestors. This is more fun for us than it is for you, I guess. We'd rather talk about the Community than eat."

This is the story the children of the Oneida Community put together for me that night:

John Humphrey Noyes was a red-headed, gray-eyed divinity student at New Haven in 1833 when the tale begins. A graduate of Dartmouth, he had begun his theological studies at Andover but an inner voice which he recognized as that of God had bade him change to Yale. It was this voice, too, which revealed to him that Christ, for whose second coming so many were preparing, had really returned to the earth some thirty-seven years after He had left it. Thus, according to Biblical prophecy, the Kingdom of God was at hand, the intervention of Christ for our sins was no longer necessary for redemption, and he who wished might live perfectly, sinlessly, in a state of blessedness. Back home in Putney,

Vermont, John's mother worried lest he be losing his mind. But John Humphrey Noyes had started to preach the new doctrine of Perfectionism and he continued telling all who would listen that surely they might live now without sin.

Doubt assailed even the mind of the fanatic preacher himself, however, when, on his arrival at Brimfield, Massachusetts, accompanied by Simon Lovett, another young advocate of the faith, he found there a group of singularly free-mannered women, "handsome, brilliant, young." It almost overcame him when Hannah Tarbell, seated beside him before the fire in her father's house, kissed him passionately.

"That night while on my bed in prayer," he wrote later, "I got a clear view of the situation and I received what I believed to be 'orders' to withdraw. I left the next morning alone, without making known my intentions to anyone, and took a bee-line on foot through snow and cold—below zero —to Putney, sixty miles distant, which I reached within twenty-four hours."

This panic-stricken flight across the snow may have saved Noyes but it left Lovett at the mercy of the adversary. Two days later Mary Lincoln and Maria Brown, fanatically inspired by the young man's preaching, sought his room at midnight. Their purpose, "by no means carnal," was "a crowning demonstration of the spirit triumphing over the flesh." "But as usually happens in such presumptuous experiments," Noyes wrote, "in the end the flesh triumphed over the spirit." Under the pitiless blast of the scandal Mary Lincoln came to believe that for her sin God was about to destroy Brimfield with fire from heaven. To avert this catastrophe she and her best friend, Flavilla Howard, set forth at nightfall to scale the neighboring mountain through slippery mud and driving rain. At dawn they threw their clothing from them as they ran to stand naked on the summit calling upon Jehovah to stay his avenging bolts.

As a result of their intercession, they afterwards said, the city was saved.

Noyes was to suffer one more defeat from the arch-enemy before the conquering revelation that was to free him and his followers. George and Mary Cragin, ardent believers in Perfect Living, had gone to stay in the house of another convert, Abram Smith, and there Mary had lived as wife to both men. Noyes, who had contracted a conventional marriage and settled in Putney, had visited the trio and rebuked them severely, urging the Cragins to leave and join him at Putney. This they did and the Vermont group were living quite perfectly until Noyes one evening took Mary Cragin for a walk. After that he realized the necessity for further divine guidance on the relationships between male and female Perfectionists.

The result of his prayers (his rationalizations, say some of his children) was the discovery that in the Kingdom of God all beings must love each other equally well—and that this law applies as well to physical manifestations as to spiritual affections. Thus Complex Marriage was born, the working basis for the world's one great experiment in human eugenics.

Putney, Vermont, has ever been a respectable, God-fearing town. Only a little more than a decade ago Putney sent a summer-theater group kiting because the young actresses appeared on its neat streets in shorts. It was a consistent gesture, for a hundred years before the good citizens had rebelled against the scandalous goings-on of the Perfectionists. That rebellion caused the removal of Noyes and his followers to Oneida and the establishment of a communist group enterprise in the center of York State.

The Perfectionists chose well when they selected the land of Jonathan Burt, Perfectionist farmer, at Oneida. It was good soil and the gentle hills around it, hiding one valley from the next, promised the liberty to live as they believed, free from spying eyes.

Many like communities began their ambitious endeavor to find a panacea for social and economic ills during the first half of the nineteenth century. Only Oneida was able to support and advance itself. The others looked to the land for survival. The Oneida group had the common sense to realize that farming was not enough. One of their number, Sewell Newhouse, invented a wolf trap better and more efficient than any previously made. At once men, women, even children, were called on to do their share in the manufacturing and marketing. The business grew until they were selling the bulk of wild-animal traps made in America, and it is still profitable, though the manufacturing interest was sold to another firm some years ago. The Perfectionists were among the first to can fruit in glass jars. Their attempts to sell it met with immediate success despite the campaign of righteous housewives throughout York State and New England to boycott a business conducted by people whom they considered immoral. They turned to making sewing and embroidery silks, to hardware and plated silver. Profits accumulated, to be used for the common good. Then began a series of discoveries, amazing anticipations of ideas that were to be thought advanced almost a century later. They found that long hours were not necessary to success when everyone shared in the labor. So they shortened working hours. They found that females could work with males if properly attired for it. So they bobbed the hair of the women, and they dressed them in short skirts with pantalettes below—a costume so fetching and so sensible that it might well be revived. They found that children were happiest when they shared in the labor, too, and so they set them to work straightening the tangled chains used on the traps.

As economic survival became assured, Noyes and his associates turned their minds to social adjustment. There were between 250 and 300 members in the Community now, all carefully selected upon application, each having given up all his personal property to be shared with his fellow members. Naturally, in a group living so intimately, friction was bound to arise. To meet it a form of correction known as Mutual Criticism was instituted. If a member of the Community seemed antisocial it was suggested to him that he present himself at the meeting held every evening in the meeting room of The Mansion. There a committee of critics would offer him a criticism which, while not overlooking his virtues, calmly and dispassionately enumerated and explained his faults. These criticisms are surprisingly like psychoanalytic reports today. Some of them are amusing and revealing character studies.

There are few people who have not known a Mr. A. and felt more exasperation with him than is expressed in the tempered judgments of these three critics:

Critic Number 1: Mr. A. is impetuous and positive in his manner, and is deficient in persuasiveness. He takes a position that you are not prepared for, and announces it without any circumlocution whatever, and though you are not sure but that he is correct, you naturally resist being jerked into the admission of it. He has a kind of honesty that strips everything of romance, and this is apt to revolt you. He might have the same independence and honesty with more tact.

Critic Number 2: The prevailing trait in Mr. A's character amounting almost to idiosyncrasy is directness. He is direct in everything he does—in his religious pursuits, his thought, his speech and his actions. This is in general a good quality, giving intensity, singleness of eye, and consequent success. But in our social intercourse this trait needs some modification. It will not do in conversation to drive straight at a topic and think of nothing else. There are many side-considerations growing out of our personal relations and the demands of social harmony. Mr. A.'s excessive directness sometimes causes him to forget everything but his subject, and leads him into unnecessary discord.

Critic Number 3: Mr. A. should make it more of an object to think and to speak harmoniously with others. Suppose that he forms an opinion which he wants to express, but has reason to think it will not fall pleasantly into C.'s mind. In such a case true consideration requires not that he should suppress his opinion or that he should agree with C., but that he should broach his opinion moderately—make some stairs for C. to descend on and not drop him right down with a jolt. All our speech should have the most delicate reference to harmony. With a quick ear for harmony and a heart that values it as God does, Mr. A. might be just as independent as he is now and yet find a way to express himself musically.

And it would be hard not to be a little bit in love with the lively Miss E., even while sympathizing with those whose tranquility she invaded:

E. is remarkably outspoken and impulsive, consequently her faults are decided and well known. She is a fine specimen of the vital temperament, has great exuberance of animal spirits, would live on laughing and frolic, is ardent in her affections, and lively in her antipathies. In the circumstances of ordinary life she would not have been corrected of her faults, simply parental authority would not have been sufficient. She would have ruled all around her, and henpecked her husband to the last degree. But the Community is too much for her, especially as she is wise enough to give herself up to its criticism.

The elderly people criticize her for disrespect and inattention. She will fly through a room perhaps on some impulsive errand of generosity, leave both doors open and half knock down anybody in her way.

Her laughing propensity is criticized. Some think she could dispense with half her usual indulgence, while one recommends as a compromise that she should cease laughing at others' calamities.

She has a touch of vanity, likes to look in the glass, and plumes herself on her power of charming.

Her wonderful exuberance, gaiety and impetuosity are her gift, the inheritances of her youth and constitution, and no one would have these qualities changed. Like many another good passion these would be bad if allowed to act under the influence of selfishness, but of themselves they are much to be prized in society.

Though E. is zealous, industrious and useful, we should miss her more for what she is than for what she does. We must cure her of her coarseness and teach her to be gay without being rude, respectful without being dull.

Mutual Criticisms met with enthusiastic approval. So beneficial were they considered that frequently members, feeling out of harmony, offered themselves for criticism, listened with humility, and returned to their duties refreshed and reinspired toward the perfect ideal. The method was even used to help people physically and the legend is still told gleefully of how the communists cured an epidemic of diphtheria with cracked ice and criticisms. The ice relieved the throats of the victims and the criticisms, made unusually hot in the effort to save, caused many a man to burst into an embarrassed sweat and so broke up his fever.

"When I was about two years old—I have been told—I was a bad little boy," said P. B. Noyes. "So my elders gathered a half-dozen other little boys of about my age around me in a room and bade them report on how sinful I was. It is said that I did much better after that."

"And when I was four," said one of the ladies, "I received a criticism for losing my enthusiasm for my work in the chain room. At first I had liked untangling the chains. Then it bored me. After my criticism I went at the work with new spirit."

Criticism was felt to have a definite cleansing value. Agents, members of the Community whose duty it was to travel about in the outside world selling its products, were clothed for their missions from the general wardrobe. When they returned to Kenwood after the defilement of association with unbelieving capitalists, it was an infrangible rule that each must take a Turkish bath (an excellent one had been established in the basement of The Mansion), receive a complete change of clothing, and submit himself to a criticism before being allowed to associate with the rest of The Family.

Life in the Oneida Community must have been rich and full and pleasant during the sixties and seventies. The sweet spirit and honesty of the communists had brought them the respect, even the affection, of many of their neighbors. Visitors were welcomed with sincerity and hundreds of York Staters made pilgrimages to Kenwood to partake of the lavish Oneida Community Sunday dinner, served at many large round tables which had stationary rims for the eaters' plates and revolving centers which passed all dishes of food in rapid succession. "This place has a sweet clean smell," said one of the visitors, and a woman communist softly replied, "It is the odor of crushed selfishness."

The land was rich with harvest. Men and women, together among the peach trees, in the factory, found work good and looked forward to the social pleasures of the evening. Sometimes there was a concert and the large orchestra, recruited from members, played from Beethoven and Bach, and there were solos, *Flee as a Bird to the Mountain, The Carrier Dove*. Sometimes there would be a play and the boards of the auditorium would feel the tread of a communist Hamlet. Most popular of all was the production of *H.M.S. Pinafore*, written by the Community's distinguished contemporaries, Gilbert and Sullivan. There are still legends of how magnificent was the performance of the communist who played Sir Joseph Porter.

And after these communal pleasures were over, came

those ecstatic practices which held in themselves the germ of the Community's immortality and of its destruction, practices misunderstood by most of the outside world and misinterpreted into a mass of pornographic folklore that still hangs like a foul mist about the environs of Oneida.

Having subscribed to the theory of Complex Marriage, in which every woman of the Community was, potentially at least, the wife of every man, Noyes began to see in it more than the Christian edict "Love one another" physically applied. With that strange mixture of vision and common sense which characterized him, he saw the opportunity for the beginnings of a superior race. The result of his persuasive arguments toward that end was a meeting of the young people of the Community at which thirty-eight young men signed this document:

> The undersigned desire you may feel that we most heartily sympathize with your purposes in regard to scientific propagation, and offer ourselves to be used in forming any combinations that may seem to you desirable. We claim no rights. We ask no privileges. We desire to be servants of the truth. With a prayer that the grace of God will help us in this resolution, we are your true soldiers.

And fifty-three of the young women at the same time subscribed to these remarkable resolutions:

> 1. That we do not belong to *ourselves* in any respect, that we *do* belong first to *God* and second to Mr. Noyes as God's true representative.
> 2. That we have no rights or personal feelings in regard to childbearing which shall in the least degree

oppose or embarrass him in his choice of scientific combinations.

3. That we will put aside all envy, childishness, and self-seeking, and rejoice with those who are chosen candidates; that we will, if necessary, become martyrs to science, and cheerfully resign all desires to become mothers, if for any reason Mr. Noyes deems us unfit material for propagation. Above all, we offer ourselves "living sacrifices" to God and true Communism.

The inspired teaching of Noyes and the co-operative acquiescence of his followers led to one of the most interesting social programs in the world's history.

Sexual intercourse at the Oneida Community was divided (as mankind has always divided it, although rarely admitting the distinction) into acts for a propagative purpose and acts for social pleasure. All sexual activities were supervised by the Central Committee of which Dr. Theodore Noyes, the founder's eldest son and a graduate of Yale Medical school, was an important member. If any man of the Community wished to share the joys of the flesh with any woman of the group, merely for the sake of those joys, he applied to the Central Committee. The Committee were lenient enough with such requests, usually acting as a go-between, sometimes saving the man the embarrassment of receiving a refusal in person. Or a woman might make such a proposal to a man through the Committee. The consent of the man or woman chosen was necessary—and approval of the Committee. These obtained, the man presented himself at the woman's door at bedtime and spent an hour or two in her room before returning to his own room for the night.

Naturally, if the eugenic experiment was to be successful,

contraceptive methods were necessary to prevent these merely social unions from bearing fruit. The system used by the communists, and ardently recommended and defended by John Humphrey Noyes, is defined by the term by which it is usually technically described—"male continence." It stipulated the avoidance of the sensual crisis, thereby usually insuring the retention of the human seed, and, it was claimed, prolonging enjoyment of the act. That this method was successful seems proved by the record of only four "unplanned" births out of a total of fifty-eight. It was attacked by contemporary scientists on the grounds that it tended to make men nervous and endangered their health, but Dr. Theodore Noyes, in a surprisingly frank and seemingly unbiased report, stated that of all the men in the community he had found but two who might possibly have been adversely affected by it.

If, however, a man or a woman wished to have a child by a chosen partner and made application to the Committee the matter was taken under more serious advisement. The Committee investigated the background and heredity of each of the proposed parents, weighed their physical and mental attributes, discussed their dispositions and talents. If the conclusions were that the offspring of the projected union would be a superior child, the Committee approved the application and the man and the woman met each night until pregnancy was achieved. During fifteen months when the stirpicultural experiment was at its height (a time coincidental with the establishment of financial prosperity), nine applications for parenthood were vetoed by the Committee, forty-two approved. In some cases the Committee recommended the mating of couples who they thought had complementary qualities which would be highly desirable in offspring.

Naturally the one defection most feared in the Oneida reproductive scheme was falling in love. "Special Love" the communists called it, and it was considered one of the more heinous sins, denying the theory of equal love for everybody and interfering with the eugenic program. There is a powerful tragedy in the still-remembered story of the young man and young woman who were most loved of all the Community, most often pointed out as models of religious demeanor and social conduct. The diphtheria epidemic took them from the world within a few days of each other and their grieving friends, disposing of their effects, found two diaries in which their guilt of Special Love was all too pathetically betrayed. The offending portions of the diaries were forthwith read before the evening assembly amid a profound hush. The shock and sorrow caused by the secret sin affected the whole Community for a long time.

The Community had a very sensible way of dealing with the problem of Special Love. One of the more well-to-do communists had been a farmer at Wallingford, Connecticut, before being admitted at Oneida. Noyes had seen the value of keeping his lands for Community use and they were never employed to greater advantage, from his point of view, than when they served as a land of exile, a kind of Devil's Island, for one of a pair of sinful lovers. Many a growing romance suddenly found itself stunted by the edict that the young man's services were needed immediately on the farms at Wallingford. One proud fellow committed the double sin of loving one girl too much and another too little. Since his feelings were obvious from his conduct, the young man one day learned that his loved one was in Wallingford and that the Committee recommended, as a sort of punishment for his sin, that he become a father by the girl whom he did not like. So strong were the sanctions of the Committee that the young man did not demur, and he and the unloved one became the forebears of some of the most attractive residents of Kenwood.

The Community also sought to avoid the sin of Special Love as applied to children. As soon as a child could walk he was sent to the Children's House where he lived and where, under the tutelage of expert teachers, his education was begun. The children, though they took the names of their fathers, were considered to be the charge of the entire Community and were not to receive special favors from the man and woman who gave them physical birth. The whole Community took an enthusiastic interest in their welfare, perhaps unconsciously trying to make up to them for the lack of the usual parental demonstrativeness. An extraordinary affection for children still characterizes life at Kenwood where golf foursomes and tea parties are made up, without condescension on anybody's part, of people ranging in age from twelve to seventy.

"We children had a happy time of it," said P. B., "and we did not miss family life as you know it. Nor, as I remember it, did our parents. I didn't have any special feeling for my father. He was a distant dignified figure, the leader of us all. With my mother it was different. I'm afraid she was guilty of Special Love once in a while, for she used to get me into her room and give me things to eat and do little things to please me. I felt a strong affection for her."

The Children's House at Kenwood not only anticipated the kindergarten in America, it was a forerunner of much that is now admirable in modern teaching. Sometimes when the children presented themselves for class instruction to the good Mr. Warne they were overjoyed to hear him announce that today would be "Walking School." Then off they would troop through glens and hills and suddenly Mr. Warne would stoop and pick up a fossil and talk about the earth and what it was made of and how it came to its present condition. Or he would point out a bird and tell them of the state from which it migrated each spring, or pluck an ear of corn and tell how the land feeds its people.

Later, when the children were ready for higher education, the communists sent their boys to the master of the wardrobe to be fitted out for college. Yale was the most frequent choice and that institution later contributed in no small degree to the ultimate dissolution and abandonment of the communal experiments. The girls were occasionally sent to New York to be instructed in "accomplishments"—singing, playing the piano, painting.

By the time the older children were of college age, however, York State moralists were in full cry. Though the Community may seem to have given opportunity for licentiousness, every evidence proves that the great majority of its members lived in it idealistically with moderation and discipline and decorum. It is surprising that in a group of its size there should have been so few exceptions to the general rule. What divagations there were, however, were seized upon by the avid orthodox. Dirtier and dirtier grew the stories about the goings-on behind the walls of The Mansion. More and more outraged became the good church people of Utica and Rochester and Buffalo. And the spearpoint of the attack was one Professor John W. Mears of Hamilton College. Up and down the state he stamped, exposing, denouncing, vilifying, demanding that the state legislature wipe out this blot of immorality and licentiousness.

"In the Children's House we learned to hate Judas Iscariot, Benedict Arnold and Professor Mears as the great triumvirate of evil," said P. B.

While outside pressure was growing constantly stronger, the young men began coming back from Yale. Noyes and his associates were no cowards, and they might have fought off Mears and those he represented indefinitely. But a more deadly enemy was at work. The college boys had drunk of the springs of Darwin and Spencer and Huxley. They could no longer believe in their fathers' Perfectionism. And questioning that, they came to question, too, the right of the Community to deny them the privilege of falling in love, or to insist on what they regarded as indiscriminate mating.

With his prophetic insight, Noyes knew that the end was at hand, and with his intelligence and wisdom he knew what to do. On the twenty-sixth of August, 1880, he spoke to the assembled communists:

"I propose that we give up the practice of complex marriage, not as renouncing belief in the principles and prospective finality of that institution, but in deference to the public sentiment . . . that we place ourselves . . . on Paul's platform which allows marriage but prefers celibacy. . . . For my part I think we have great cause to be thankful for the toleration which has so long been accorded our audacious experiment. . . . Especially are we indebted to the authorities and people of our immediate neighborhood for kindness and protection. It will be a good and gracious thing

for us to relieve them at last of the burden of our un-
popularity and show the world that Christian Communism has self-control and flexibility enough to live
and flourish without complex marriage."

By the end of that year it had been decided to give up
nearly all phases of the communistic experiment. Conventional marriages were effected—with the purpose of advantage to the children held uppermost. The communal
property was divided as evenly as possible among the 225
members. The businesses conducted by the Community
were put in control of a stock company, the stock also
justly divided. And all these changes were accomplished
with so much honesty and impartiality that there has never
been a lawsuit by a member or even a complaint as to the
fairness of the procedure. Probably this was due in part to
the fact that only two members of the Community got
from it at the time of the Break-Up less than they put into
it. These were Noyes himself and the former owner of the
Wallingford farms. Disappointed but bravely adhering to
his beliefs, John Humphrey Noyes left Oneida with a few
followers and took residence at Niagara Falls in Canada.
His life ended in 1886, and his body was brought back to
Kenwood to lie beside those who had died believing in him.

"And when did the last member of the Original Community die?" I asked P. B. Noyes.

"They aren't all dead yet," he said. "One man and seven
women are still alive. Their ages range from seventy-six to
ninety-two. I've been trying to get Auntie Norton, who was

a member of the Central Committee, to say she'd talk to you. She'll see you tomorrow."

"She's still living here?"

"Lived in The Mansion practically all of her life. She won't tell you much about it, though. She is one of the women who, as they got older, were convinced that my father was wrong, and that they had been martyred in a fanatical experiment."

"They didn't think so when it was going on," said Dr. Hilda Noyes decisively. "There is basis for the belief that at least some of the women welcomed the variety of lovers."

"And what about the offspring?" I said, turning to her. "Eugenically speaking, was the experiment succesful?"

"Unfortunately, the records of fifty-eight children don't prove any general conclusions," she said. "Fifty-eight are too few specific cases. But, whether it's eugenic heredity or environment or chance, we children don't die—there are forty-seven of us still alive after the fifty-five years since the Break-Up—we don't have diseases, we're big and we're vigorous. Compare our record with the normal expectancy of death in New York State calculated by the insurance companies, and we're almost incredibly healthy and long-lived."

"Well," I said, "of course you had a good business left to take care of you." They all smiled.

"Not exactly," said P. B. "After my father died a group of spiritualist members of the Community controlled the company. They said they were in daily conference with my father and that he was directing them in the administration of the business. I was selling silver in New York then and making occasional visits up here. I heard complaints. One old stockholder summarized them all when he said, 'Spir-

itualism can't can corn.' So, with the minority, I put up a
fight for control of the company. It was a narrow squeak.
I thought I'd lost when I went to bed the evening the stock-
holders voted. But one woman who voted her dead father's
stock against us because he hadn't liked me, voted her own
stock for us, and we won. Since then we've been getting
along."

"Did the communistic idea go out completely with the
establishment of the stock company?" I said.

"Not exactly. We've had a liberal, perhaps I should say
radical, tradition to uphold. The idea here has been to pay
the bosses more than the employees—but only a little more.
We have depressed top wages in order to raise those at the
bottom. During the World War and immediately after,
when the cost of living was increasing rapidly, we instituted
a High Cost of Living wage paid in a separate envelope.
Whenever Bradstreet's Index showed a twenty-point advance in prices the worker received a one-percent increase in
his weekly wage."

"What happened when the war boom ended?"

"We had to give up the idea, but we established instead
a method of profit-sharing called the 'contingent wage.' We
turned over to our employees each year half the earnings of
the company after all obligations, including seven-percent
dividends on common stock and surplus, had been fulfilled.
One year the workers got almost a half-million dollars. We
paid a service wage, too, giving automatic increases with increasing length of employment. But all that was wiped out
by the depression. Now we're starting all over again. We
shall have profits to share with our workers and we will
share them. Why shouldn't we? Before the depression, we
had paid seven percent on our common stock for twenty-

five years, besides several stock dividends which amounted in all to over three hundred percent. It pays to share profits, pays everybody."

"How many of your workers are descended from the members of the Community?" I asked.

"Practically none, except in the executive positions. But most of them have been with us a long time. We've helped them buy homes in Sherrill, just across the creek. We've owned the land, and so we've been able to protect them from unscrupulous merchants who would like to start stores there. But we have welcomed honest merchants. There are, too, many recreational clubs, under the general title of Community Associated Clubs, in Sherrill. Every member of the Associated Clubs pays ten dollars a year and the company pays into the treasury a sum equal to the total of the dues collected. And in addition to taxes in Sherrill, we've contributed until they have as fine a school as you'll find in this section. We've got every worker covered with group insurance until he's sixty-five. Then he gets an annuity. I think you'll find that our workers have a good deal of faith in us. During the depression I finally had to tell them that every worker's pay must be cut a third. They greeted the announcement with a storm of applause."

My visit with ninety-two-year-old Auntie Norton the next day was almost as fruitless as prophesied. The little white-haired, blue-eyed lady who had once been on the Central Committee looked at me shrewdly, told me she would be glad to tell me anything I wanted to know about the old days, then skillfully evaded answering my questions.

"Life then was well ordered," she said finally. "We worked hard and on a schedule. Mr. Noyes was a distant man and he was quite strict. I never saw him laugh much. He saw to it that the place ran smoothly. I guess it was a little *too* well arranged—but then in a community like ours it *would* be, wouldn't it?"

I said it would.

"And life here was fanatic, too," she said, eying me severely. "It would be that, too, wouldn't it?"

"Yes," I said.

"I'll tell you one story about it, and then I'll have to go to bed, because I've been working hard today.

"There was a nice young man—I'll not tell you his name —and he was guilty of Special Love—for me. He used to try to see me and make love to me when no one was around. They found out about it and sent him to Wallingford. He was gone a long time—as much as two years, I guess. Then, when he came back, we were afraid to be seen together, and we hardly spoke when we came upon each other, but walked on quickly looking straight ahead. One afternoon I was in the cellar going toward the laundry, and in a long narrow hallway we met. He stopped, and I took one look and hurried by him as fast as I could. But as I passed him, he suddenly grabbed my hand. I tried to move on, but he kept hold—and he took my hand in both of his and raised it to his lips and kissed it. Then we both walked away—very fast.

"And now, young man, if you'll excuse me, I'll go on to bed. I enjoyed talking with you."

I sat in Fat's diner—eating an egg sandwich. I said "Fat, you've got the lowdown on what these Sherrill people think of their bosses. You hear 'em talk it every day at lunch and most nights after work. How about it?"

"They like the joint," said Fat, stomping over from the counter with the chili sauce. "They know the bosses mean what they say. They've seen the bosses take pay cuts and share the grief and they know that when there's money they'll be gettin' some of it."

"Aren't any of 'em dissatisfied?"

"They kick like any other gang o' workmen, if that's what you mean," said Fat, "but they stick just the same. Say, listen—I hear it all right here in this dump. My beer loosens up their tongues. Some of 'em are a tough lot—I've had to kick out one or two of 'em. But they think the bosses are O.K."

"Even the tough ones, eh?"

"We're sort o' proud o' being tough in these parts. A young feller come in here one day, said he was lookin' for work, but he heard we was kind o' tough customers. '*Tough*,' I says, an' I grabs the meat knife, 'I'll show you how tough we are.' "

Fat grabbed the long meat knife from the back of the counter, raised it high and brought it down with terrific force. It stuck quivering and bending in his leg.

I gasped.

"It's my wooden one," he said a little apologetically. "You know that lad ain't stopped runnin' yet.

"Yes, sir, we're tough around here, but the bosses are O.K. Why I went to New York with Mr. P. B. himself once to see the Dempsey-Firpo fight. We stayed at the Hotel Commodore. When it was time for dinner P. B. says, 'Let's go in,' and started for the dining room. I says, 'You go ahead, but I ain't goin' in there an' be waited on by some goddam sissie in a dress suit.' P. B. says, 'O.K.,' and we went out an' found a dump like this one only bigger and got some corn beef and cabbage. No airs about the bosses round here, I tell you."

"Do the workmen here know much about the old Community life," I said, "or don't they think much about it?"

"They know enough to know that plenty went on up at The Mansion."

"What do they think of it?"

"'T' tell the truth they're sort o' proud of it."

Before I left Kenwood, I walked with a friend past The Mansion and down across the railroad tracks and finally up a winding little road to the Community cemetery.

From the outside it looked like any other graveyard. The usual uninspired designs of the monument-makers recorded such data as are found on gravestones. But inside the circle of more recent marble balls and urns and crosses stood a sturdy phalanx of white stones, an army of thick-shouldered little slabs, not quite two feet high, each one identical with its neighbors save for the carving on it.

"They didn't care any more for death than they did for man-made conventions," said the man who was with me. "It was not important to them. And since every man living the Perfect Life in the Kingdom of God was of equal importance, they didn't believe in any fancy business about tombstones. Look at the names. You may find one you know, the name of a man who organized the living of over 250 people so well that for thirty-eight years there was no scandal, no divorce, no prostitution, no illegitimacy."

In the middle of a row I came finally upon a stone undistinguished from the rest which bore the name: JOHN HUMPHREY NOYES.

20

The Woman
Who Died Twice

"WHEN I WAS A YOUNG MAN IN DRYDEN," MY white-bearded grandfather once said to me, "I was a carpenter and they sent for me and some others to come over to Starkey on the west side of Seneca Lake to build a couple of houses for strange folk. They were religious people and followers of a woman prophet who had died some years before. We builders were all young fellows and lived in a barn loft while we were at Starkey. I can remember we nearly starved to death because the man who hired us was supposed to give us our keep and didn't make a very good job of it. Finally one morning I spoke to him about it. He looked sort of funny and said, 'I will ask The Friend.'

" 'Who's The Friend?' I said.

" 'Our spiritual leader in Christ.'

" 'But she's dead,' I said.

" 'She has left time,' he said, 'but I can talk to her and to God.'

"Then he went down by the shore of the lake and looked up into the sky and began making gestures upward and talking. By and by he came back and said that The Friend and God had told him we were to have codfish and potatoes for dinner.

"That was pretty lucky" my grandfather said, and he laughed, "because that was all he had in the house."

My grandfather's story was the first I had ever heard of the Jemimakins—popular name of the followers of The Friend. But years later I remembered it and it led me to the village of Penn Yan standing at the head of the placid waters of Lake Keuka and to the hospitable doorway of Arnold Potter who was kinder to me than I deserved and allowed me access to manuscripts and evidences never before offered to those who would tell the story of a vessel of human clay which had two successive tenants and suffered two deaths separated by over forty years.

When Jemima Wilkinson was eighteen years old in 1776 she caught a plague spread by the discharged British prisoners of the American Naval Ship *Columbus* and died. Her young body soon lost the fever's head and stiffened in cold rigor, then grew warm again and arose from the bed in which it lay. A mouth that had once been Jemima's spoke saying that Jemima Wilkinson of Cumberland, Rhode Island, had left the world of time's reckoning, that her earthly form had been chosen to serve as the vehicle of that Spirit of Life from God who should be known henceforth as The Publick Universal Friend.

The body served its new tenant well. It stood above medium height and it was straight and graceful. The Spirit of Life from God looked out through sparkling dark eyes set in a strong face which blood currents colored delightfully. Her hair, parted in the middle above her broad forehead, was thick and dark and fell in curled profusion upon her shoulders. Above it rested a broad-brimmed, low-crowned, white beaver hat, and from her strong neck, encircled by a white knotted silk scarf, hung an unconfined robe of white linen.

When The Publick Universal Friend in this garb spoke the messages of God to the sinful states of Rhode Island, Connecticut, Pennsylvania, there were crowds to listen. Her appearances were the more dramatic in that she was accompanied by her two apocalyptical witnesses—Sarah Richards, who professed to be "the prophet Daniel operating in these latter days in the female line," and James Parker, dressed in prophet's robes and proclaiming himself inspired by the spirit of Elijah. Sometimes Sarah Richards fell to the ground with a great writhing of limbs and heaving of the breast, and then arose to tell that she had had a "view" of heaven and now knew more clearly the will of God. And often James Parker drew his robes about him and prophesied solemnly. Standing between the two, The Universal Friend pleaded earnestly and spiritedly. Her graceful gestures and her dark beauty led many of her hearers to believe so thoroughly in her mission that they identified The Spirit of Life from God as no other than that of the returned Christ. This she did not affirm or deny and her failure to do the latter brought upon her charges of deception and blasphemy from the members of established religious sects about her. She held her own against them, however, for many of those who came to believe in her were persons of respect and importance. Judges, financiers, people of wealth and culture were among her friends and converts. For the first fourteen years of what she called her ministry she traveled about the northeastern states calling on their citizens to lead Christian lives and to place the love of God above all human affections. She became a forerunner of modern thought in her lack of respect for marriage bonds, frequently influencing her followers to leave lawful spouses who were not completely devoted to her and her teachings. This and her disciples' sincere conviction of her divine nature accumulated so much antagonism finally that she gave heed and sought a place of peace where she and those who wished to be with her might live holy lives.

She sent scouts into the Genesee country of New York State to seek a section in which she might direct the building of a New Jerusalem. They returned with stories of a land of thin blue lakes lying among wooded hills, a soil made rich by leaf mold and the waters of little streams. Then James Parker, with the courage and the robes of Elijah, set out, accompanied by a group of The Friend's followers, for that land and made a settlement there. A year later The Spirit of Life from God wrote him a letter:

The Woman Who Died Twice

Now if you have found a good country where you can live together and desire me to come live with you . . . there I should be willing to dwell what few remaining days I may spend in time for my soul hath long dwelt with them that hate peace. I am for peace but when I speak they all prepare for war. . . . I desire there might be a town where I may dwell and no one hold a possession there any longer or upon other terms than that of being true friends. . . . Those that are raising themselves up in opposition to me . . . if there is such already there I do desire them to depart . . . and dwell with those that walk the same round. Let them know I am determined not to dwell with revelers for I am weary of them. . . . I don't forget faithful souls. I bear them in my arms continually. But rebels and traitors and whatsoever loveth and maketh a lie I cannot abide.

So it was that The Publick Universal Friend ordered built for herself an open coach, the body of which was shaped like an upturned half-moon, and the seats of which were covered with a golden tapestry. From its top, held above her by slim rods, hung richly colored curtains and on panels in the front were engraved the letters U. F.

On the rear seat of this equipage The Friend rode from Philadelphia to the new house her people had built for her on the west side of Seneca Lake. There she lived and directed their living during the early days of her colony. On a beautiful horse, her saddle and stirrups studded with silver, the wide brim of her famous beaver hat tied down by a cord under her chin, she rode about the newly cleared lands, advising and correcting the 260 pioneers who had entrusted their lives and their souls to her guidance. Sometimes she dismounted and lent the strength and grace of the body that had been Jemima Wilkinson's to the swift alternations of the crosscut saw.

So richly did her community prosper that by 1791 they bought six square miles of land from those early real estate developers, Phelps and Gorham, and called their new township Jerusalem, the name it still bears. Soon a new dwelling for The Friend was under construction, a big, beautiful house in the New England tradition with fan windows over its fluted doorways, and large, stately rooms. It stands on a hilltop to the west of Lake Keuka whose waters are just visible from its windows. In its upper story was her boudoir made luxurious by her mirror with the carved letters U. F. on its elaborate frame, her clock, her armchair, her medicine case (a masterpiece of wood inlay), her silver salver, her warming pan, her perfume bottles. Seven girls, all young and pretty, waited upon her eagerly, jealous of the privilege of approaching the divine one.

But those who had been closely banded in adversity lost their unity as abundance came. The lands held communally became so valuable that those who lived on them coveted individual ownership. Some of The Friend's most trusted disciples left her, including the berobed Parker. Others, who in poverty had been willing to follow her doctrine of celibacy (the only point at which she differed in creed materially from most Christian evangelism of the time), married and had children. Serenely she went about among her flock, counseling the puzzled, nursing the ill, comforting those who were "leaving time" (her phrase for dying). Many an entry in the diary of Rachel Malin, her closest confidante, reads: "She left time in the arms of The Friend." And many another tells of the sacred visions of the writer, her associates, and The Friend herself as they sought guidance from God. Rachel writes poetically of a pure white rainbow in the north extending from east to west across the heavens and she records The Friend's vision that "the Son of Man spake with all the feathered folk."

Now the number of The Friend's enemies was growing. Settlers were filling the Finger Lakes country rapidly, and their churches attacked her with bitterness. Pioneer women who envied her luxurious way of life and her possessions spread evil tales about her. And James Parker, fallen angel of her Paradise, swore out a warrant in Canandaigua for her arrest, charging her with a blasphemous assumption of her own divinity. Twice she avoided apprehension, once through the speed of her horse and once through the stout resistance of her women companions who belabored the deputies to such advantage that the latter fled. Then she voluntarily appeared in court for her trial.

Unhappily, no complete record of that trial has been preserved. It might prove a strange parallel with the account of that other ordeal of a woman who saw visions and was burned for it in Rouen centuries before. For the story is that The Friend was beset with ensnaring questions and she answered them simply but so cleverly that she confounded her persecutors. The end is happy, however, for, turning to the spectators, she preached them so godly a sermon that the indictment was dropped and the judge, adjourning the court, said, "We have heard good counsel; and if we live in harmony with what this woman has told us, we shall be sure to be good people here, and reach a final rest in heaven."

This vindication did not stop the spread of tales maliciously intended to harm The Friend. It was rumored that she was neither man nor woman but had sexual characteristics of both. It was reported that once when she had spoken to a group of Seneca Indians, Chief Cornplanter had answered her in his native tongue and when she had said she could not understand he had turned from her in disgust, saying, "Jesus can understand all languages and if He were in you He would have replied to me."

Another unverified but popular chronicle tells how a man of the community climbed a tree at night to peep into The Friend's chamber but she saw him, ordered him down and sentenced him as penance to wear a cowbell tied about his neck for six weeks.

Most popular of all the malicious apocrypha about The Friend is the story still widely told of her alleged claim that she, like Jesus, could walk upon the water. She made the announcement, so the raconteurs of Yates County say, and set a Sunday afternoon for the time, a spot on the shore of Seneca Lake for the place. A great crowd of believers gathered to see this evidence of her divinity. The Friend drove up in her crescent-curved coach and stepped down upon the sands.

"I cannot do this thing unless ye have faith that I can," she said. "Have ye all faith?"

With one accord they all responded, "We have faith."

"Then if ye all believe that I can do this," she said, "no evidence is needed," and she returned to her coach and drove away.

Years were passing over the head of The Publick Universal Friend now and the body that had been Jemima Wilkinson's had begun to age. It swelled with dropsy and, despite the advice of her follower, Elizabeth Walker, who prescribed three or four wine glasses a day full of a strong solution of saltpeter, each to be followed by "twice the quantity of old strong cider strongly impregnated with scraped horse-radish and rolled mustard seed," it grew steadily weaker. The Friend was distressed, less with the disease than with her loss of physical charm. She became sterner in her insistence on chastity, more wrathful when her disciples gave unmistakable proof of their sins by having children. She allowed a Canandaigua artist to paint her portrait but was so disappointed in its realism that she forbade its being shown. In the presence of younger and prettier women she even gave some evidences of jealousy. But the faith of her people never wavered. Many of them, believing her immortal, were sadly surprised when The Spirit of Life from God at last departed its earthly residence. Their grief was pitiful, for their dependence had been not so much on formal creed (since they had been taught none) but on The Friend herself.

The day after The Friend left time was a Saturday, "meeting day," since she had adhered to the Hebrew Sabbath observance. Service was held as usual and as her people shook hands at its end, their usual custom, many of them were in a state of great exaltation, believing that after two more days their leader would rise from death. Hopefully they passed by the cherry-wood board on which The Friend's body was laid, pathetically they gazed on the calm face of her whom they looked upon as their Savior. Another service of prayer and devotion was held on Sunday. While it was going on four strangers in Quaker costume, two men and two women, drove up to the big house in a carriage that had evidently come a long way. After the shaking of hands, one of the two women mounted the horse block in the front yard and began to speak a solemn prophecy: The Friend's colony, she said, was a flight of steps supported by a single beam; now that this main prop had been taken away, the whole structure would collapse and come to nothing. Then the strange four climbed into their carriage and drove away.

When the third day had passed the body of The Friend was interred in the cellar of her house in a vault that had been built to receive it. There it rested for some time but there were those among her people who remembered that she had said she wished to be buried as Moses was, where no one might know her grave. On a black midnight two men came to the door of the big house on the hilltop. When they left they bore a heavy burden into the darkness. Now the resting place of the body that died twice is unknown save to two men, descendants of the two who committed it to the earth.

All this happened a long time ago. The Publick Universal Friend left time in 1819—but to this day, though the descendants of her people fulfilled the Quaker woman's prophecy by failing to observe her teachings, she is a live influence in the countryside around Seneca and Keuka lakes. Perhaps she lives most vigorously in the pretty village of Penn Yan where more than a score of families boast descent from the "Jemimakins." There live the Wagners and the Potters, the Baldwins, the Beaumonts and the Sheppards, the Barneses, the Botsfords and the Ingrahams, the Stones, the Sissons, the Hazards; the Millers, the Luthers, the Spencers, the Norrises; the Comstocks, the Gurnseys, the Dains, the Shearmans, the Hartwells and the Briggses. Speaking ill of The Friend—or ridiculing her—is not a wise thing in the pleasant, quiet town. A few years ago a man struck Arnold Potter's father in the face because he was under the mistaken impression that the elder Mr. Potter had moved the bones of The Friend. Naturally there are people in Penn Yan who believe that Jemima (as most of the town call her) was a charlatan and sometimes little feuds grow up—even after so many years.

I had been warned by a friend that the descendants of The Friend's people honored her memory by respecting too literally her desire that little should be known of her after her death. Therefore I was a little timorous when I presented myself at Arnold Potter's door. My perturbation waxed when he said:

"Come in. I know an Alabamian who wants to shoot you for what you wrote about his state."

His homemade grape brandy and the gracious presence of his sister, Mrs. Pierce, soon established, however, a cordiality that grew into friendship.

"Why don't you show him the portrait?" said Mrs. Pierce.

"I was waiting for your permission," said Arnold Potter.

So the canvas was brought down and I sat gazing at an unknown artist's reproduction of the spirited brown eyes, the strong nose, the firm chin, the body that was no longer slender and strong. Then they showed me her medicine box, her mirror, her perfume bottle.

"There's just a faint musk odor about it," said Arnold Potter.

"You can tell she liked nice things," said Mrs. Pierce.

Then we got into my car and drove into the country to a barn behind a farmhouse and there in the carriage shed was her crescent-moon coach with U. F. engraved on the front panels and the tapestries faded and rotting away. After that we went to the house on the hilltop, still sturdy, still occupied—and we walked over the slopes near it until we came to The Friend's burying ground. Here in the middle of a grove of hickories were many small field stones, one at the head, one at the foot of each grave—and no marks on them to tell whose body lay below.

"The Friend believed the marking of a gravestone a sign of vanity," said Arnold Potter.

We found one, though, on which with painful uncertainty some loving mourner had tried to inscribe a name, and others of a later period, after The Friend's death, which bore names and dates.

Finally we went back to Arnold Potter's home and read many letters and documents—strange relics of mystic visions, arguments over possessions, religious creeds. At last I found myself gazing at an oval piece of glass.

"It was the window over her face in her first coffin," said Arnold Potter, and I suddenly realized that he is one of the two who know the place of the secret burial.

"She is well taken care of," he said, with a smile.

21

The Magic Hill

IN THE COUNTRY AROUND THE QUIET TOWN OF Palmyra many drumlins rise steeply to their rounded tops. Like formal cones in a cubist drawing they give the land a curiously geometric appearance, at the same time artificial and mysterious. I have never had the same feeling about a country except once when, in the effort to understand a young woman of a past century, I went to Domremy where she was born. Like that far French province, this region of the glacier's molding is a land of shadows. And like the girl who lived in Domremy, one who lived here heard voices that are not of earth.

To this country out of the higher hills of Vermont once came a man and woman, tall, dark, "like a pair of splendid gypsies." They were Joseph and Lucy Smith. On their wagons rode four children. Descendants of soldiers in the American Revolution, these people were typical of the restless, pioneering spirit that followed it. In the quiet of the drumlin country they found some answer to the mysticism that was inherent in their souls and they settled themselves there upon a farm. The pioneer mystic, however, was not a successful husbandman. The activities of his speculative mind too frequently interfered with his plowing. And so this family, gradually increased by six more children, was poor in material things.

When they came to Palmyra their youngest child was Joseph, a sturdy ten-year-old with a sensitive face and dreaming blue eyes. He liked York State better than Vermont. Here were hills not too high for climbing and it was not long before his bare feet found their summits. Clothed in ragged jeans, held up by suspenders improvised out of sheeting, and a calico shirt, with his unkempt yellow hair sticking out from the holes in his torn hat, he wandered the country about his home and a feeling came to him that long ago other people had found these lonely hollows. He discovered that a witch-hazel twig held in his hand would bend down sharply when he held it over water, no matter how deep in the earth it lay. He felt magic in the rocks and, boylike, dreamed of buried treasure to which a stone of strange color and shape might lead him.

When Joseph was fifteen the hills around Palmyra echoed to a great shouting. The Methodists and the Baptists and the Presbyterians, feeling the influences that in this region cause men emphatically to proclaim their creeds, began a war of words. The farm lad listened gravely as they argued, and took the problem of his own belief out into the valley woods. He came from them white and shaking to tell such a story as had not been heard since the days of the prophets.

"Thick darkness gathered around me and it seemed to me for a time as if I were doomed. . . . I was ready to sink into despair and abandon myself to destruction—not to an imaginary ruin but to the power of some actual being from an unseen world. . . . Just at this moment . . . I saw a pillar of light exactly over my head, above the brightness of the sun. . . . I found myself delivered from the enemy which held me bound. When the light rested upon me I saw two personages whose brightness and glory defy all description, standing above me in the air. One of them spake unto me, calling me by name, and said, pointing to the other—'This is my beloved Son, hear Him.' "

Then the second being spoke to the boy, forbidding him to join any religious sect, saying that all their creeds were an abomination in his sight. When he had ceased Joseph came to himself. He was lying on his back, looking up into heaven.

Three years passed before Joseph again heard a voice from another world. Then one night in his little bedroom in the Smith farmhouse a light began to grow until it had surpassed the brightness of noon. In it, his feet not touching the floor, stood an angel wearing "a loose robe of most exquisite whiteness . . . a whiteness beyond anything earthly. . . . He had no other clothing. . . . I could see into his bosom. . . . His whole person was glorious . . . and his countenance truly like lightning."

The Angel said that his name was Moroni and that he had come to tell Joseph of a buried treasure, a book written upon plates of gold "giving an account of the former inhabitants of this continent." Beside it, he said, lay two stones in silver bows, fastened to a breastplate. These had been the magic talismans by whose power men had become seers in ancient times, and with their aid Joseph might read what was engraved on the golden surfaces. All these precious objects, Moroni said, lay beneath the earth at the summit of the hill of Cumorah, the highest of the drumlins near the Smith home.

Three times that night Moroni told this tale to the eighteen-year-old Joseph and on the next day while the boy worked near his father in the fields the Angel came again to repeat it.

So Joseph left the field and went to the place where the Angel had told him the plates were buried. On the west side of Cumorah Hill, near the top, he found a stone of considerable size, its center visible above the surrounding sod. Joseph dug the earth away from the edges and with a lever pried up the stone and tipped it on its side. Then his wondering eyes beheld that it had been a cover for a stone box. In that box now at his feet lay the gold plates and the stones in the silver bows just as the Angel had said. He would have picked them up and carried them away but Moroni appeared to him once more, saying that if Joseph would meet him at this spot and at this time each year for four years, the plates would then be released to him and he might make a translation of their contents.

In those next four years Joseph Smith grew taller and more powerful than most men. Few dared oppose him in tests of strength and bodily skill. None defeated him. And as each autumn began the youth and the Angel met on the summit of the high hill.

At last the fourth September came and Joseph and the Angel spoke together. After sunset, Moroni said, Joseph must come to the summit again and take up the book, and return to his home.

There was no moon that night, and the darkness was intense as the eager climber stumbled up the side of Cumorah. But people living as far as fifteen miles away saw a strange light in the heavens, a light that changed constantly, forming countless human shapes. From the northwest the watchers saw them coming, great armies marching diagonally across the black sky into the southwest and on out of sight.

Joseph lifted the gleaming plates from their box and bore them down the hill and away to the farmhouse where he lived. Then he began to decipher the oddly formed symbols cut into the gold. The letters were Egyptian in character and Joseph could not read them but when he put the stones in the silver bows before his eyes the English translation appeared below them.

It was a book of many words. The yellow pages (fastened together by three gold rings running through them near the edges) were eight inches long and seven inches wide and, though they were almost as thin as paper, the volume was half a foot in thickness.

It told a strange story. At the time of the confusion of

tongues and the dispersion of the peoples, it said, the followers of Jared wandered away from Babel and came at length to an ocean. On its shores they constructed eight barges and in them they set out upon the vast waters. The barges were crowded and would have been dark had they not been lighted by miraculously luminous stones which the voyagers had found in the sand as they embarked. For over eleven months the boats were afloat and then the colony landed on those shores which now are known as America. Here the Jaredites flourished for a time. Then came dissension that led to a great civil war. It ended with a battle on Cumorah Hill in which the opposing armies completely destroyed each other.

At about the time of this suicidal struggle, 590 B.C., the chronicle told Joseph, a Jewish prophet named Lehi, of the tribe of Manasseh, landed on the western coast of America with his followers. He had left Jerusalem about ten years before, had followed the shores of the Red Sea, then turned eastward across Arabia. At the Arabian Sea he and his colony had built a boat in which they embarked on a voyage that took them across the Indian Ocean and over the Pacific.

In America this colony, too, had met with dissension. Lehi had died and rival leaders strove for supremacy. Nephi, duly appointed successor to Lehi, led his followers into a prosperous, cultured, civilized existence. But Laman, oldest son of Lehi, and those who accepted him as prophet, fell under the curse of God. They became dark-skinned and nomadic, poverty-stricken in spirit, united only in their hatred of the Nephites. And again the hill of Cumorah saw the destruction of a people. In a great battle that surged about its summit the Lamanites massacred the entire

Nephite nation save one. Moroni alone escaped and it was he, "wandering for safety from place to place, daily expecting death," who, having completed the abridged history of his people begun on the golden plates by Mormon, his father, hid the chronicle beneath the earth at the very place where its subject had come to an heroic end.

Behind a curtain by which he had divided a downstairs room in the Smith farmhouse, Joseph finished dictating to his friends on the other side the story that is related in the *Book of Mormon*. Moroni had instructed him that the plates might be shown to no other human eye. He relented, however, before the book was returned to its resting place, and Joseph was allowed to show it to three of his best friends and later to eight witnesses who said, "We have seen and hefted, and know of a surety."

When the work of translation was finished Joseph and his friend Oliver Cowdery, instructed once more by Moroni, carried the book back up the hill of Cumorah. And when they had climbed a part of the way the hill opened and showed a cave in which there was a vast room made bright as day from some invisible source. There was a large table in the center of the room and on it they laid their golden burden. The floor of the room was piled high with other golden plates, "more than probably many waggon loads."

After the two men had come out of the hill into the sunlight the great cave closed silently behind them. The mission that Mormon had entrusted to his son, Moroni, had been accomplished.

This is the story as it is told by the people who live in the drumlin country. The members of the Church of the Latter-Day Saints—churches in Palmyra and Rochester and

The Magic Hill

Niagara Falls and Buffalo and many another York State town—can tell much more of it than their neighbors. They know the sequel, too, how Joseph formed the beginnings of their church out of his conviction that the *Book of Mormon* should be considered an addition to the revealed gospels of the Christian Bible and how he led those who believed with him westward away from the sneers and persecutions of an intolerant countryside. These are history. The story of Joseph and Moroni, true or false, is a folk story, as are all the narratives on which religious creeds are built. But the history is quite as fantastic as the mystic tale. The young dreamer, coming down the lovely green hill of Cumorah for the last time, could hardly have pictured himself in a lieutenant general's gold-braided uniform fourteen years later, riding a white charger at the head of his Nauvoo Legion of five thousand men. He could not then have foreseen that sultry June twilight in Carthage, Illinois, when the black-painted faces of a mob hysterical with hate and fear were the last images his eyes received as a storm of bullets flashed through his big body. Nor could he then have raised up in his youthful fancy a vision of the great six-towered temple beside an inland sea which was to be a shrine to his memory and to the story of his boyhood among the green drumlins near Palmyra.

I climbed the hill of Cumorah on an early summer day. Maud was with me and we laughed as we scrambled up the last few feet, arriving quite out of breath. Then we grew silent as we stood in the shadow of a tall mysterious figure. At the very summit long sheets of gray canvas flapped in the breeze veiling something that pushed far into the sky above us.

"Hello," said a hearty voice.

In a little hollow beneath the gray, ghostlike something stood a small tent with an awning in front of it, and beneath the awning sat a smiling, freckled, sandy-haired young man.

"Hello," we said and we walked down to him.

"Sit down," he said, and gave us camp chairs. We sat.

"I'm a missionary," he said, "sent here with a lot of others to work until this statue of Moroni is unveiled next week. I'm Elder Brooks."

"You aren't exactly what I thought a Mormon missionary would be," I said.

He laughed.

"I don't know what you thought but perhaps you didn't know that all the young men of our faith are brought up and educated with the idea that they will give up two years of their lives to missionary service. That's one reason why we're the fastest-growing Christian organization in the world. No other church can compare with us in the number of recent converts. I suppose you're acquainted with the gospel on which our belief is based?"

"Yes," said Maud in unbecoming haste. Elder Brooks looked at us ruefully.

"In that case you might be interested in reading it in full

in the *Book of Mormon*. I have some copies here I'm allowed to sell for a dollar."

"I'll take one," I said.

"I wonder if you're aware," said Elder Brooks, "that the members of our church are the healthiest people in the world. We have the highest birth rate and the lowest death rate. Did you know that we have made greater strides in education in Utah in the last quarter-century than has any other state in the Union? Do you realize that the members of the Church of the Latter-Day Saints have the highest percentage of homeowners of any people in the world? And has anyone told you that the number of divorces among us is only six a year per ten thousand?"

"No," I said faintly, "no one ever told me."

"You'll agree with me, I'm sure," said Elder Brooks, "that that religion is best which produces the best people."

"Oh, surely," said Maud, casting an anxious glance at me.

"Well, then," said the young man triumphantly and somewhat as if he were speaking by rote, "the Latter-Day Saints, according to the testimony of scholars, moralists, and statesmen of international note, are a healthy, industrious, intelligent, prosperous and virtuous people." He paused, then said solemnly, "By their fruits ye shall know them."

Maud and I were silent.

"There must be some questions you'd like to ask," said Elder Brooks briskly, his face lighting up with an enchanting freckled smile. "I seem to have been doing all the talking."

"Yes," I said, "how does Mormon account for the American Indians in his interpretation of what happened in America before Columbus came?"

He looked at me reproachfully. "I'm afraid you haven't read much about us, sir. The Indians are what is left of the

Lamanites—the fierce and degenerate people who destroyed the Nephites right on this very hill."

"Of course," I said, a little abashed.

"The Indians are only one of hundreds of corroborations of the *Book of Mormon* that have been made by modern anthropologists," said Elder Brooks. "They have found that horses existed on this continent before the coming of Europeans, just as the book says, that cement was used in building, that there are similarities between the ancient Hebrew and the languages of the American Indian, that——"

"May I ask a question?" said Maud eagerly.

"Why, of course," said Elder Brooks, smiling again.

"What about your underwear?" said Maud.

"What?" said Elder Brooks.

"Your underwear," said Maud gently.

"It's a phobia of hers," I said apologetically. "She collects underwear to finish her hooked rug."

"That wasn't what I meant at all," said Maud indignantly.

Suddenly Elder Brooks began to laugh and then Maud, too. I joined in but I didn't quite see why.

"You must mean the sacred garments," said the young man to Maud finally and with dignity.

"I suppose so," said Maud. "When I was in college we used to have assembly speakers who shouted about the menace of the Mormons and how they still practiced polygamy secretly and how you never could tell whether even your best boy friend was a Mormon and likely to betray you if you didn't contrive some way to get a look at his underwear." Again we all laughed.

The Magic Hill

"Well, there's a little more to it than you think," said Elder Brooks, his eyes dancing. "The orthodox Latter-Day Saint has worn a special undergarment approved by the heads of the church ever since the days of Joseph Smith. Then it was like a union suit—long arms and legs—the kind of thing a pioneer needed on the long trek west. But with prosperity and the coming of modern styles of dress the leaders have had visions which have allowed them to modify the holy garments. Now they're quite suited to the use of any healthy young people and not very different from what's in general use everywhere."

"We'll have to go," said Maud, rising. "Coley will be hungry as a bear by the time we get back and Tammany will never forgive me for leaving her alone so long."

"But you'll be back in two weeks for the unveiling," pleaded Elder Brooks.

"We'll try," I said.

"Look me up when you come," he said, and smiled again and waved his hand.

On the way home we decided we liked Elder Brooks.

The day of the unveiling was pitilessly hot. When I arrived a large field near the bottom of the hill was covered with countless automobiles left in orderly rows. Hundreds of them bore Utah license plates. I parked my car and rushed to a seat in the tremendous outdoor auditorium constructed on the flats below the summit on which the veiled statue stood. The canvas drooped listlessly in the still heat. The merciless sun shone on the faces of the audience. Thousands held newspapers over their heads for protection.

As I sat down four white-clad figures appeared at the foot of the towering canvas far above us. They raised long gleaming trumpets and stood silent for a moment in sharp relief against the blue sky. Then they began to play.

When they had finished a bearded, largely proportioned man who had somehow the look of a prophet stood up on the platform before us. In a deep resonant voice he announced a hymn and as the audience sang it I saw that beside him stood other big men of strong features and dignified bearing. I thought—these people have come back here to a country I have known a long time, in whose little towns I played ball games when I was a boy, a country I have always taken as a matter of course, an ordinary, folksy section. I thought of Mecca and Bethlehem and I suddenly realized that the minds and emotions of a million people over the world were turned at this moment to this hillside just out of Palmyra in York State.

The big crowd were all singing lustily now, led by a choir on the platform:

> When I leave this frail existence
> When I lay this mortal by,
> Father, Mother, may I meet you
> In your royal courts on high?
>
> Then at length when I've completed
> All you sent me forth to do
> With your mutual approbation,
> Let me come and dwell with you.

After the last chord crashed out there was a hush and suddenly the canvas fluttered down and flattened out on the ground, and high in the air above us stood a gleaming bronze Moroni clasping a book to his breast with his left hand and pointing heavenward with his right.

Then the big bearded man who had announced the hymn stepped forward and spoke:

"We stand on holy ground," he said.

22

Words through the Trumpet

WHEN THE JOHN FOXES MOVED IN 1847 FROM Rochester into a little frame farmhouse about thirty miles away at Hydesville, Arcadia Township, several of their neighbors felt called upon to warn them that their new dwelling was haunted. Indeed, Mrs. Fox must have heard more than once the story of Lucretia Pulver who had been hired girl for the John Bells when they lived there. Lucretia had told it around confidentially that one day a peddler came by with a pack of shining dippers and pans and beautiful dress materials and that Mrs. Bell took that moment to dispense with her servant's services. She was sorry, she said, but she did not need Lucretia any more; however in return for having wounded her feelings by discharging her so unexpectedly, she was buying for her a bright-colored piece of cloth which the peddler would deliver to her home the next day.

So Lucretia went home and waited but the peddler did not come to her house—nor did he, so far as anyone knows, ever rap at another door. In a few days Lucretia got a message from Mrs. Bell saying that she had changed her mind about not needing a hired girl and would like to continue their former arrangement.

Lucretia came back and went to work. A few days later the Bells decided to drive into Palmyra and spend the night with friends there. At midnight Lucretia was awakened in her second-story room by the sound of a slow, regular tread on the ground floor. Thinking that the Bells might have come home, she arose and peered down the stairs just in time to hear the footsteps pass the stairway and to realize that the walker was not visible. Panic-stricken she returned to her bed and, lying in it, heard the footsteps slowly descend the cellar stairs. Then there was silence. The next day the Bells returned and sent Lucretia on an errand to the cellar. As the trembling girl was obeying, her feet sank beneath her into a hole only partially filled with soft earth. When she reported this upstairs, Mrs. Bell said the hole had probably been made by rats.

The Bells did not stay in the little house long. But before they left, Mrs. Bell had told Lucretia "that she often heard footsteps of a man walking about the house all night," and that she had become "sick of her life."

After the Bells had moved away the Michael Weekmans took the place, so the Hydesville housewives told Mrs. Fox, but not for long. Great raps that fairly shook the house would come upon the outside door late at night, but no matter how quickly it was opened, there was no one there. And the little Weekman girl more than once ran screaming through the darkness to her parents to tell them how a cold hand had passed over her face as she lay in bed.

But the Foxes were good Methodists and unimpressed by these tales of the supernatural. They did not believe in ghosts or haunted houses and, since it was already mid-December, they busied themselves in the house preparing a happy Christmas celebration for little Margaret and Katherine and, possibly, grown-up Leah if she and her husband could come out from Rochester.

It was after New Year's Day that Mr. Fox first heard light knockings in the bedrooms late at night. When his wife and children heard them and asked about them, he explained a little uncomfortably that a cobbler lived next door and he must sit up late pounding at his shoes. But on the awful night that fearful groans sounded throughout the house and it seemed from the noise that a heavy body was being dragged through the rooms and down the stairs to the cellar whence came the gruesome scrape of a shovel, the Fox parents did not try to explain. They told the frightened little girls to ignore the strange noises as they themselves intended to do.

Another month went by and the knockings continued. Then, on the evening of March 31, 1848, came a discovery that has since puzzled hundreds of thousands of people. Little Katherine had become so used to the knocking that she jested with it, calling out gaily, "Here, Mr. Splitfoot, do as I do," and snapped her fingers three times. Three distinct raps sounded on the wall nearest her. Then she held out four fingers and said, "How many fingers am I holding out?" There were four raps and Katherine cried out, "Only look, Mother, it can see as well as hear."

Then Mrs. Fox asked the ages of the children and the strange intelligence counted out the years. Finally she said, "Are you a man?" and there was no response. "Are you a spirit?" she said, and there was a storm of rapping.

Then they called in the neighbors and the spirit rapped

replies to them. It was neighbor William Duesler who, Hamletlike, was the first to suspect that the spirit's return was occasioned by the nature of his taking-off. Having formed a simple code by numbering the letters of the alphabet, he learned through the rappings that the spirit's name was Charles B. Rosma, that he had been a peddler, that he had been murdered for his money in this house and buried in the cellar. Mr. Duesler thus reported his later research:

> I went into the cellar with several others and had them all leave the house over our heads, and then I asked, "If there has been a man buried in the cellar, manifest it by rapping or by any other sign." The moment I asked the question there was a sound like the falling of a stick, about a foot long and half an inch through, on the floor and in the bedroom over our heads. It did not seem to rebound at all; there was but one sound. . . . We all went upstairs and made a thorough search but could find nothing.

The next day digging in the cellar began, but the heavy rains of spring flooded the workers out. It was begun again as soon as dry weather came and under one of the walls the diggers found a plank covering a small depression. Under the plank they found human hair; part of a human skull, and quicklime, and the tale of the haunted house had reached its end.

But to many Americans the ghost story was the least impressive part of the narrative. Gradually it dawned on their excited minds that here in this little farmhouse, after centuries of skepticism, lay proof of human immortality and of the ability of mortal men to converse with those who had preceded them out of earthly life. A little girl had bridged the chasm of the grave. Again, after an interval of centuries, a Jewish wanderer who had been cruelly slain had returned from the dead to speak to a living woman.

Grown-up sister Leah hurried from Rochester to Hydesville. In her own account of the events that followed, the spirits forced her and her little sisters to give public demonstrations by refusing to continue to knock for them unless they could knock for the world at large. At any rate it was not long before Leah was exhibiting the children and their communications with those in the world of spirit. In Rochester their demonstrations led to a riot in Corinthian Hall during which "torpedoes" were exploded and the performers barely escaped the mob storming the stage. In Buffalo a number of learned physicians discovered that if the feet of the little girls were placed on separate chairs in front of them and their knees were firmly held, no raps could be heard, but Leah explained this by saying that the spirits were horrified at such brutal treatment of the children and that they refused, therefore, to perform.

Then came New York and the two little country girls were plunged into a highly interested world. James Fenimore Cooper, William Cullen Bryant, Alice Carey, George Bancroft, Bayard Taylor, all came to see them, were won by their natural charm, puzzled by their strange gifts. And Horace Greeley was so enchanted by them that he undertook to finance little Katherine's education in a private school.

In Philadelphia with her mother one autumn day in 1852 for the purpose of arranging a course in Spiritual Manifestations, Margaret met Elisha Kent Kane, thirty-two-year-old Arctic explorer, already famous for his expedition to relieve

Sir John Franklin in the ice-bound wastes. Though the girl was but eleven, Kane was at once strongly attracted to her. He followed her to Washington and back to New York. Her manager-sister opposed him strongly, but through his own sister's efforts he succeeded in having Margaret sent to Crookville School near Philadelphia. He had an artist paint her portrait and he carried the picture with him throughout his remarkable explorations in Grinnell Land in 1853. When he returned, despite the disapproval of his own family and of Leah, he continued to see Margaret often and finally persuaded her to go through an unconventional self-created marriage ceremony with him. Soon after this he made a trip to England and thence to Cuba in the hope of obtaining a rest and guarding his failing health. He was in Havana awaiting the arrival of his seventeen-year-old bride and her mother when, at the age of thirty-seven, he died.

Margaret was heartbroken. Out of respect for her dead husband's wishes she gave up her spiritualistic demonstrations and joined the Roman Catholic Church. She wore heavy mourning for the next fourteen years. By the end of that time, however, Kane's family having refused her funds the explorer had wished her to have, economic necessity forced her to return to her old ways. For a time she became the high priestess of a Spiritual Mansion established in Philadelphia in the interests of psychic research by Henry Seybert, but her benefactor soon died, leaving a fund for the testing of mediumistic phenomena. The first act of the administrator of the fund, Dr. Howard Horace Furness, famous Shakespeare scholar, was to investigate Margaret Fox and to declare her a complete fraud.

After that it was harder to obtain money from séances. Margaret and Katherine went to England for a while and, during their visit, Margaret demonstrated her psychic powers in the home of Thomas Carlyle.

Then the sisters, playing both ends against the middle, announced on their return to the United States that they would expose the methods by which they had become saints of the Spiritualist movement. And in New York at the Academy of Music, October 21, 1888, Margaret Fox gave a demonstration of the rappings by which she and her sister had given thousands belief in immortality and the hope of the renewal of their associations with loved ones beyond the grave. With her right foot bared, she showed the vast audience how she had made these noises with her big toe.

When she and Katherine were little children, she said later, they had been so amused by the story of the haunted house in which they lived that in their bed at night they had frightened their parents by dropping apples on the floor and snatching them back under the sheets by means of strings tied to them. Then each had discovered that she could make similar rapping noises by snapping the first joint of the big toe on her right foot. The older sister, Leah, Margaret continued, had taken advantage of their extreme youth and innocence to frighten them into prolonging the deception in the interests of increasing gate receipts. Then both she and her sister had been strongly influenced to keep their secret by the wonder and adulation in which they were held by the crowds before whom they performed.

These revelations did little to stem the tide of spiritualistic fervor that had been sweeping the country for forty years. There were now too many other mediums who claimed supernatural powers, too many thousands of people willing to testify to the truth of their revelations. The Spiritualists forgave Margaret and Katherine Fox their desertion.

They brushed aside the defection by explaining that the sisters were in desperate need of funds and that the spirits will not perform for those who use them to gain material ends. So to their deaths the Fox sisters remained among the Spiritualist elect, and now the little haunted house where they lived as children has been moved from Hydesville to the great Spiritualist camp at Lily Dale near York State's western border. It is the holy of holies, the Mecca of all good Spiritualists, the shrine of those who believe that we may talk with those who shall live though they have passed through that experience known to men as death.

I drove to Lily Dale from Chautauqua. The distance is only twenty miles or so and the road traverses a pleasant stretch of hills and valleys. In many ways Lily Dale is like Chautauqua: it is an enclosed settlement beside a little lake; a fee must be paid for the privilege of entering; the cottages line shaded streets, many of which afford no glimpse of the water.

I arrived at eleven in the morning and the man who sold me my entrance ticket told me I would find a public séance in progress at Inspiration Stump. Then pressing into my hands a printed program of the summer's activities and a newspaper entitled Dale *News,* he informed me that there were a lot of mighty nice folks living at Lily Dale this season and waved me onward through the gate. I parked my car in a field inside and began my walk toward the séance. Many of the Lily Dale cottages are bungalows, not so pretentious nor so high as the two-story Victorian summer dwellings of the Chautauquans. They squat beneath the leafy maples in so much shade that they seem to be in a twilight even in the middle of a clear day. In almost every window there is a card with big black letters on it announcing the name of the resident and below it such legends as Trance Medium, Psychic Reader, Trumpet Medium, Independent Slate-Writing, Psychometric, Clairvoyant, Clairaudient, Spiritual Healer. Feeling that I had completely shut myself off from any world I could conceive, I turned into a narrow trail through thick woods that led, so a sign informed me, to Inspiration Stump.

In less than five minutes I came to a clearing surrounded by very tall trees. In the center was a large stump about three feet high, and in concentric circles around the outer edges were a half-dozen rows of benches partially occupied by about fifty people. A bespectacled and rather sallow young man seemingly in his middle twenties was speaking. I slipped into a seat in the third row and listened.

"Now I get a vibration," said the young man, suddenly pointing a lean forefinger at a kindly-looking woman of middle age in the front row. "Does the name John mean something to you?"

"Yes," said the woman. "I had a cousin named John."

"And he's now in the spirit world?" asked the young man triumphantly.

"Yes."

"I seem to connect him with some kind of uniform," said the medium. "Was he a soldier?"

"Well, no," said the woman hesitantly, "but he used to wear a lodge uniform when they paraded."

"That's it," said the medium quickly. "I thought it was a lot fancier than a soldier suit. He died sort of early in life, didn't he?"

"I guess so—for our family," said the woman. "It was around sixty."

"And just before he died he had a lot of trouble breathing—his chest sort of filled up and his throat was congested—he had trouble breathing?"

"Yes," said the woman. "I wasn't there but that's what they told me."

"Well," said the medium, "he's standing right beside you now dressed in his lodge uniform and he says something about some business or other—something connected with some property or land and there are some papers about it—do you know what he means?"

"Yes."

"He says to go ahead the way you've planned. Don't let anybody change your mind. Just go ahead and everything will be all right. Understand?"

"Yes."

"And there was a special piece of furniture in your family—a chair or table or a clock—that everybody put a lot of store by—and you've got it. Am I right?"

"Yes, a table."

"Well, he says to hang onto that table. He says it's getting more valuable all the time. So you just hang onto it. Understand?"

"Yes," said the woman, and the young man walked to a bench and sat down.

Immediately a wiry, pleasant-looking man with a deeply seamed face rose and advanced to the stump.

"We all have been tremendously impressed this morning," he said, his voice booming out cheerily, "with the truth and depth of Brother Porter's message. We are indeed fortunate in having with us so many distinguished mediums from many parts of this state and from Florida and elsewhere. The next messages will be delivered by Sister Smith of Utica."

Sister Smith was a thickset woman and she was around forty-five—facts the obviousness of which she had apparently tried to modify by a long corset beneath her ripply black silk dress and by a henna rinse for her thick hair. She had young eyes, black and flashing. To my extreme dismay she pointed a finger directly at me and began to speak.

"I've been watching you," she said. "I've been seeing the thoughts chase through your head. You're wondering whether we mediums are fakes or whether we get our messages from spirits. You've been wondering whether we're just good guessers or really have psychic power. Now, I'll tell you something you don't know. You have as much psychic power yourself as any medium here today. In the contours of your face and forehead I can read that if you had chosen a few years ago to be a medium you would now be more successful in giving spirit messages than anyone here. Now I'll tell you something else. I see an old white-haired lady standing beside you, your mother?"

"My mother is alive," I said.

"Your grandmother," said Sister Smith decisively, "and

she has a little child, a girl, by the hand. Do you know who that is? Have you a little sister in spirit?"

"No," I said.

"Perhaps she had a little girl who passed on into spirit?"

"I don't know."

"Well, that's what she's telling me. The little girl is your aunt in the spirit world. And your grandmother is speaking to you. She says if you only believed the way she believed when she was on earth you'd be a happier man today."

Sister Smith turned and pointed at another man in the audience:

"Now I get a vibration," she said—but I was too confused by the suddenness of her descent upon me to follow her next reading. By the time I had collected myself the chairman of the meeting was again on his feet.

"We must close our message meeting now," he said, "in order to give us time to walk to the auditorium for the Reverend Mr. Taylor's inspiring talk at eleven-forty-five."

As the group filed out of the benches and took the path through the woods I fell in with Brother Porter, who introduced himself to me, and a woman he presented as Sister Maxwell.

"I hope you weren't annoyed by being selected so soon," said Porter. "It's sometimes a little embarrassing the first time."

"How could you tell it was the first time?" I said.

"A true psychic can feel these things," said Sister Maxwell.

"And do you agree with that medium that I am psychic?" I asked.

"Certainly," she replied calmly. "The shape of your forehead definitely proves that. Of course, being the type isn't enough to make you a successful medium. You must develop your powers and acquire your controls. The perfect medium, you know, has thirty-six controls. They go in bands of twelve spirits each. There are very few mediums here who have three complete groups of a dozen controls. You might have acquired them, though. Your face shows it. Of course one must never go into mediumship for commercial reasons. If you do you lose your psychic power. But I wouldn't be at all surprised if you went into it you might be a really important medium and work up to as much as three dollars an hour."

Sister Maxwell left us when we came out of the woods and Brother Porter and I strolled through the streets toward the auditorium.

"How many controls have you?" I asked.

"I'm really only a beginner," he confessed, "and I have only three—an aviator who was killed in the Great War, an Indian and a little girl. When I go into a trance and she's my control they tell me I talk in the little girl's voice, high and shrill. She used to be an awful nuisance, though, because she lied so. People would ask her questions and she'd answer any old thing that came into her head or sometimes deliberate untruths. I've argued with her and got my other controls to argue with her and now she's doing ever so much better."

The auditorium was a large frame structure and its seats were well filled by several hundred people when we arrived. A florid, rotund man made several announcements, including dates of ball games, a swimming meet, a "Bingo" game and a masquerade ball. Then with many respectful phrases he introduced Dr. Henry A. Taylor. Dr. Taylor was a distinguished looking gentleman of medium height and sturdy frame. His gray hair, quite short, stood straight on his head in a sort of brush cut. His eyes, deep-set behind double-lens glasses, gave him a strange look that emphasized his claims to psychic powers. He gave a good talk. On the whole it was quite as logical and certainly more skillfully delivered than any of the sermons I had heard at the auditorium in Chautauqua.

He spoke of the many evidences of spiritualistic truth in the Bible—of Daniel and of Joseph and of Moses who had interpreted to their people the conversations they had had with those in spirit, of Saul who had become a Christian through spiritualistic revelations, of Jesus, "the greatest medium of all times," who had not only interpreted messages from the spirit world but had Himself, after having passed on into spirit, returned in visual form to reassure His followers.

All Protestants may be Spiritualists, he said, and the Protestant churches are coming to believe in Spiritualism more and more. Some churches are even setting aside rooms in which their members may converse with their loved ones who have passed on. Then by some strange transition he began a discussion of colors. Green, he said, is the color of rest, violet the color of progress (he cited the violet-ray machine as an example), and yellow is the spirit color. The color of the spirit world is, fittingly enough, a bright golden yellow, and in this radiance our friends who have passed on live and move. Then he concluded in a pulpit-hammering burst of oratory. Spiritualism, he shouted, is a science in which revelation has followed revelation until now only those who refuse to see are unconvinced. It is a science, not a religious dogma, a science of rules and observation like any other science. And it is bringing peace and comfort to thousands upon thousands of people who had come to think that the grave was the end of life.

Dr. Taylor rested for a moment after he had finished and wiped his beaded brow. Then he walked swiftly to a table on which lay a brass salver covered with white slips of paper. He selected one of these and walked down to the front of the platform.

"I will now begin the message service," he said. "I want those of you who put these ballots on the tray at the beginning of the meeting to speak up immediately, as soon as I call out signatures or initials you signed. I must insist on this, for a loved one may be waiting to speak to you and a spirit may return for only sixteen seconds at a time. So hold up your hand and speak out at once when I call you. The first ballot is signed E. A. W. and it asks for a word from any loved one on the other side. E. A. W., where are you?"

A hand rose from the midst of the audience and a feminine voice said, "Here, Dr. Taylor."

Dr. Taylor strode toward the side of the platform, his right hand cleaving the air in a swift arc.

"I see a flash of light over here," he said, "and a young woman is standing here beside me. She's a brunette, rather stout. Does the name Gertrude mean anything to you?"

"No, it doesn't, Dr. Taylor."

"Think hard. It will—because this woman says her name is Gertrude and she used to know you well. That's what she's telling me."

"There was a family of Joneses lived up on the hill back of us when I was a girl," said the feminine voice. "I think Mrs. Jones' name was Gertrude."

"Right," said Dr. Taylor. "This woman says her name is

Gertrude Jones and she used to know you well when you were a little girl playing along that hillside. And she says to tell you she is more alive where she is than you are here and she sees many of your old friends in spirit and they are all happy. You understand?

"And now," said Dr. Taylor, striding to the salver and picking another slip of paper at random, "here's a ballot signed Emily. Is Emily here?"

A young woman in the front row held up her hand.

"You also wish to converse with a loved one who is in spirit?"

"Yes, Dr. Taylor."

"Does the name Frank or Franklin mean something to you?"

"No, Dr. Taylor."

"Are you sure?"

"I never knew anyone named Frank that I know of."

"Well, maybe you don't know now, but it will come to you, Frank or Franklin, or maybe it's Fred or Frederick. I can't hear this spirit very well."

"No, I never knew a Fred either."

"You'll remember before long. You *must* have known somebody like that, maybe a Francis?"

"I did know a Francis Edredge once."

"There—I knew it—because that's what he's been telling me. And now he's telling me something else. He carries a tiny child in his arms and he says he's helping it along in the spirit world. Just a few months ago you lost a baby girl, didn't you?"

"Yes, oh, yes," the woman's voice rose in an hysterical cry.

"And I'll tell you something more"—Dr. Taylor's voice

was loud and increasingly emphatic—"right there in your lap, in your pocketbook, you are carrying a little something from your own baby's crib. *Am I right?*"

The woman babbled incoherently, waved a tiny shoe in the air, and collapsed. Her long-drawn sobs were painfully audible in the still hall.

Dr. Taylor looked about him. "This will end the message readings for this morning. It is very tiring for me to exercise for a long time this gift a kind God has endowed me with."

Porter and I walked out into the sunlit square beside the auditorium.

"I'm going to the hotel to get some lunch," I said, "and after that I'd like to arrange for a séance with the very best medium at Lily Dale. Will you tell me who it is?"

He looked a little frightened.

"Well, my opinion is that Mrs. Ingram is the best. I'll write out her address for you and I'll tell her you're coming this afternoon."

"Will you join me for lunch?" I said.

"No, thanks," he said hastily. "I'll just go over and tell Mrs. Ingram you're coming."

While I ate a good lunch at the Leolyn Inn I read the Dale *News*. Its items were not unlike those of the Chautauqua *Daily*. Plans for celebration of July Fourth were complete. There would be a baseball game and the Erie County District Attorney would speak. A bridge tournament was under way. A noted harpist would give a concert. The Ladies' Auxiliary now had exclusive headquarters near the beach. An editorial headed "Do Guides Leave Mediums?" stated, "Spirit guides are more charitable than those people who so easily declare that they desert sensitives." There were the usual motion-picture and department-store advertisements from nearby towns. But on the back sheet were thirty-five advertisements for mediums and one which read: "Standard Trumpets, Students' Size $2.75 —Professional Size $3.50—Leatherette Case $4.50—Lumonous Bands $.50." I decided I must attend a trumpet séance before I left.

When I rapped on the door of Mrs. Ingram's white cottage a motherly-looking, middle-aged woman appeared at the door. She was taking off a large apron and peering at me through her spectacles at the same time. She smiled.

"You're the young man Brother Porter told me about. Won't you come in?"

Her parlor was neat and quite Victorian. I sat in a Morris chair and she in a rocker. She asked me my name and the date of my birth, both of which she recorded on a tablet. Then she looked at me keenly.

"I see an old white-haired lady standing beside you. A little child is beside her holding her hand. Do you recognize these people?"

"The old lady must be my grandmother," I said, "but I don't know who the child can be."

"Your family home is near here," she said.

"Not very."

"You were born not far away."

"More toward the center of the state."

"Around Ithaca."

"Yes."

"In McGraw or Ludwig or Varna?"

I shook my head. "I was born in Cortland," I said, "but my family home was Dryden."

She smiled.

"There now," she said, "that's what comes when I forget and use my own mind instead of letting the spirit talk through me. I was guessing. My control would either have told you the truth or told you nothing. Now the spirit tells me you've had a hard time but things are better now. Correct?"

"Yes."

"And I seem to see you wearing a badge—some sort of symbol of authority. And I see a big building like some sort of Government house. You are employed by the Government as an officer of the law perhaps?"

I laughed.

"No," I said. "I can't think of anything less likely."

She seemed a little hurt.

"At least you're some kind of an investigator," she said.

"Well, yes," I said. "I guess so."

"And I still see a uniform near you."

"I've been up north visiting some state troopers on the Canadian border," I said.

"That's right," she said, "for now I can see a state trooper standing beside your chair. You knew someone killed in the Great War."

"Yes."

"His name is Gordon. He is standing beside you."

"I don't remember a Gordon. But let me ask you a question. All the people I've heard mediums talk about today are recently departed—people who have been personally known by the listeners. How far back in the years can a medium go?"

"Whom do you want to talk to?" she asked promptly.

"My great-great-great-grandfather."

"He was a soldier in the American Revolution. Am I right?"

"Yes."

"I thought so. Now I can see an oxcart coming over a hill. In the cart is an old trunk and on it sits a woman. A man walks beside the oxen carrying a wooden goad. Is he the one you mean?"

"He might be."

"He is coming from Connecticut and he is crossing the York State hills."

I was silent for a moment at this. The man I had asked for was, so far as I knew, my only great-great-great-grandfather who had not come from Connecticut. He had been born a Knickerbocker Dutchman and had migrated to Dryden around 1780 to settle among Connecticut Yankees.

Suddenly Mrs. Ingram jumped to her feet. Her face was strained in agony, her hands were twisting in front of her.

"My stomach," she cried. "I've been shot in the stomach." Then she turned and said to me curiously, "Were any of your ancestors shot in the stomach?"

"Not that I know of," I said.

"Think," she said impatiently. "Are you sure you don't know?"

"Well," I said, "it might be my great-uncle Charlie. I never knew where he was shot."

"That's it. He says his name is Charles Carmer and he says he sees an aunt of yours frequently; did you have an aunt who was a teacher?"

"Yes."

"I have a pain in my knee, now. Was any of your family shot in the knee?"

"My grandfather Henry."

"Yes, his name is Henry Carmer and——"

"His name was Henry Lamson, my mother's father."

"Well, he says he just didn't want to be left out."

Mrs. Ingram seemed to be getting weary. Her hand sought her forehead.

"Before I go," I said, "do you mind telling me how you became a medium?"

"Not at all," she said. "My mother had the gift but she never used it. After I had grown up and married and left her she sent me money one day because she had had a vision that showed me with a hole in my shoe. I never needed money so badly."

"And that started you investigating?"

"No. But after Mother passed on I used to wake up at night and see a little girl dressed all in white floating around the head of my bed. Then one day while I was doing the washing I was suddenly surrounded by a sort of white cloud-like substance—it's called ectoplasm in books. Then my mother spoke to me and gave me good advice. Since then I've been developing my gift. That little girl who floated around is one of my controls. Another is an Indian. I only wish I could have begun my mediumship earlier so I could have done more good in the world."

"Is it true," I said, "as I've been told here today, that a perfect medium has three groups of controls, each band having twelve members?"

"Somebody got that from a book," she said. "I only tell what I know from experience."

"Tell me, do these controls have a definite individual existence and do they enjoy it?"

"My, yes. Why, just a little while ago I was going to a meeting of mediums in a grove and just as I got there my little girl control and three other girl controls of other mediums drove up on a yellow sport roadster (visible only to a psychic, of course) and all the controls left the car and went into the meeting to join their mediums."

"I must be going," I said.

"Now do come again," said Mrs. Ingram. "When you get a medium who can do you good and is compatible, you should stick to her. You and I have had a nice time. We like each other—and I'm able to get psychic results for you."

"And what do I owe you?" I said, a little embarrassed.

"Whatever you choose to give," she said.

"Would a dollar and a half be about right?"

"Just right. It's what the spirits told me you would give me. You'll come back?"

"Yes," I said as I walked down the steps. "Good-bye."

"Good-bye, and remember all I've told you."

Just to be sure that I remembered what Mrs. Ingram told me I bought a tablet and pencil at a store in the park near the auditorium, went to the pleasant little Marion Skidmore Library and wrote down as quickly as I could all that she had said. The shadows under the tall trees were lengthening when I had finished and the afternoon light was fail-

· 248 ·

ing. The time for my visit to the haunted house had come.

The Fox Cottage is well kept and it stands in the midst of Forest Temple Park. I was welcomed at the famous door, on which the great knocks had sounded so many years ago, by Miss Flo Cottrell, a sweet-voiced young blonde woman. I paid her a quarter and she showed me the many relics of Spiritualism with which the little house is crowded. There were slates on which unseen hands had drawn pictures, photographs developed from unexposed plates, paintings whose colors and design had not been conceived by human talents but had appeared automatically on their canvases, and a number of those chocolate-colored busts of American Indians which used to decorate Victorian parlors. I saw the upstairs room where Lucretia Pulver had cowered in terror the night she heard the invisible walker down below, the cellar steps down which the body of the murdered Charles Rosma had been dragged.

A man and two women had entered and Miss Cottrell suggested that we would like to hear the rappings that had been the beginnings of American Spiritualism. She sat in a straight-backed chair just to the right of the stair doorway and we sat facing her. After we had taken our places she said to me:

"Did you see that arm appear out of the stairway?"

"No," I said.

"I saw it," said the woman sitting next to me.

"It was an arm in the sleeve of a Confederate soldier's uniform," said Miss Cottrell. "Now about the knocking," she continued. "One rap means 'no,' two means 'yes,' three means 'we don't know' and four means 'cordial greetings.' Will you ask the spirits a question, sir?"

"I'd like to know whether they have a sense of humor," I said.

Immediately two sharp knocks sounded below Miss Cottrell. I was not sure whether they seemed to come from the floor or from the legs of her wooden chair.

"Don't they ever disturb you?" I said.

There was a sharp, angry rap, apparently from the floor. Miss Cottrell laughed.

"They are usually very considerate," she said. "Sometimes I wake in my bed upstairs and hear them knocking softly but sometimes they seem to be racing around the room as if they were playing a game."

While I was in their presence, however, the rappers did not choose to race around the room. They stayed close to the presence of Miss Cottrell. Once she rose and stood in the stairway.

"They always sound louder here," she said, and the invisible rappers proved her statement with several sharp echoing blows. As I left the house I asked Miss Cottrell if it would be possible for me to attend a trumpet séance.

"There will be one this evening in the octagon studio," she said, "and I am sure you will be welcome."

At supper in the Inn I almost gave up the idea. I had been wearied by the most fantastic day of my life. As I walked up the path toward the little octagon frame house I was forcing myself to take each step. When I arrived, a number of people were already seated in the small octagonal room which formed the interior of the house. Soon there were no seats left. In a clear space near the middle of the floor sat a glass bowl nearly full of water, a vase of roses, and a trumpet. The latter was apparently made of aluminum. It was about three feet long and in three sections so arranged that they could be telescoped into one.

While I was gazing about, the lights went out and the crowd sat silent in complete darkness for about ten minutes. Then a man began to sing the hymn, *Jesus, Lover of My Soul*, and everybody joined in. A moment after the song ended I was suddenly aware that the trumpet was suspended above our heads. Three shining strips about it gave sufficient light for it to be recognizable and I now understood the "lumonous bands" of the Dale *News* advertisement.

A cracked male voice came from the trumpet. "John," it said, "John," and finally a man's voice below it said, "Yes, father."

"Trouble may come to you through a dark, foreign man, trouble of a business nature. You must be careful."

"Yes, father."

Then a woman's voice came out of the trumpet as it swung about in the air.

"Carl," it said, and I cursed myself for having given my name to Porter and to Mrs. Ingram.

"Yes," I said.

"We are with you," said the woman's voice, "and we are helping you. God bless you."

As the trumpet called another name I rose and stepped quickly outside. I walked, almost ran to my car and I did not feel better until the engine was racing and I was hurtling over the dipping, climbing road to Chautauqua.

23

The English Dude
and the Prophet

CLAD IN GORGEOUS BLUE BROADCLOTH, A HIGH SILK
hat on his distinguished head, gloves and a gold-headed cane
in his hands, a heavy golden chain across his waistcoat, Mr.
Oliphant descended from the railway coach. No one in the
farm village of Brocton, resting on the white sand shores
of Lake Erie, had ever seen the like, and a talking arose as
the wagon Mr. Harris had sent for him rolled out of the
town and along the road beside the lake.

A greater uproar was rising over England in the wake of
Mr. Oliphant's departure. About his empty seat in Parliament swirled a storm of wonder and surmise. For the nation's favorite young man, gallant, witty, dashing, urbane,
had murdered a most promising career "at the bidding of
a crazy fanatic." British gossips recalled that Laurence Oliphant's father had been Attorney General of South Africa
when the lad was born there. They repeated the stories of
the boy's precocity in the law, how at nineteen he had already been engaged in twenty-three murder cases on the island of Ceylon. They chuckled over his reports on America

· 252 ·

when he was a member of Lord Elgin's embassy, his conclusions that in President Franklin Pierce intellect did not
exist and that "in the hands of a skillful diplomat, liquor
is not without value." They remembered his reckless soldier-
of-fortune enlistment under the blue and white banner of
the American filibuster William Walker, President of Nica-
ragua, and his arrest therefore by his own cousin, Admiral
Erskine, his wounds received defending the British Embassy at Tokyo from infuriated Japanese, his gay journeying
to Corfu in the company of the Prince of Wales, his triumphal election to Parliament.

But their imaginations failed in the effort to conjure up
some vision of Thomas Lake Harris whom Mr. Oliphant
had now traveled so far to see, the strange man who had
met him walking on Piccadilly some years before and who
had "talked to him as never man talked before."

In a large frame farmhouse near the lake Harris awaited
his distinguished English disciple. Rich tapestries draped
the walls of his room, and a thick carpet silenced footsteps.
He was a large man and his thick hair fell in streaked waves
of gray and shiny black almost to his shoulders. Far back
beneath his bushy, overhanging brows his eyes shone "like
revolving lights in two dark caverns." His grim mouth and
strong chin were partly hidden by a luxuriant mustache and
a long gray beard.

Harris' parents had brought him from England to New
York State when he was five years old. An inquisitive and
receptive youth, he had been greatly influenced by Spiritualism and later by the teachings of Swedenborg. While a
young man he had become pastor of the Independent Christian Congregation of New York City and had preached to
its members a sermon which he said was dictated to him by

angels. So effective had it been that it caused Horace Greeley to organize a public meeting for the establishment of
the New York Juvenile Asylum.

"I read that discourse," Harris wrote, "on Sunday morning to my great congregation; read it in the mystery of vi-
brating intelligence, quivering with love, calm as the stillness of a great night in midsummer; while from eye to eye
it seemed as if the hushed melted audience diffused an
atmosphere to hold the dew of tears."

Later Harris was a traveling lecturer and poet, still de-
pending on the angels for his trance-composed works. Then,
gathering a few of his followers about him, he established
a little colony called the Brotherhood of the New Life in
the village of Wassaic in Dutchess County, New York. The
group moved first to the larger town of Amenia, four miles
away, and then, with the conversion of Oliphant and Lady
Oliphant, his mother, in London, and the accession of much
of their wealth, acquired lands at Brocton on the far western
border of the state. Here Harris had taught them humility
and the desire to perform such labor as God saw fit to require of them. With this idea in mind he had renamed his
colony The Use and, with Lady Oliphant already in residence, had granted her son's request to be allowed to for-
sake the world and live a new life.

The countryside still chuckles over the English dude's
first night at The Use in a loft with but one mattress between his finery and the barn floor, and with empty wooden
boxes as the only furniture. The next day he was set to work
cleaning the manure out of a cattle shed. This was the beginning of a slavery so distressing that it cannot but have
had its effect on Oliphant's mind and spirit. He was forbidden to talk with anyone, and all other members of The

Use, including his mother, were enjoined not to speak to him. A silent messenger brought him his food. As an inexperienced teamster with English ways he found himself the butt of many a Yankee countryman's practical jokes. When he came home at night after a long day of hauling cordwood from the southern hills (often through the deep snows of winter) he was obliged to spend two more hours drawing water for household use.

And while Oliphant worked painfully and in silence, while his aged mother, accustomed to the pampered life of the British nobility, mended and washed the clothes of the farm laborers, while his friend Dr. Buckner, former president of a Southern college, delivered milk from door to door —Thomas Lake Harris, prophet, sat in his luxurious room and received the homage of the faithful, governing them by the divine revelations offered to him in his spiritual trances. He spoke his people well, calling them by the secret names he had given them—Steadfast, Golden Rose, Woodbine (Oliphant's title)—but he ruled tyrannically and without question.

Legend has it that he declared his second wife insane (his first wife had died before the Wassaic colony had begun) and incarcerated her in a room of the old house while he took unto himself his "spiritual wife" and secretary, the rich and cultured Jane Waring. Jealously he separated families, declaring that the individual must love God and God's prophet to the exclusion of earthly affections. Fanatically he dragged references to the sexual into his every discussion. Complacently he smoked his daily dozen of twenty-cent cigars while denying tobacco in any form to the young men of the community.

That revolt was so long in coming is strong proof of the

earnestness and sincerity of the members of The Use. For fourteen years the spirited Oliphant allowed Harris complete control of his every action. The Englishman is reported by his second wife to have told her of his one defection:

> There were times when I felt I could no longer bear it. I remember one evening I was driving home a load of potatoes in a farm wagon. Suddenly I felt as though something in me would break if I did not have some sort of outlet. I threw the reins on the backs of the horses . . . and whipping them into a mad gallop . . . we went down the road at break-neck pace, I shouting at the top of my lungs. I am told that prisoners sometimes break out in this way and warn their keepers that the frenzy is coming. . . . I never enjoyed a better quarter of an hour. . . . The neighbors, hearing the commotion, ran after us in an ever-growing crowd, and when the affrighted company reached us, my intelligent team had raced, unguided, into the stable yard where they belonged, without grazing a gate-post, and I was calmly feeding them.

Oliphant was finally promoted from the stables when Harris decided to build a restaurant near the railroad station to help in the sale of the wines the community was now making from its extensive vineyards. It was part of his work as manager of the restaurant to board trains when they stopped at Brocton and sell fruits to the passengers who were delighted to buy strawberries hawked by an English M.P.

As a reward for his commercial success with the restaurant and for using his influence to bring twenty distinguished Japanese gentlemen to The Use for study of the Harris gospel (among them men who later became ambassadors to England and France), Oliphant was given permission in 1870, his period of probation over, to go abroad to become London *Times* staff correspondent with the French armies during the Franco-Prussian war. In Paris on that mission he met a beautiful English girl, Alice Le Strange, fell in love with her and wrote Harris of his desire to marry her. His only reply was a letter from Miss Waring, the spiritual wife, to Lady Oliphant:

> Harris never dreamed of Oliphant's loving anyone until they had been thoroughly tested by the discipline of life. . . . If this dear girl can give him up utterly to God and enter upon what discipline is before her to prepare herself for the place and use in God's new kingdom, He will bring them together when and as He will, if they are for each other.

Two years of trial followed. Oliphant, ever obedient to his distant Master, begged Alice to submit fully to all of Harris' decisions, and she agreed. At last Harris allowed them to be married, in June, 1872, and on condition that Alice give her entire dowry and property to him. Perhaps the strangest part of the love story is that, due to the influence of Harris, this wedding of two who had been so long devoted to each other was not consummated. Again Oliphant speaks in the writings of his second wife:

> If one is not the master of powerful passions, one is bound to be their slave. . . . Hence I learnt self-control by sleeping with my beloved and beautiful Alice in my arms for twelve years without claiming the

rights of a husband. . . . I am a passionate lover and so it was difficult, very difficult, but it did not prove to be impossible. . . . Presently when my health failed for a short time, my physician ascribed my breakdown to my continence.

"I do not believe you," I said to him, "but even were it true, is it not high time for men to be willing to suffer a little in order to prove that passion can be bridled, when thousands upon thousands of helpless women have been broken down, and have even died, because passion is so often unbridled?"

Even when, on their return to Brocton, Harris separated the loving couple and sent the husband back to Europe they made no complaint. But others in the colony were beginning to murmur and Harris was a wise man. He called all the members of The Use together and announced that in a trance he had had a vision of a new and more blessed community in California. Obedient to heavenly behest he was leaving Brocton to make this prophetic dream come true and, since it involved a more sacred community and more comprehensive holy revelations, he had been divinely directed to take with him only the select few who would provide a sympathetic environment. The list of those whom God had suggested that he leave behind included the names of all his disgruntled critics.

When Oliphant in England heard from his wife she was in California and his mother was still doing the mending at Brocton. By the time he had returned, Alice had left Harris and was teaching a school for miners' children. He begged the prophet to allow him to call on her but was refused, and docilely he went back across the Atlantic.

The English Dude and the Prophet

Then came the news that Lady Oliphant was desperately ill of cancer. Oliphant rushed to Brocton and set out with her for California in the hope of obtaining divine aid through Harris' intercession. The dying woman and her son were received coldly. As she was leaving the Harris home in despair, she saw on the finger of Miss Waring a ring which Lord Oliphant, her husband, had given her and which Harris had required her to give up as an evidence of worldliness put by. Suddenly, with death upon her, she lost the faith that had given her the strength to endure hardship and loneliness in a strange country. All that she and her son had trusted to for many years turned to bitter disillusion. And when she died and had been buried in the California earth, her son at last shook off the strange shackles that had long bound him. He successfully sued Harris for the return of his Brocton property and took his wife far away to a community of the Brotherhood of the New Life at Haifa in northern Palestine.

Here the story of the English dude and the Prophet really ends—but there are addenda for the curious. Harris continued his work in California, and after his wife died, married Miss Waring. For the last fourteen years of his life, which ended in 1906, he lived in New York, the close friend and associate of the American poet, Edwin Markham.

Laurence Oliphant was once more to have a connection with an American community. Alice died after three years' residence in Haifa and her grieving husband on his return to the United States at the age of fifty-nine became greatly interested in Rosamond Dale Owen, granddaughter of Robert Owen, the wealthy Englishman who had brought his followers to America and settled them in a communistic colony at New Harmony, Indiana. Oliphant persuaded her to join him and a group of his friends on a journey to Palestine and when their boat arrived in England he married her. Two days later he collapsed from cancer of the lung and five months after that he died.

Part Five

Down the
Bear Path Road

House on the Square, Hamilton, N. Y.

The country here has the very look of the old romances that I love best. . . . In every direction narrow, lonely "dirt roads" wind through faraway valleys and over remote hill-tops, leaving behind them, as their perspectives diminish, that peculiar thrill that seems to come down to us from the generations. . . . It is an impression that has to do with horsemen journeying, inn-lights beckoning, journeys' ends coming to lovers, to tramps, to hunters, to camp-followers, to adventurers, to the life-weary Dead. . . .

. . . This vague sense of old-world romance . . . can only appear under particular conditions in the history of any landscape and it requires a particular kind of landscape for it to reveal itself at all. These conditions are precisely fulfilled in the hilly regions of "up-state" New York. . . .

. . . The presence of both stone walls and hedges gives this landscape, combined with the bare grassy uplands between the wooded hills, a look sometimes, especially in the winter, that stirs up in me feelings that must revert to far-away impressions of my Salopian ancestors of the Welsh Marches.

From *Autobiography*, John Cowper Powys

24

Chenango People

THE STORY IS THAT A MAN OF GOD RODE INTO THE
Chenango Valley and tried to start a church there. He
preached loud and he preached long but he could not get
the people to give him enough money to build the church.
So he mounted his horse and rode on. When he got to the
top of the ridge on the far side of Unadilla Creek, that
marks the Otsego County line, he turned back in his saddle,
lifted a hand and cursed the land of the Chenango. Never,
he said, should people gather in the valley, it should never
hear the wheels of industry nor feel the happy prosperity of
busy cities, it should always dwell darkly in the displeasure
of his God.

The curse came true in part—for Pierceville, where he
meant to build the church, faded completely away. Stream
and highway pass through it now and people do not even
know a town was there. There has never been a big city in
the whole county. In the folds of the Chenango hills the
shadows lie deep and dark—nowhere darker than on Nine
Mile Swamp where the outlaw Loomis brothers dealt in
robbery and murder. Most families in the region live far
apart, avoiding each other and the villages, picturesque little
huddles of red grocery stores, white churches, gray garages
and yellow homes. But the people live contentedly and, if

the old preacher's God is still displeased with them, they do not know it.

It was DeVere Card, source of pocket money to the farmer's wife, antique dealer to the rich folks of Syracuse and Utica, who helped me to know this country. Antique dealers are good friends for writers about people to have, for they know everybody and have been in everybody's house.

I came to Hamilton in early summer. The village green, with the finely proportioned white-pillared Colgate Inn at one end, stores down one side and houses down the other, was a happy York State memory of New England. And the tall iced drink my host of the tavern sent to my room as an arrival gift was most welcome. Card, florid, stocky, his white shirt open at the throat, one of the legs of his tweed knickers fallen toward his ankle, met me in the lobby.

"I hope we'll have some tennis while you're here," he said. "I don't get much in the summertime when the college isn't in session. And in the fall I spend most of my time shooting."

"I'm not very good," I said.

"You don't have to be. We're all too good shots to be much at anything else. Know anything about guns?"

"Very little."

"You'll have to learn if you're going to talk to folks in this section. It's all the men argue about—except politics."

"Why all the emphasis on guns?" I said. "Does Colgate——?"

"The college hasn't anything to do with it. But I don't believe a boy grows up in this country without knowing how to handle a rifle. Maybe it's because we've got room to shoot in. Maybe we've got more woodchucks than most sections. At any rate, if I was in a war I'd hate to be fighting a regiment from Madison County."

"There must be other reasons," I said.

"Well, yes," he said thoughtfully. "We've had some sort o' game to shoot since before the Revolution—and no cities to harness us with regulations. We have to go a little north for deer now, but a chuck still makes a good target. When I was a kid our whole gang used to go out of town about a mile to see Randy Cook every night we could sneak off after supper. Randy would talk guns to us, guns and horses. He didn't have much use for modern firearms but he'd get us pretty excited with his gun stories. Randy taught a lot of us to shoot with his old muzzle-loader. He was the kind of old man kids go crazy over."

"I'll have to hear more about him," I said.

Card laughed.

"You couldn't miss it," he said. "Everybody in Hamilton has a different story to tell about Randy. Hardly a night goes by but somebody over at the filling station or at the drugstore corner doesn't get started on him. Somehow he sort of fits people's ideas about this country, he and his guns and horses. And gettin' back to guns, I guess Pop Risley's got a good deal to do with our liking 'em, too."

"Who's he?"

"Just about the best gunsmith there is. He used to do all the metalwork on the Bob Owens rifles. Some of 'em sold as high as twelve or fifteen hundred dollars. Yes, I guess Pop has had really more to do with Madison County's liking guns than anybody—even Randy. We'll drop out to see him Sunday when everybody else goes."

Pop Risley's shop was a low, red-board building beside the road that runs along the east side of Nine Mile Swamp from Sangerfield to Hubbardsville. Next to the steps that led to the white-trimmed porch were several dog kennels and a crate which housed a yellow duck. On the wall of the porch were drying ears of deep yellow Indian corn. The door usually stood open and inside, hanging on the walls, was a collection of Revolutionary muskets, Civil War pistols and freak firearms. A sign, "Please Do Not Touch the Machinery," hung above the belts and wheels of his lathes.

You could hear Pop coming, for he was heavy with the heaviness of a strong-muscled man of middle life. His curly black hair was touched with gray. His face was round and full, a strong setting for his steady gray eyes. His arms were brawny and thick as a smith's should be and his belly was thick, too, as though accustomed to hearty food.

"Glad to meet you," he said to me. "I hear you want to know the story of the Loomis gang. They've made most of the talk around here for years, they and Randy Cook and the Cardiff Giant. You can hear 'most everything about those three stories round here. Everybody my age and older knew some of the people in 'em. Now I knew Plum Loomis pretty well, and Randy, o' course, and I've heard folks talk about the Cardiff Giant. I'll be glad to tell you what I know—and what I tell you will be true."

"Let's go up to the house," said Card. "Maybe some of the folks on the porch will help out."

As we walked up the rise toward Pop's farmhouse two setters greeted us enthusiastically and the yellow resident of the crate waddled toward us, quacking conversationally. Pop picked the duck up and tucked her under his great elbow, head down, where she hung complacently. I scratched the backs of the wiggling dogs.

"What are their names?" I said.

"Martin Van Buren and Zachary Taylor," said Pop.

"What became of Natty Bumpo?" said Card.

"Sold him last year."

"What do you call the duck?" I said.

"Andrew Jackson," said Pop.

The Risley farmhouse is large and rambling and comfortable. It follows no period pattern. It has been added to from time to time to suit the convenience of the Risleys. From the knoll where it stands, most of Pop's rolling acres can be seen.

"We've had this land a long time," said Pop, as we moved up toward the side porch. "My folks came here soon after the Revolution. My great-great-grandfather was in that fuss. It was his son took this land here—the one that shook hands with George Washington."

"How did that happen?" said Card.

"They had a big celebration in New York," said Pop, "and George Washington rode through a big arch of triumph. My great-grandfather was a little boy then—but his father held him up above the crowd and George Washington saw him and shook hands with him. My great-grandfather lived to be an old man and I knew him well. I've shaken his hand often. I've shaken the hand of a man that shook hands with George Washington." Pop paused for a minute. "I guess I'm prouder of that than anything else," he said.

The long porch of the Risley house was pretty well occupied with people when we arrived. There were Pop's wife and his pretty daughter, a white-haired man from Utica who had dropped in to talk about guns, a farmer from down the road who had come to see how Pop was getting on repairing his shotgun, and three young men from Hamilton.

"Pop," said the pretty girl, "I think the cow's got down in the swamp again. I thought I heard her bell a minute ago."

"Too hot to tell me that," said Pop, "and it's Sunday besides." He spoke seriously but the well of laughter in his eyes was deep. "One thing I can't stand is a naggin' woman. Send me after that cow an' I might do like old Mr. Marsh did."

The farmer from down the road laughed uproariously and the white-haired Utica sportsman leaned forward.

"I haven't heard that one," he said.

"Old Mr. Marsh married a naggin' woman. She used to git him down the country most the time. One day she wanted some wood for the stove an' she says, 'You go git me some oven wood an' don't be more'n twenty years about it neither.' Mr. Marsh, he went out and he didn't come back, jest plain disappeared. They gave up lookin' for him after a while. After about five years his wife decided he was dead and she married again. Well, sir, twenty years to a day from the time he left she was in the kitchen baking bread and she heard the door open. She looked up and there stood Mr. Marsh. He had an armload o' short-cut logs and he walked over and dumped 'em beside the stove.

" 'There's your goddam wood,' he says. He runs her second husband off the place and settled down there with his wife and lived there till he died not so long ago. And the moral o' that is—don't send me after no cow. I'll tell Fred to get her out o' there in a few minutes."

"You'll never get her if you're countin' on that Indian," said Mrs. Risley.

Chenango People

"Indian or no Indian, he better get her," said Pop. "Folks around here never cared much for Mohawks anyhow. Fred! Oh, Fred!" Pop walked into the house. We heard snatches of loud conversation. Suddenly a door slammed and we were all looking into the blazing eyes of the Mohawk.

"I ain't wadin' through water up to my goddam belly for any goddam cow," he said and his clear white teeth seemed to bite off his words. "I ain't riskin' pneumonia and typhoid fever for nobody. The boss says, 'Take your choice—git that cow or quit.' Well, I quit," and he started in a swift loping walk down the hill toward the shop. Pop came out the door looking very mild and undisturbed.

"He'll be back," he said calmly. "Now let's see what we can tell you about the Loomises. You see that tumbledown barn over there across the swamp?"

When Pop had finished, aided by many interpolations from his hearers, the sun was behind the hills. Nine Mile Swamp, dark tangle of cedars and vines from which a few sycamores lifted white despairing arms, had become a mystic, spell-ridden retreat, refuge of evil.

Card and I left before suppertime. On the way back, rolling over the low hills and following the curves of a little road that traces the line of the farmhouses, I said:

"Pop's an unusual man."

"No," said Card, "he's not unusual. Most of the farmers around here are like Pop. He's just a little more the way he is than any of them, that's all. I mean, I suppose, he's the type that represents this section."

"A sort of survival of the old Yankee, American Revolution spirit, eh?" I said.

"You can call it survival if you want to—providing the word doesn't imply weakness or decreasing numbers. All the farmers round here feel pretty much the way Pop does. This country has done pretty well by them. They've been here a long while. They love the land and their possessions. They love the sharp competition of their neighbors."

"Sounds conservative."

"Well, it isn't. It's independent. They figure things out for themselves. Pop never had much education but he sent his daughter to college. He's mighty proud of her but he doesn't accept her judgments because she's formally educated. He reads a lot and he thinks for himself. Some of his opinions on religion or philosophy would sound pretty radical even in a university. You ought to hear him argue with his daughter. When she pretends to get mad and calls him an 'ignorant old hillbilly' he laughs because he knows he's won."

"What about economics and politics?"

"As I say, he likes the competitive system—gets a real kick out of it. He's one of the best gunsmiths in America. He knows it and likes to dicker over the price of his work. His friends like to dicker, too. How do you think you can ever reconcile Pop, blacksmith physique, Yankee traditions and all, with all those little New York City men I saw last week carrying red banners and hysterically screaming the *Internationale*?"

"I don't know," I said.

I went back to see Pop often after that. Sunday afternoons were the best time to sit on his porch. Then you could hear the stories of the region with plenty of interruptions for amendment. I am telling a few of them in the following pages.

25

The Loomis Gang

GEORGE WASHINGTON LOOMIS TRIED TO KISS RHODA Mallet when she was churning and Rhoda slammed the hell out of him with the plunger. Soon they were married.

Rhoda bore George Washington twelve children before he died in 1851. Everybody always spoke kindly of George Washington Loomis. He was a nice, easygoing man, they said. Of Rhoda and her brood (nine of them lived to maturity) there were differing opinions. These became more pronounced after the father's death—particularly when storekeepers began missing things. It did not take the merchants long to note that this usually happened after the visit of one of the Loomises. It was rumored that Rhoda beat the children who did not bring back anything useful after a visit to town.

Wash was the oldest and his brothers were Plum, Grove, Wheeler, Denio. Cornelia, Eclista, Alucia and Charlotte were the girls. On the three-hundred-acre farm above the swamp the children grew tall and strong and handsome. Their good blood asserted itself in the perfection of their bodies, the alertness of their bearing, the winning charm of their manners. They learned to ride horses like cavalrymen and they explored the strange watery ways of the swamp until they knew every vine-choked passage, every still morass, in its labyrinthine depths.

The first story that most folks tell about the Loomises is the only one they laugh over. Cornelia and Charlotte Loomis went to a dance one winter's night at Hubbardsville. They were the prettiest girls in Madison County with their pink cheeks, bright eyes, and figures that a life in the saddle had made lithe and rounded. They danced joyously and with many partners. But after the fiddler had played *Home Sweet Home* a terrific hubbub arose in the room set aside for ladies' coats. Not a single muff could be found. Lady after lady sternly demanded that her escort "do something about it" while her hoopskirt bobbed up and down with the sobs she strove to repress. But a tearless minx saved the evening. Approaching Charlotte Loomis, she suddenly gave her a quick push that landed her on a sofa. With a shameless gesture the artful detective lifted Charlotte's widespread skirt—and there snugly stowed above and below each shapely knee were many muffs. It was but the work of a moment to discover that Cornelia was similarly accoutered and the young men of the party with a hearty good will began the work of reclaiming the furs and distributing them to their rightful owners.

The next inkling that Madison County people had of the intent of the Loomises toward their neighbors was more serious. One morning a farmer seeking to water the pride of his life, a sleek Morgan mare, found the stable empty, his new shiny black buggy with red wheels gone from the carriage barn, the harness with the silver trimmings no longer hanging on its accustomed nail.

The Loomis Gang

On his way to town he stopped by the Loomis place and told Wash and Plum about it. They were much concerned and said many unpleasant things about horse thieves. They offered to ride in pursuit of the scoundrel if his track could be found. Nevertheless, the farmer rode on with the helpless feeling that within a few rods of him in the silent swamp lay the end of his search.

Other horses and wagons disappeared and there were mutterings of angry men along the Chenango Valley. A hired man tending a sick calf at three in the morning reported that he had heard hoofbeats along the road and peering out from the cow shed he had seen five horsemen pass and three of them were leading extra horses. They were tall men, he said, and they rode well. A farmer who had been robbed of a horse said they were Loomises. The next night his barns burned to the ground and he lost all his hogs and cows and chickens. After that suspicions grew, but no one had the courage to voice them. A man who lived in Nigger Hollow recognized his own saddle on a horse Wash Loomis was riding but he did not dare claim it. Farmers lost sleighs and blankets, butter, cheese and chickens, and fearfully said nothing. Strange men from other counties were seen driving small groups of horses along the west side of the swamp. The talk was that the Loomises received the horses, changed their markings by the use of dyes, and sold them in Albany.

For ten years the Loomises took tribute from their neighbors, living like graceless feudal lords on the gleanings of others, and no one dared raise a hand against them. Then a small sandy-haired man named James Filkins was elected constable of the little town of Waterville. He said quietly he was "goin' to clean up the Loomises." The answer to that was a charge of buckshot that crashed its way through a window, narrowly missing Officer Filkins as he sat reading in his home.

Things happened fast then. A tin peddler, his shiny cargo of dippers and pans glistening in the sun, set out along the west road from Hubbardsville to Sangerfield. He did not reach Sangerfield and no one ever saw him again. A Negro farm hand working for the Loomises told a friend he was leaving them because he never got any pay. The next day he was dead, his jugular vein cut. The Loomises said he fell on his scythe. A serving girl at the Loomis place, made pregnant by one of the brothers, was shot through the stomach. Her death was reported a regrettable accident resulting from the cleaning of a gun. One afternoon a farmer's wife heard a timid knock on the front door. She opened it and in stumbled an hysterical girl. When she could speak she said she had been working for the Loomises, had begged to be allowed to quit, and had been forced to stay on against her will. She had pretended to go berrying that day and had run across the fields in terror. One of the children of the house to which she came was a wide-eyed witness of her panic-stricken entrance and it is she, now a gray-haired lady, who told me of it.

The swamp and its low-rising banks had become an abhorred place. The mutterings of the angry men subsided into silence—but it was the waiting silence of desperation. They knew what to expect from the Loomises—seizure of their property, dishonor to their women, death to their friends and perhaps to themselves. And suddenly during the silence the enraged countryside struck.

The story is not a pretty one. When the midnight raid of masked avengers was over, Wash Loomis lay dead in his woodshed, "the back part of his head smashed in and his face so disfigured that it was almost impossible to recognize him." Grove lay senseless in the kitchen, his face marred by brutal kicks, his clothing afire from a grain bag which had been soaked in oil, ignited, and thrown upon him. Only the heroic efforts of his sister Cornelia saved his life and kept the house from burning.

No one knew who the disguised raiders were. It was natural that Officer Filkins should be suspected of having had his hand in the affair and he was arrested and indicted for the murder of Wash Loomis. But the efforts of the prosecution were scandalously lackadaisical. Filkins' bail bond of $10,000 was signed by no less than twenty-eight prominent citizens of Sangerfield and Waterville.

Then, while he awaited trial, Filkins got the chance he wanted—with the law on his side:

I got information yesterday that some horse thieves whom I had been after for a long time came to Loomises' last Friday night. I left Waterville for the Loomises' about ten o'clock Saturday night. Four other men and I formed our party. All of us surrounded the house a little after daylight Sunday morning. Mrs. Rhoda Loomis, the mother, was at the back door feeding ducks. As soon as she saw us she halloed out to the men in the house, "Here is Filkins and a lot of men." We then entered the house and went upstairs. Conger and I started to go up the garret stairs together, Conger a little ahead. At this time someone, I cannot positively say who, stood at the top of the stairs with a gun and said, "Go back, G—— da—— you, or I will shoot you through." Conger advanced and the unknown man struck him with the gun, inflicting an ugly wound on the head. I now being some fifteen feet from the unknown man, shot at him with a revolver, do not know whether I hit him or not, but I aimed at his breast. The man now attempted to strike Conger again, and I shot at him a second time, taking aim at his head; do not know whether I hit him or not. Someone then fired a gunshot down the stairs; do not know that anyone was hit. As Conger and I started to go downstairs we met a stranger, who, upon being asked his name gave it, but I now forget it; Conger put the handcuffs on this man. As Conger together with his prisoner and some of our men went out of the house toward the road, the party in the garret fired on them several times. The prisoner was hit on the shoulder and breast with buckshot, wounding him considerably though not dangerously. Conger and his party then went away for help. I stayed there with the others to watch the house. Soon we saw a man come out of the house with a gun and start for the woods. We followed him and he fired at us with a repeating Minie rifle several times and at last hit me, inflicting a wound in the arm and one in the leg; I do not know who the men were, I do not remember much after this.

That happened on a June Sunday. Despite Officer Filkins' modest asseverations that he did not know whether or not he hit anyone, friendly visitors to the Loomises on Sunday afternoon reported two upstairs beds soaked with blood, and a man lying between them "writhing, groaning, and vomiting by spells" and wearing the pitiful disguise of a woman's sunbonnet.

The Loomis Gang

A week later came the dramatic end. While Officer Filkins, seriously wounded, lay in his bed, a company of about a hundred men approached the Loomis homestead, men from along the Bear Path Road and the Alley-Out, men from Clocksville and Munns and Siloam and White's Corners. It was just daylight on a Sunday morning when they surrounded the house. Old Rhoda was the first to see the danger and she gave fight like a cornered panther. She threw herself on the first men to reach the doorstep but she was quickly subdued. The rest of the Loomises looked out on the leveled guns of their besiegers and surrendered. Sullenly they sat in irons watching their home and their big barns blazing fiercely toward the blue sky, hearing the screams of their six beautiful horses burning to death in their stalls, the pop of hidden cartridges exploding with the heat.

Then a rope was thrown over the limb of a maple tree and the first to feel its terrifying pressure about his gullet was "The Dutchman," one of the Loomis servants and companion in crime. Suspended for a few seconds, he gestured frantically to be let down and when the rope was loosed he told all that he knew of the crimes the Loomis gang had committed.

Then it was Plum's turn. He stood up straight while they adjusted the noose. Then he said quietly, "If I confess you'll kill me, and if I don't confess you'll kill me. So kill me anyway."

They pulled him up and held him there until his eyes bulged and his face was a dark red. Then they let him down and asked him if he had anything to say. He said no. So they pulled him up again. When he was almost unconscious they let him down. He said he would say nothing. When they let him down the third time he slumped forward on his face and he was senseless for a long time. When he came to, he sobbed and said if they would let him live he would confess everything. When he had finished, his brother Grove took up the narrative. He had seen enough hanging that day to be glad to talk. One by one the brothers told of their other crimes. But there was something about the Loomises, something that compelled admiration, even a grudging affection in the face of hatred. When they finished they had admitted enough to send them to prison for life. Yet all their captors demanded of them was that they promise to sin no more. Only Plum was arrested that day, and then for the crime of having stolen a cap from a drygoods store in Canastota the winter before.

On the following Thursday the Waterville *Times* carried an editorial which began:

After many long years of fruitless endeavors to bring to justice the infernal gang which has so long cursed this town, and, in fact, all this section, the wearied and harassed people have in their despair taken the law into their own hands, with the fixed determination that THIS HELLISH GANG SHALL BE DRIVEN FROM OUR MIDST. The act committed last Sunday morning was illegal, we admit, but it no more deserves the name of a mob or the condemnation of the people than did the revolution by which our forefathers rid our land of British tyranny and robbery. The cases, except in magnitude, bear a similarity to each other. Both were appeals to force, by respectable, virtuous and well-disposed citizens, in disregard of existing laws, to rid themselves of unbearable oppression and wrong which all legal means had failed to reach. . . .

The Loomis Gang

The Loomises kept their word after that awful Sunday. Some of them moved away. Cornelia, "The Outlaw Queen," married and went to Syracuse to live. Plum stayed on the old place and made a fair living out of it. He died a natural death not so long ago.

There is only one Loomis gang story left to tell. It is Pop Risley's story and this is how he tells it:

"A few years ago an Irish peddler came through here carryin' a pack of tin things. I remembered him because he used to do odd jobs around this part o' the country. He did some work for the Loomises at one time. Well, he got to talkin' and by and by he says, 'Ye know the very year Plum Loomis died I was walkin' along the other side of the swamp with a lad who's a friend of mine. We come to Plum's place and we spoke to him civil and he spoke to us civil. An' I says, "Do ye mind if we look around a bit?" And Plum says, "Go right ahead." So we walked about the place for a while and come back an' Plum says, "Ye didn't see nothin', did ye?" An' I says, "No, we didn't see nothin'." "Well," he says, "ye don't know where to look. Just come along with me." Ye know how the ground rises back o' where the old house stood before they burned it? We walked up the rise a bit and Plum says, "Now watch," an' he puts his foot on a clod just under him. I thought I was drunk for it seemed like the side of the hill in front of us began to move. A slab o' land the size of a double barn door began to slide upwards and inwards an' there was a hole big enough to drive a team o' horses and a surrey in and have room on all sides. The lad an' I was pretty scared but Plum walks in and we follows along. Soon's our eyes got used to the light in there I seen it was a cave as big as two carriage

· 279 ·

barns in one. And all around the outside walls was the prettiest gear I ever seen in my life. There was buggies and traps and coaches and surreys so black and shiny that the light they reflected from the big door behind us fair blinded our eyes. There was saddles with silver mountings and saddles with gold mountings. There was black harness and harness of a pretty light brown color and all the rings of it was polished silver and the check-reins hooked on silver hooks and there was special plates of silver on the blinders. We must 'a' stayed in there about an hour lookin' at all that gear. It was a horseman's heaven. And when we come out Plum says, "I don't need to tell you to say nothin' about this," an' I says, "No, ye don't need to tell me." Then Plum steps on the clod again and the piece o' hillside rolls down in place an' ye couldn't see where it joined on to the rest. Plum died jest a few months later an' nobody else knew about all that stuff bein' hid there. It's bound to be there yet and I want ye should go over there sometime with me and help me find the clod to step on.' "

Pop says he said, "I've got to go on to Hubbardsville right now but I'll be back and then we'll both go over there and find that stuff."

"But he never came back," says Pop, "and I never believed any of his tarnation foolishness anyway."

THE STORY OF OLD BILL IS TOLD IN A STRANGE LITTLE BOOK of printed folklore entitled *Joshua, A Man of the Finger Lakes Region.* Its title page calls it "A True Story Taken from Life by Charles Brutcher." In his introduction to the book the author writes: "William Rockwell [the Old Bill of my story] was the father of John, who was destined to become one of the world's most powerful business men."

Mr. Brutcher also states that Old Bill sometimes aided the Loomis gang in their illegitimate horse dealings but other historians say that he ran his own show and was not even in Tompkins County at the time the Loomis boys were operating.

26

Biography of an American

ACCORDING TO RANDY COOK'S OWN TELL HE WAS born down on the east branch of the Delaware River near Fishs Eddy. His father wanted him to be a lawyer but when Randy was a little boy he heard a tramp fiddler play *Money Musk* and the old tune with swing and jump sang its way into his heart. He made a cigar-box fiddle using horsetail hair for strings—and he just naturally took to fiddlin'. Fact is when he was just a little fellow he took his fiddle up the Shinhopple Road one night to play for a pretty girl and a few months later he heard the sound of many horses' hoofs on the road across the flats and knew he had better be leaving Delaware County for a while. The cliff back of the Cooks' house was nigh to two hundred feet high and just a sheer wall of rock. No one had ever climbed it, no one ever *could* climb it, but Randy, his cigar-box fiddle tied over his shoulders, went straight up the side that winter night, leaving beneath him a surprised family and a large angry group of moral-minded men from Shavertown and Chiloway and Harvard and Cadosia.

Then the little boy fiddled his way southward until the earth was warm to his bare feet. And one day he came upon a great city of tents and a great crowd of men in blue uniforms who surged around him to hear the fiddlin'. After it was over, a bearded man with gold stripes on his sleeves and shoulders said to him:

"My boy, after we get through the day's fightin' come to my tent and play for me."

So after the day's fightin' was over Randy went to the General's tent and played for him and he slept there that night.

In the morning the General took Randy up on a high hill and pointed out the Confederate Army all spread out for battle and his own army all spread out, too. The General said, "Well, Randy, what do you think?" And Randy said, "General, it's your fight." "But," says the General, "are you sure, Randy?" "Sure as I'm standin' here."

"All right, if you're *sure*," says the General and he waved to his men and shouted *"Charge!"*

After that Randy and the General were walking along between the lines looking at the fighting when all of a sudden they heard a rebel yell and a lot of Confederate soldiers came running toward them with fixed bayonets. The rebel officer did not have a bayonet, though. His hands were high above his head as he ran and just as the General shot him and he pitched forward dead and his men ran away, Randy saw that he held a violin and a bow. They flew out from his uplifted hands and Randy, running forward, caught them.

"Nice catch," said the General. "By the rules of war they are yours."

That is how Randy Cook got his Stradivarius, his first real violin, and the first of his collection which was later to number a half dozen or so.

The tale of how he obtained his second violin is quite as interesting. Having left the General, Randy started back North. One cold evening he stood under a street lamp in the city of Washington fiddling hopelessly as people passed him without dropping pennies in his cap. He was ragged and dirty, he was shivering, and there were tear marks on his cheeks. A shiny black brougham drawn by a spanking team of roans rolled down the street. Suddenly the tall-hatted coachman pulled up the horses beside the little boy and a fine lady, dressed in velvets and furs, stepped out. As Randy extended his cap for pennies she bent above him and kissed him and asked him his name. She took him back to her hotel and there she told him to play for her. When he had finished she said that she was a concert violinist and asked him if he would like to travel with her—"carry her trail" on the concert stage and play violin "demonstrations" on her programs.

So Randy Cook of Fishs Eddy became the page and companion of Camilla Utsell, "one of the greatest lady violinists of her day." In a black velvet suit he carried her "trail" and played on his fiddle in many of the courts of Europe. It was after a concert before the Queen of England that Camilla gave Randy his Cremona. His playing had been so magnificent that night that she took the most prized instrument of her collection and offered it to him on the condition that he would never leave her. He promised, and he used the Cremona more than any other violin of his collection in his later life, fiddling at country dances and county fairs.

Acting as a page, holding Camilla Utsell's "trail" and "giving demonstrations on the violin" were irksome to a young man of Randy Cook's democratic American temperament. Europe and the applause of crowned heads bored him. And so one foggy night after a London concert he forgot his promise and with his two violins under his arm slipped away from his hotel and down to the docks. He earned his way across the Atlantic by fiddling and, once arrived at New York, he set out inland.

The big tents of Barnum and Bailey's circus rising in the morning mist beside the Ohio River lured him. He found Mr. Barnum in the cook tent and came out smiling. He had a job in the after-show "demonstrating" on his violin and then playing his own accompaniment while he recited *The Face on the Barroom Floor.*

He left the show at Little Rock. He was weary of the bustle and excitement of circus life and he needed rest and peace—one of the high moments of his career was almost upon him. He went to live in the hills with an old man. Randy has described this period in his life to many of his friends—the sunny lazy days, the nights of lying out under the stars, the wish to make up a tune of his own on his fiddle. It was in the Ozarks while he was still a dreaming boy, he said, that he put together note by note, bar by bar, word by word, *The Arkansaw Traveler.*

It was in eighteen seventy-two
in the early month of June
I landed in Hot Springs one
sultry afternoon
Up steps a walking skeleton and
gives to me his paw
Inviting me to his hotel, the
best in Arkansaw.

I rose quite early next morning
to catch an early train
He says you'd better work for me
I have some land to claim;
I'll give you fifty cents a day,
Your washing, board, and all
You'll find you are a different man
when you leave Arkansaw.

I worked six weeks for this gentleman
Jess Harold was his name
He stood nine feet in his stocking
feet as tall as any crane
His hair hung down in ringlets
o'er his lean and lantern jaw
He was a photograph of all the gents
that were raised in Arkansaw.

He fed me on corn dodgers, such
beef I couldn't chaw
Till all my teeth got loosened
and my knees they got the knocks

I got so lean on sassafras I
    could hide behind a straw
I tell you boys I *was* a different
    man when I left Arkansaw.

"This is the way I wrote it," Randy used to say, and then he would talk it and fiddle it, "and this is the way it goes now since some damned miscreant stole it on me."

The life of Randy Cook is naturally divided into two periods: the days before he came to the Chenango Valley and those afterwards. I have told the first period much as he told it himself thousands of times to eager listeners in Hamilton and Pratts Hollow and Solsville and the other Madison County towns. The second is in the memories of hundreds of those listeners. All of them speak of Randy with a crinkling of the eyes, a suddenly enriched tone of the voice. Frequently they speak in the present tense for, though Randy has been dead now for about twenty years, he is still very much alive in the mind and heart of everyone.

Randy had saved up quite a bit from his fiddling when he came to Madison County and decided to settle down. During his first few years of residence there he added to it rapidly, for he was a handy fellow, pretty good at 'most any job, and everybody liked having him around. Now he began to think of fulfilling an ambition. Ever since the days when the family nag provided the strings of his cigar-box fiddle he had loved horses. He could afford to own a horse at last and horses joined fiddles in the category of the ruling passions of his life. In the years that followed, folks could tell when county fair season had started all right by watching for Randy, seated on his high-wheeled sulky behind his jogging horse, rolling along the central New York roads. Brookfield and Dryden and Moravia and Cortland came to expect him as surely as the fairs themselves and their people used to roar down at him from the grandstand when they heard his high-pitched yell as he urged his faltering trotter down the straightaway and under the wire. The rumor can still be heard here and there that he began this habit of yelling in the stretch just after he had taught his first race horse that whoa! meant to extend himself to the utmost. As the horses rounded the last curve it is said that Randy would begin yelling "whoa!" at the top of his lungs and his horse would trot faster than ever while the other horses, hearing the cry, would slow up and Randy would win.

Years went by, and the demands for a handy man became fewer. So did the purses won by Randy's trotters. But Randy never got too poor to own a horse after he first bought one. Sometimes when he had had a bad season he could not even pay his entry fee. It was then that his old friend, the fiddle, came to his rescue. At the Syracuse State Fair one year he needed five hundred dollars to be allowed to enter. Approaching the filled grandstand he placed his old hat down before him, lifted his fiddle, and began to play. Thirty thousand people rained down on him such riches that he was able to enter his horse, pay his feed bill, and get back home though he won none of the prize money.

He told this story one evening in his home in Hamilton before a group of that town's leading citizens. "I was so broke before that happened," he said, "I 'most thought o' sellin' this here Cremony. I could git nigh ont' eight thousand dollars fer her. Now that Stradivarius over there, the one I got out'n the Civil War, that's wuth around ten thousand. What you puttin' them figures down on that paper fer, Jim Shepard?"

"Jest been elected assessor o' the town," said Jim. "Guess we'll have to tax you on them valuable articles."

"Shucks," said Randy, "I got 'em both from Sears, Roebuck and you know it."

Gradually through his years of experience with racers Randy became a known authority on horse trading. The rules of this game, though never written down, were hard and fast, and Randy, like David Hannum over in Homer (prototype of Edward Noyes Westcott's *David Harum*), obeyed them implicity. He bore the respect accorded him as a competent judge by other horsemen with dignity and he strove to deserve it. Many were the fine distinctions he drew between justifiable deception, the basis for all worthwhile horse trading, and damnable dishonesty. Revealingly characteristic of the traders' code is the story of the parson's mare, still quoted as precedent in the diminishing horse circles of Madison County.

It begins with the day Randy saw the mare hitched to a post near the water trough where Charlie Kilts used to fill the village sprinkling cart. The parson had unhitched her and was washing his buggy beside the trough. She stood with her feet bunched together under her, her head hanging down between her front legs, her lower lip sagging away from her lower jaw, her rat tail standing out and down—with a sharp dig at the end, her eyes glazed, and her ragged hide tight-drawn over her protruding bones.

"A great ruin, elder," said Randy.

"Maybe," said the parson, "but remember my master rode into Jerusalem on an ass."

"Same horse, elder," said Randy.

Randy's animadversions stung the parson. He remembered that Dan Stokes had persuaded him to buy the horse with such ambiguities as "A woman can drive her as well as a man" and "You'd be pleased to see her draw a load." So he sued Mr. Stokes for misrepresentation, and that worthy had Randy subpoenaed as a witness.

The night before the trial the cleric's lawyer made a point of seeing Randy, giving him a cigar, having a talk with him.

The next day Randy testified that so far as he knew the horse was sound and gentle.

"Didn't you tell me just last night," shouted the parson's lawyer wrathfully, "that that horse was windbroken and had stomach trouble, to boot? Didn't you say her teeth was bad and her feet was sore, she was so spavined and ringboned, she was over on her knees and down on her off hip, she had skin disease and was a switcher and hugged the reins and kicked if they got under her tail and would squeal and lay down in the shafts?"

"Last night I was talking horse," said Randy. "Today I'm swearing."

"Well, didn't you say that you knew for a fact that that horse was deaf from putting mud and snow in her ears to start her when she balked?"

"Maybe, but that could be cleared out."

"How?" thundered the lawyer.

"Well, if you want to know, you first stop all the orifices, except the ears, then you put a little red pepper up the nostrils. Then if you have closed the orifices right, the sneeze and cough that have got to come must take place inside the horse, and the wind so generated would be forced out her ears. All the mud and snow and other foreign substances would be blown out leaving her ears clean and dry."

"Your honor," said the foreman of the jury, "could we

have an adjournment? I want to see if a man across the street has got any horse medicine left in a long-necked bottle over there."

"I'll go with you," said the justice.

The seasons went by too fast for Randy. "Never get time to do nothin'," he would complain. By the time he got his spring planting done and his house fixed up a bit the first "summer meeting" was at hand and the starting judge would be ringing the bell insistently and calling down from the tower, "Take your horses back, gentlemen. Bring them down together. Make room for that pole horse, *make room, I say!*" Then the shout "Go!" and the close squeak at the turn, the settling into the backstretch, once around and under the wire and it was anybody's race, the brushes in the backstretch this time as the horses behind challenged the leader, the maneuvering for position at the last turn and the final yelling, whiplashing finale with the grandstand a mass of jumping, roaring maniacs.

And when the last county fair was over in October—usually it was the tiny "Hemlock World's Fair"—Randy turned, like all the rest of Madison County, to the joys of hunting. He felt that his experience in the Civil War, while chiefly musical, had given him prestige and authority on the subject of guns and he remained in this respect steadfastly conservative. He preferred a muzzle-loader to a "britch-loader" and he frequently referred to shiny new guns with modern attachments as having "globe and tossel" sights—though no one ever knew what he meant by that. Hunting season always added a new group of narratives to be included with his horse stories when winter finally came and the long evenings of talk beside the stove began. And as the hair on Randy's head grew whiter and more sparse, the number of his listeners grew greater. Mothers of small boys in Hamilton knew full well what enchantment made their offspring forgetful of time and the distance from Randy's little hilltop house to their homes.

"Tell us just one more, Randy," the little boys would beg, forgetful of the advance of moonshadows along the crusted snow outside. "Tell 'em 'bout the time you shot the pigeons." This from a father who ought to know a boy's bedtime but would explain tomorrow by saying he "clean forgot."

So Randy would tell how once, persuaded against his better judgment to try out a double-barreled "britch-loader," he went out along the towpath and stalked a flock of pigeons feeding there.

"I crep' up on 'em," said Randy, "an' all of a sudden I riz up an' a whole cloud o' pigeons riz up an' I let go with both barrels. Knocked me flatter'n a pancake an' twice as senseless. In a couple o' minutes I come to an' I begun pickin' up pigeons an' countin' 'em as I picked 'em up. An' the last one was number ninety-nine."

"Whyn't yuh make it an even hundred while you're about it, Randy?" a friend always asked when the tale had progressed this far.

"Think I want to make myself out a goddam liar for one pigeon?" said Randy.

And last of all the gun stories Randy always told a story on himself. He thought it was the funniest of the lot.

"Ye know how the grass grows greener in front of a woodchuck hole," he would say. "Well, I was tryin' out a new rifle one day an' I seen a patch o' that bright green 'bout eighty rod away. Jest fer fun I ups with the gun an' drawed a bead on that spot and by the Lord there sits a chuck—plain as day against that new grass. So I brings the gun down on him an' squeezes the trigger. I lowers the gun an' by God I missed. He ain't there no more. I raises the gun agin in a minute an' there sits Mr. Chuck agin. This time I takes extry pains 'fore I let 'im have it. But it don't do no good. When I takes the gun down he's back in his hole again. Ye know I wasted four shots at that goddam chuck 'fore I seen he was nothing but a potato bug roostin' on top o' that gun barrel."

And so, though he could "never get nothin' done," Randy's life in Madison County was a happy one. Few griefs can mar the serenity of a man who loves music and horses and hunting. Occasionally a "female" clouded his sunny sky but only for a brief interval. He had learned a lesson climbing the cliff back of his house when he was a little boy. For some years, though, his friends tell, he lived, without benefit of clergy, with a woman whom he affectionately termed "The Mustang" because "she had to be broke all over again every time yuh got her in harness." Finally another man persuaded the Mustang to elope with him—"done me the best turn ever been done me," said Randy.

Randy's only real sorrow was the death of a horse. When one of his trotters died he was inconsolable for weeks. He dug the graves of his favorites out in the sun-dappled pasture and he put markers over them on which he inscribed farewell verses. Old Shackleback was the first to go.

Here lies the remains of Old Shackleback
The cause of his death I'll tell right away
He was kicked into the stream by Asa Tibbitt's gray.

And when Bingo died Randy wrote:

> Here lies a trotter of R. C. Cook
> Many a horse-race has he took
> Here lies his bones—among the best
> May his soul go to heaven to trot with the rest.
> Bingo. Time 2:16.

Randy's best-loved racer, however, was Husky Harry. He never tired of telling of that trotter's speed and stamina and he would consider no biography of himself complete that did not include some reference to Husky's attainments. Due to certain sharp practices on the part of his former owner, the horse had been outlawed by the National Racing Association and it was a state's prison offense to enter him in a race. Moreover, since Randy claimed for him a world's championship mark of 1:59 and since therefore he was much too fast to be entered in the trotting races at most upstate fairs (which seldom scheduled races for classes lower than 2:14), Randy found himself in a dilemma. If he entered the horse at all he would face two prison sentences— one for entering an outlaw, one for entering a horse in a class much slower than that in which he rightfully belonged.

Randy took a chance on the first penalty. But on the second he was most discreet—always holding Husky Harry back, slowing him down just to win out at the wire. That is, until one heat at the Dryden Fair. That day Husky Harry, entered in the 2:40 trot, got the bit in his teeth, was out ahead by sixteen lengths at the first turn, and Randy realized that if the horse were allowed to continue at this rate his driver would be sent to the penitentiary for the rest of his natural life. When he told this story Randy would inch his chair up to the stove and put his feet out along the guardrails just as if they were along the thills and he would stretch his arms out just as if he held the reins on the horse's swinging rump. Then his voice would rise to the familiar high racing pitch and shake with emotion.

"There I sat—facing *death or dishonor!*" his body would be bumping up and down now as if he were in the sulky seat.

"I chose death! I pulled Husky Harry into the fence. There was a crash and we come through like it was paper. All the grandstand folks jumped up to see. Husky stumbled an' fell an' I jumped clear jes' when the sulky turned over. Husky got on his feet an' I turned the sulky right-side up. The headstall was busted an' I tied it, I put the bit back in Husky's mouth, I buckled the in-chin latch, an' clim' aboard. We turned around in the lot, went back through the hole we jest made an' lit out —an' by the *Lord*, sirs, we come in *second. Time o' the mile—two-forty and one-half.*"

When Husky Harry died—on the road to Moravia Fair —Randy was an old man, but he sat up all night beside his dead. In the morning he said that when he was buried he wanted Husky's likeness carved on his tombstone. He had not long to wait. Randy timed his last race from the judges' stand at the Smithfield Fair. He had driven horses for fifty years on that track. The day before he had timed nine heats while the trotters' hoofs slapped the soft mud and the drivers' faces were contorted by the sting of a slanting rain. Now, on the last day, the sun shone down hot but Randy shivered even in his overcoat. His straw hat was tilted down over his eyes and his chin rested on the rail of the stand. He pushed the pin of his stop watch as the winning horse reached the wire. Then he sat back, his long face drawn, his eyes dull for the first time. A few days later he was dead.

Now when a visitor comes to Hamilton his hosts never fail to take him out Madison Street to the cemetery. There they point out a large gravestone from which a stone horse, slim-limbed but sturdy, stands out in deep-carved relief. Above the graceful curve of his back one may read in clear-cut letters, HUSKY HARRY, and below his eager feet, RANSOM C. COOK, 1849-1928.

27

The Cardiff Giant

STUB NEWELL NEEDED A WELL OUT BEHIND HIS barn. He told Gid Emmons and Hank Nicholas about it and they said they were pretty busy but they would come over after supper if the moonlight was good and get it started. It turned out to be a clear night so they went over to Stub's place—it was near Cardiff on the Tully Center road— and fooled around with a hazel twig for a while in order to find a place where they would be sure to hit water, and then they began to dig. They had dug a hole about six feet deep when Gid's shovel brought up on something hard. He and Hank thought it was just a rock at first but pretty soon they realized it was a lot bigger than most rocks you find around there and they got sort of curious. In a little while they had dug all the dirt off the top and there in the moonlight, looking mighty white and strange, lay a naked man, a damn sight more of a man than either Gid or Hank had ever seen in their lives. He looked over ten feet tall and he was sort of scrooched up a bit at that, and everything about him was in the same proportion. His right arm was bent at the elbow so that his right hand rested on his belly and the back of that hand was at least an inch over half a foot across. But it was more than his size that was queer about this fellow. He was as hard as stone. By God, he *was* stone, so far as anybody could tell, although there wasn't any rock like what he was made of in York State.

Gid and Hank called Stub. He got pretty excited about it and somehow by morning most of the people round about had heard about it and came by to see what the stone man looked like. Stub said he might as well charge them a little something to look at it, seeing as how so many of them came that they kept him from working around the place, and it was only a little while before he was taking in over twenty-five dollars an hour.

Of course, people got to speculating about where the big fellow came from and what he was. Stub said he figured that giants must have lived in this section a long time ago before the Indians, and this was one of them that had died and got petrified somehow just like some shells do and pieces of wood. Almost everybody agreed with him until an Indian from the Reservation just a few miles away showed up and he said he had heard tell from his own father about stone giants that lived in these parts and made war on the Onondagas. The Indians used to dig pits and cover them over with foliage and leaves and then lie in wait until one of them came by. If he fell in the trap they did away with him quick enough. This Onondaga said he thought the stone man must have been killed that way and laid there in the pit ever since.

The Cardiff Giant

Then some students and teachers from the colleges near by began to arrive. One of the professors of geology began shouting around about the stone giant being a fake and a "preposterous imposition" and that made Stub sort of mad —so he said, "I'm goin' to get the leadin' authorities on this kind of thing down here and let them see it free of charge and ask them to say what they think about it."

So he asked Henry A. Ward, who had a museum of his own in Rochester, and Lewis Morgan, who knew more than anybody else about the history of York State Indians, and the Chancellor of the State University in Albany, and the Secretary of the same place, and the State Geologist, all of them to come have a look. They all came and Stub had everybody run out of the tent covering the exhibit. Then he sent all those experts in there and refused to let anybody else in for a whole quarter of an hour. When the five of them came out they all looked very serious and stroked their chins and teetered up and down on their toes. Chancellor Pruyn said he had nothing to say, but Secretary Woolworth said he was "gravely impressed with this probable creation of the Jesuit missionaries." Professor James Hall, the State Geologist, cleared his throat and said, "It is the most remarkable object yet brought to light in this country and although perhaps not dating back to the Stone Age, is nevertheless deserving of the attention of archeologists."

Everybody agreed that these reports made the giant pretty important even if they did not say anything very definite. Stub said they could never make him give up the theory that the big fellow was alive once and that his flesh had petrified. "Just look at the pores in his skin," he would say, "and the hairs on his leg. Nobody with a chisel could make those things." The crowds agreed with him, too, and they had become so big they were hard to handle.

Then a scholarly-looking young fellow from Harvard University named Alexander McWhorter came by and looked the giant over with a magnifying glass. He got very excited at seeing some scratches under the big stone arm. He copied them down and said they were Phoenician words meaning "Tamur, god of gods" and that Phoenician explorers must have left this religious image there when they passed through Cardiff long before the days of Columbus.

About that time Stub got an invitation to bring his unexpected guest to Albany and set him up there in the Geological Hall. As soon as the details of how much they would charge at the door and how much of that Stub would get were settled the job of moving began. All the men who could get their hands on the giant grunted and strained but they could not lift him. Fnally they hoisted him with a block and tackle and he got a ride to Albany. The gate money doubled there and people came from most of the states in the Union to see the human giant that had turned to stone.

Mr. P. T. Barnum had heard of the giant by now and he went up to see Stub about buying him. He went as high as a hundred and fifty thousand dollars but Stub refused to sell. He had got a few fellows in on the deal with him, one of them being David Hannum over in Homer, and they planned to take the giant on a tour of the United States. So Mr. Barnum went away looking pretty sly.

When receipts began falling off a bit at the Geological Hall, Stub had the giant loaded on the Albany-to-New York Hudson River boat. There were crowds at every landing on the way down trying to get a look at the big passenger and the whole trip seemed like a triumphal procession.

When Stub and his party reached New York, though, they got a bad surprise, Mr. Barnum had gone off to Syracuse and got Professor Otto to make a plaster of Paris giant the same size as the stone one. He had had it shipped to New York and it was already on exhibition on Broadway at Wood's Museum as "the only original giant." Stub had his giant carted to Apollo Hall just two blocks away and hired a barker to outshout the one down the street. Then the fun began.

"We offer the magnanimous reward of a thousand dollars, ladies and gentlemen," Mr. Barnum's man shouted, "to anyone, man woman or child, who can prove that ours is not the only simon-pure original giant. Beware of imitations, ladies and gentlemen. Do not be deceived by the calcareous humbug of the Albany showmen. Our claims are based on scientific fact alone. I appeal to you as intelligent Americans. Enter and behold the most stupendous contribution to the world's history ever discovered."

"Don't be fooled by counterfeits," Stub's barker yelled. "Enter and see the only petrified giant— lying there so natural you'd think he was alive. See the pores in his skin, the hairs on the back of his hand—all turned to stone. See the grand old sleeper taking his nap of the centuries. The intelligent man and woman will not be deceived by spurious and cheap duplicates, ladies and gentlemen. See the only original stone giant just as he was found in the York State earth."

Both shows were doing a big business when an upstate professor named O. C. Marsh, who had been doing a little detective work on the kind of stone the big fellow turned into, found a man out in Fort Dodge, Iowa, who said he "got up that giant" out of a block of Iowa gypsum. The professor relayed the news and Stub said he guessed the jig was up. He said he had had the giant shipped east to Binghamton to his cousin, George Hall. He and George and a twelve-year-old boy had buried the big fellow in the middle of the night after he had been brought to Cardiff on a wagon drawn by four mules and four horses. Then York State folks began to laugh. They laughed and laughed while the professors and geologists got red in the face and looked straight ahead or tried to explain just what they had meant a few months before. Stub's giant got more popular than ever. Everybody wanted to see him—so they took him on a trip to let folks all over the United States laugh, too. The whole country bent just about double over Stub Newell's giant and how he fooled the professors—and six million people went to look at him.

The Cardiff Giant is still taking in the money after sixty-six years. For twenty-three of them he rested in a warehouse in his old home at Fort Dodge. Then some businessmen dusted him off and sent him on a tour of the Midwestern fairs. Last year the Syracuse, New York, chamber of commerce tried to "beg, buy, borrow or rent" him. He came back as a loan and spent the week of State Fair on exhibition just fourteen miles from where he was found that moonlit autumn night in 1869.

And around Cardiff and Pompey and Tully and Vesper there are still folks who think the giant was once human flesh and blood. Ask Ed Calkins who runs the hotel over at Jordan and was around when it was all going on.

"Stub Newell and the rest agreed to call him a fake when they found out they'd make more money that way," Ed says. "There's talk about him being made of gypsum. That's wrong. He's more like granite. He doesn't sound like gypsum when you hit him with a hammer and he weighs the same as he ever did. Gypsum would be light and porous by now. Mark my words, you haven't heard the last about his being a petrified human giant yet."

28

Cockfight

SOFT RAIN WAS HELPING THE DUSK BLUR THE Hamilton village green when I heard a knock on the door of my room. I turned from my window.

"Come in," I said, and DeVere Card, shiny in a green slicker, stepped inside.

"You're about to see an example of the most popular indoor sport of the upstate farmer," he said.

"I don't believe it," I said. "And besides, what about the state police?"

"They'll leave us alone unless somebody gets onto it and complains to them."

"Where do we go?" I said, buckling on my slicker.

"The pit is in Norwich. We're taking a couple of Colgate boys with us. This is a hack fight—not a main between two big owners—and they've got a chicken they want to enter."

"Where did they get him?"

"Well, his brother ran away in a fight over at Auburn. The owner wrung his neck and the necks of all his family trying to stamp out the breed. That is, all but this cock. He was on a walk taking care of the hens that belonged to the father of one of these boys. The boy said he'd kill him but instead he brought him down here and he and his whole fraternity have been feeding, running and flirting him for the last two weeks."

"Flirting?" I said.

"Tossing him in the air to make him flutter and kick his feet. Good exercise."

A few minutes later we drew up before a large stone house. Card sounded our horn and we saw the door open and heard a chorus of male adjurations coming from the yellow glow of the hall. Two young men appeared at our streaming windows and I opened the door to the back seat. They climbed in, handling gingerly a large burlap sack from which came an occasional quick inquiring note.

"What makes you think this one won't turn out to show the dunghill just like his brother?" said Card.

"We're just takin' a chance. This Spangle was as carefully bred as any cock in these parts. Sometimes a runner is just one cowardly exception in a good strain."

We drove into Norwich, had dinner and a few drinks. The rain was beating a heavy tattoo on the top of our car when we climbed in again.

"We take the second road over to the right and turn east along the railroad tracks," said Card.

In a few moments he said "Look sharp now for cars without lights. Must be a lot of 'em back of one of these houses along here."

I swung the driving wheel to the left and as I did so our headlights picked out a field about fifty yards away filled with parked automobiles. We drove into it and were soon

Cockfight

sloshing through the mud toward the dark towering mass of a huge barn. Through cracks between the boards of its walls light filtered in strong rays. There was a heavy humming noise, the voices of hundreds of men talking in controlled tones.

We paid our entrance fee, two dollars apiece, and stepped inside. The glare of the light was blinding. It came from one source only, the center of the floor space where three big bulbs hung under a wide reflector. Gradually I was able to see that this illumination was focused on a round plot of worn carpet surrounded by a wooden baseboard about a foot high. And I saw that the barn was not really a barn at all but a circular theater. Ten tiers of seats, movie-theater variety, rising on a steep slant, surrounded the baseboard circle. And nearly all of them were filled. At first the faces seemed a series of round white blanks to me but as my eyes adjusted themselves to the light I saw that the people before me were unmistakably farmers. Many of them were in overalls and flannel shirts. Some wore sweaters and khaki pants, a few of the younger ones were in windbreakers, riding pants and high-laced boots. An elderly, white-haired man, stocky and with a swelling waistline, stood in the center of the pit. His shirt was painfully white in the glare of the bulbs above him. His face creased into sharp weatherbeaten lines as he talked earnestly to a lanky, sandy-thatched fellow in a khaki shirt and blue overalls.

"We'll be seeing you later," said one of the college boys. He was a slight, brown-eyed fellow with wavy brown hair and a sweetly serious expression about the eyes. He looked a little pale and bewildered. But his tall loose-jointed blond companion for the first time in the evening seemed perfectly at ease. He had been silent and awkward at dinner.

Farm near Ithaca

Now there was a sparkle in his gray eyes and a sureness about the way he swung the burlap sack.

"Who's handling for you?" said Card.

"I'm doin' it myself," said the tall boy. "First time—but I've seen a lot o' handlers work."

They left us to climb the stairs to the loft and we looked for seats. Some farmers in the third row moved over to give us two together.

The white-haired man in the pit stepped to the center and raised his hand.

"Please have your cocks heeled and ready on time," he said. "I'm asking the handlers not to ask for too many handles. I'm asking you not to talk to the handlers and not to make too much noise. We can begin now as soon as the first pair is ready."

Down the stair from the loft came two men. Resting quiet in the curve of each right arm was a cock. The men moved toward a scale set on a table near the pit.

"They have to weigh within a couple of ounces of each other to be paired," said Card. As he spoke a wave of betting swept over the crowd. "Ten dollars on the White Hackle," said a voice. "Taken," and a hand was raised from across the pit. "Twelve on the Muff." "Done." "Six to four on the Hackle."

Their cocks weighed, the men presented them before the white-haired man who took a pair of scissors from the table and clipped something from the back of each cock's leg. Then he said:

"Bill your cocks."

Still holding the birds in their arms the men advanced toward each other. Suddenly the contestants became aware of each other. They stiffened in their handlers' arms. Their beady eyes, which had been shifting, bulged and took on a set look. One stretched his neck and delivered a lightning blow at his antagonist. Two feathers floated lazily toward the floor. Three times the handlers let the birds see each other and strike. Both birds pecked furiously.

"Pit your cocks," said the white-haired man. At the same moment each handler gently lowered his charge to the floor, faced him toward his enemy and let him go. What happened then is hard to describe, for my eyes were scarcely fast enough to follow. In a flash the cocks were in mid-air a yard above the center of the pit. The hackles about their necks stood out in angry ruffs. Their feet moved at such incredible speed that I was aware only that they were in motion. It was not until after the birds dropped to the floor that I saw the shining chromium cuff about each leg and the inch-and-a-quarter gaffs protruding from them like heavy steel needles. And as I saw them they rose again, striking so swiftly that their blows seemed no more real than a shimmer of reflected light. Suddenly a bird sprawled grotesquely on one side.

"Handle?" said one of the men in the pit with a sharp upward inflection. The white-haired man nodded and began to count slowly while each handler clasped his bird to his chest. They stroked their birds gently. One looked into the eyes of his cock, blew into his face, stroked his rear and thighs, and ended with a long, gently straightening gesture down his legs to his feet.

At the referee's count of ten the handlers set the cocks down and again they rushed at each other. But the bird that had fallen did not get high above the ground this time and his antagonist was above him, cutting furiously.

As he settled to the floor, the injured cock hopped upward. It was a feeble jump but it was enough. Blood covered the head of his enemy.

"Blinked him," said the man sitting on my left. "Took his left eye out."

"Handle?" came the quick cry.

The handler grabbed the half-blinded bird and took its whole head into his mouth—nursing the wound with his tongue. I turned to Card.

"I don't believe I could do that," I said. He smiled.

"You'd get used to it," he said. "It's the way to get results."

"Ten," said the white-haired man, and the cocks were at each other again. There was a sharp flurry—a staccato note. A murmur rose from the crowd. "Got him that time. He squawked." The white hackles of the blinked cock were turning red. "Cut his throat," someone said.

When the handler put down the White Hackle after the handle the cock did not move. The Muff staggered toward him, got a bill hold on the back of his neck, and flailed viciously with his gaffs. Suddenly the White Hackle hopped and struck.

"Handle? Handle?"

"Yes." After the count both birds stood irresolute. Neither moved toward the other.

"Handle your cocks and breast them," said the referee and began again his slow counting.

This time the handlers placed the cocks breast to breast, beak to beak. As they did so the White Hackle pitched forward on the floor. The counting began again but it stopped as the handler picked up the bird. "He's dead," he said, and walked away.

Cockfight

"I can't see them strike," I complained.

"Neither can anyone else," said Card. "It's said to be the fastest blow in nature. Even the slow-motion movies can't catch it accurately."

"When do our college boys get their chance?"

"Third."

The next fight ended soon and with tragic suddenness. A stalwart Pyle, perfectly white save for one black eye, was pitted against a Shawlneck, a white-legged, black-breasted red cock with very heavy hackles falling full on his shoulders. After the first wild flutter the Shawlneck suddenly turned and ran in a long curve around the inside of the pit, viciously pursued by the Pyle. The audience began to shout and jeer.

"Dunghill," they called. "Wring his neck."

As the Shawlneck reached the edge of the pit, however, he turned and leaped into the air. The white cock fell like a bag of feathers—a crimson stain flooding the white softness of his hackles.

"A wheeler, by God!" said the man next to me. "Saved me five dollars and me shoutin' dunghill at him."

The tall blond college boy came down the stairs carrying the Spangle. He brought him from the scales to the pit and set him down. The cock stepped high and proud and his neck was curved like that of a race horse under a short checkrein. His comb had been trimmed close, making his head look sharp and giving his bright eyes more prominence. His breast, as red as a robin's, was wide and flat, well filled in with muscle, and his belly was small and held up tight. Over his curving throat fell a cascade of mottled hackles that glinted in the strong light like changeable silk. His thighs were long and strong and he stood on his toes, nervously looking about him, softly uttering quick syllables.

"What's his name?" I asked Card.

"They call him Calculus. Hard to down."

The other cock was in the pit now. He looked bigger than Spangle, and he was all of one tone of dark red. "He's a Mugwump," said the man on my left, "and, boy, can they *fight*! Ten to five on the Mug!"

"Bill 'em," said the referee.

The tall boy picked up the Spangle tenderly. I saw him flash a look at his brown-eyed partner who sat close to the pit, so close that when he bent forward his head was over it. His face looked drawn and pale.

Three times the two birds silently exchanged blows. They were bundles of ferocity. They meant to kill each other and they were happy in the intention. In their eyes shone malignancy that transcended all other impulses, all other motivations of their existence, a will to murder bred into them for generations until no other will was left.

"Pit 'em."

For a moment it seemed as if both birds had somehow been caught up in a little whirlwind such as spirals the dust of country roads on windy days. Above the center of the pit they circled with incredible rapidity, their wings making a wild drumming, their legs moving as swiftly and as silently as flickers of heat lightning. Then they were on the floor, rolling and kicking desperately. The tall blond boy stood watching them patiently, looking long and white beside the stout bronzed farmer handling the Mugwump. I looked at the other college boy. His eyes were glittering and his whole body was tense. A sudden spurt of blood from the neck of the Spangle almost reached his face as he bent over the pit and I saw him draw back in horror and repulsion.

"Handle?" said the tall boy mildly.

"The Mug give him a rattle that time," said the man on my left.

The blond boy was gently massaging the Spangle's throat. He put his mouth to the cock's beak and blew smartly. The referee's counting seemed fast.

At "ten" the birds shot from their pitters' hands and were again in the air. They both came down on the floor flopping awkwardly.

"Handle?" said the stout pitter, and without waiting for the referee's nod he bent over and grabbed the Spangle below the knee of the right leg. "He's hung in the Mug," he said, and very gently withdrew the Spangle's gaff from the Mugwump's wing where it had been caught.

As the birds were pitted the Mugwump rose the higher and suddenly the Spangle staggered. "Coupled," said the man on my left. "I guess he's done for."

"Handle?" begged the tall boy, but the referee shook his head. The Mugwump leaped upon the Spangle, caught him with his beak on the back of the neck and flailed with his gaffs.

"Handle your cocks," said the referee. This time as the tall boy set the Spangle down the cock pitched forward and lay tilted against the floor. But his tail stood up and his eyes sought his opponent with a cold fury. Again the Mugwump leaped upon him but somehow the Spangle tipped him off and, striking sideways, ripped him across the base of his throat. As if heartened by this he began to move then, staggering crazily about the pit.

"He's a runaway," said a voice.

· 311 ·

"Like hell he is," said the man on my left. "He's got a brain blow. May be all right in a minute."

The Mugwump dashed in on the Spangle again and the latter failed to rise in the air. His left eye was a bloody socket.

"Blinked," said Card. "Looks as if our boys aren't in the luck. The Mug is cutting their cock to pieces."

After the handle the Spangle did not move and once more the Mugwump leaped upon him.

"Handle your birds and breast them."

The tall boy breasted his cock with the blind eye toward his opponent.

"He's lost his head," said the man on my left. "He should have got somebody with experience to handle for him. Well, it's money in my pocket."

Again after the pitting the Spangle could not strike a blow. His one eye glared hatred, but he could not see its object, for once more his handler placed him blind-side to his foe.

"He's got a twenty-count against him," said the man on my left. "I guess he's a goner. Here's his last chance."

"Breast 'em," said the referee. And this time the boy placed the Spangle so that the wicked eye saw his inexorable enemy bearing down on him. Possibly the Mugwump had grown careless without opposition for two rounds, possibly he did not realize what reserves were left in the limp body of the cock before him. His jump was low and there was something above him, a feathered fury, a winged messenger of death.

"Handle?" cried the stout farmer frantically. But when he picked up the dark red cock a wide arc of brighter red was staining his hackles, a red that streamed down their gleaming length and onto his shoulders. The Spangle had almost decapitated him and he was dead.

Blinked and coupled, struck to the brain, the Spangle lay on his side and it seemed to me that cold triumph gleamed in his one eye. With a desperate effort he rolled to his feet, lifted his head in a high arched gesture, and crowed. Then the blond boy snatched him to his breast and took him away. I saw his brown-eyed partner standing now, smiling as he took money from many hands. It seemed as if half the men in the place had bet with him.

"I've had enough," I said to Card. "I'm a hopeless neurotic from now on."

"We haven't started yet," he said. "This show ought to last until at least ten tomorrow morning."

"Do you think we could get the boys to go back now?"

"Sure. They've got a lot of money to distribute around that fraternity house."

On the way back along the rain-spattered roads the blond boy carried the Spangle tenderly in his arms.

"You ought to kill him. He'll die anyway," said Card.

"He *can't* die," said the brown-eyed boy. "And from now on he's a symbol—a lesson in pure unadulterated honest-to-God *guts*."

"We'll fix up a schedule when we get back to the house," said the blond boy. "Every man will take an hour of nursing him from now until he's well." Then after a pause he said, "Gee! I'm glad the troopers didn't come."

"Are there many raids?" I said.

"No, they leave us alone unless they're ordered to raid us. Then there's hell to pay. Sometimes the town police raid us. A deputy in Auburn got to be sheriff through a raid over there."

"How's that?" said Card.

"They raided the pit and impounded about twenty birds right there in the crates they were brought in. Left a deputy to guard 'em. When they went to get the birds for evidence they found a fat peaceable Plymouth Rock rooster in each crate. The judge let everybody go, of course. No use pretending they were pitting Plymouth Rocks. The deputy got elected sheriff next term."

"That's as funny as the time some women asked Gould Marshall for a donation to the church fair in Canastota," said Card. "He gave 'em a pair of cocks that had weathered some tough battles. Thought they were goin' to eat 'em. But they put 'em in cages next to each other and showed 'em. 'Bout nine o'clock in the evening a serious-looking fellow came by and when nobody was lookin' he unlocked the cages. One minute later Canastota had one of the finest panics ever staged in a town of its size. Women screamed and fainted. Strong men cheered. And the hullabaloo never died down 'til one of the cocks decided there wasn't a better place than a church to die in."

"Now, I'll tell one," said the blond boy. "Over in the Genesee Valley, Trooper Jerry Van got orders to raid a cockfight at Hornell. The boys over there thought they had a perfect layout. Their pit was in a big barn on an island in the river. There was just one bridge for traffic and they had that guarded. Trooper Van let 'em get started and then he dressed in overalls, and drove a big truck full of beer barrels down to the bridge.

" 'Here's the beer for the boys,' he said.

" 'O. K.,' says the guard.

Cockfight

"So the trooper drives the truck up to the barn and backs it up to the main entrance, closing it up completely. All of a sudden six troopers jump out from behind the barrels and the raid is on.

"The only way out was by a single back door that led to the manure dump. There was a little ditch in front of that full of water and manure. The first man out was a fat man from Rochester. He fell in the ditch and the man behind him used him for a bridge. So did all the rest. Every time he tried to get up another fugitive from justice would jump on him and back he'd go into the mire. They say you couldn't tell him from the manure pile when he finally got up."

We rode in silence for a while. The wind blew in little gusts that sent flurries of raindrops bouncing across the concrete roadway. Finally Card said to the blond boy:

"Why don't they fight 'em at Oneida these days?" The boy grinned.

"Sheriff's sour on it. Put two of his best cocks out on walks of hens that belonged to a farmer. In the middle of the winter the farmer run out of meat. Stood it as long as he could, then he ate one of those cocks. Mighty good eatin', you know. Then he waited a month or so hopin' to save the one cock left. No use. His stomach got the better of him. So now the sheriff's turned grim on us. Raids every fight he hears about."

"Here's the house," said Card. The boys said good-bye and left us, the blond one carrying his burden tenderly. Just as we got started the door of the house opened and as we drove away a hearty man-voiced roar sounded out to us across the rain.

Listen for a Lonesome Drum

SOME OF THE NAMES THAT AMERICAN FARMERS HAVE GIVEN to strains of fighting cocks are both amusing and revelatory of rural life. I am listing here a few of the more picturesque titles:

Arkansas Traveler
Bell Skyrocket
Black Devil
Blue Falcon
Brassback
Bushwhacker
Claret
Corsair
Crazy Snakes
Cripple Tony
Cuckleburr Gray
Fardown
Gee Dom
Gray Tormentors
High Flyer
Hustler
Indiana Rattler

Jersey Devil
Jungle Shawl
Kansas Sluggers
Killer Roundhead
Leopard
Merry Kelly
Mortgage Lifter
Mountain Angel
Mountain Eagle
Mugwump
Mule Stable Gray
Mystic Warrior
Oil Driller
Pig Iron Gray
Pit River Warrior
Racehorse
Red Hornet

Rough-House Blues
Short Circuit
Smoke Ball
Southern Athlete
Steel Driver
Strychnine Grays
Stone Fences
Swamp Fox
Tarheel Banker
Texas Ranger
Two Step
Tumbler
Warhorse
White Mules
Wild Cat Blues
Woodbine
Yellow Jacket

Part Six

The Land of Frozen Flame

House North of Malone

A pine tree stands so lonely
  In the North where the high winds blow,
He sleeps; and the whitest blanket
  Wraps him in ice and snow.

From *Ein Fichtenbaum steht einsam,* by Heinrich Heine

29

Road-Monkey
and Whistle-Punk

THE HONEOYE POSTMASTER SENT WORD UP BY LET
Washburn that the rural carrier had left a letter for me in
the Dugans' box down at the corner a mile from the house.
Coley and I walked down through the snow to get it. I read
it aloud at dinner.

"You can't get any idea of the Adirondack country if you
go there in the summer when it's full of people who wear
shorts all day and dinner clothes in the evening. Now I've
been talking to the Goulds at Lyons Falls and they say you
can go into their lumber camp (it's nineteen miles in from
the Fulton Chain Road at McKeever) for as long a stay as
you wish. I suggest your starting next week while there's
still plenty of snow. Besides I told them to be expecting
you."

"Well," said Coley, "you asked for it. If you think it's cold
here, I don't know how you'll get along up there."

"You can get lumberjack clothes in Utica on the way,"
said Maud unfeelingly.

"I can drive you as far as McKeever on Monday," said
Coley. "What do you do then?"

I consulted the letter.

"Look up Joe Gordon at Forestport and get him to take you in the rest of the way on his snowmobile taxi. There isn't any road for those last nineteen miles. I hope you will be heard from again reasonably soon. If not we'll look for you after the spring thaws."

"I tell you what," said Coley excitedly. "When you come out I'll pick you up at McKeever and we'll go on up to Malone to visit the state troopers. Captain Broadfield wants me to come any time I can get away."

"And leave me here alone?" said Maud. The masculine silence that always greets this query settled upon us.

"Perhaps I could visit Peg in Rochester," said Maud, and the dinner ended merrily.

Coley and I set out early and at noon we were in Utica where I busied myself collecting apparel. By one-thirty we had eaten our lunch and I looked very like a dummy we had seen in a store window—the only other figure on whom I had ever seen a complete new outfit of lumberman's clothes. I had even placed the contents of my suitcase in a duffel bag. The hills north of Utica looked dreary and cold as the snow blew across them. From the downward slope of Genesee Street they seemed full of bad omen. I felt a little frightened and depressed as we drove across the bridge over the New York Central tracks, on over the frozen Mohawk, and started on the long upgrade that led toward McKeever.

Soon we were passing through the old Dutch town of Barneveld, and I looked back for a moment at Mappa Hall, one of the loveliest of York State's old stone houses. Then Remsen, neat little town, with Evan Evans and William Williams and other repetitive names on the store-fronts.

"This is the Welshman's American haven," said Coley.

"They tell the story of a Welsh girl-immigrant looking for the first time at the New York City skyline and saying, 'If this is New York, just think what Remsen must be!' Have you ever attended an eisteddfod?"

"No," I said.

"They have one every year in Utica. Contests in singing and speaking, and in writing and reading poetry. Your typical Welshman gets really intense about his culture."

The white banks along the sides of the road were deeper now. Driving the car became more difficult, for under about six inches of snow was a coating of ice that glazed the cement surface of the road. No matter how carefully Coley drove, we slid around curves. We were both glad when we could see the little village of Forestport. Joe Gordon was not hard to find.

"I've been waiting for you," he said briskly, as he put on his coat and gloves in the hall of his home. "One of the jacks is going in today. We'd better get started soon if we're going to get to camp by suppertime. Jump in my car. We change to the snowmobile at McKeever."

A half hour after saying good-bye to Coley I climbed to the front seat of a strange vehicle and sat down beside Joe.

"It's part Ford, part Dodge, part tractor and part ski," said Joe, "and it's narrow enough to follow a woods road."

Behind us in a dark cavern lined with benches and looking very much like a police wagon sat the one lumberjack. There was a coughing noise, then a steady roar. I leaned out to peer at our conveyance. In the place of back wheels, caterpillar treads moved swiftly over the snow; in the place of front wheels, skis slid along easily.

"How long will it take?" I asked.

"About two hours and a half for the nineteen miles," said

· 321 ·

Joe as we turned into the woods and began to follow a trail no wider than our taxi.

"I hear you brought Jim out yesterday," yelled the lumberjack.

"Yep," said Joe. "Had kind of a hard time 'cause he was foolish all the way. They tell me he had a fever of a hundred and four. He kept tryin' to get out and run. Made it hard drivin', holdin' onto him and steerin', too."

"I heard Henry cut himself," yelled the jack.

"Brought him out three days ago," said Joe. "He wasn't hurt so bad. May lose a toe."

I remembered the ominous look of the hills beyond Utica.

"Just where are we?" I said. "And where are we going?"

"We're in the Moose River country south of Stink Mountain Lake," said Joe promptly, "and we're going in toward Kitty Cobble."

"Oh," I said, and we lurched along without talking for a while. I could see by the height of the snow around the tree trunks that there was about six feet of it under us. Once, as we went down a rather sharp grade we made a sudden stop and teetered perilously, almost turning over.

"Close call," said Joe, and we went on more slowly. The woods grew thicker and darker as we moved into them. Occasional gusts blew white veils of snow from the spruce branches and enveloped us in tingling mist. Despite the warmth of my clothes and my fur-lined cap I began to shiver.

"Gettin' colder," said Joe. "Must be around fifteen below."

Over an hour later, when I had begun to wonder if my feet could really have frozen, we passed a little shed. Then there was a sudden wide clearing and down at our left I could see a great pile of logs edged by rough, snow-dappled ice. We puffed and chattered up a little rise and stopped beside an unpainted two-story shack.

"This is your headquarters," said Joe. "Young Mr. Gould'll be around here some time soon. You'll know him because he looks more like a jack than a jack does." .

"You're going to stay in overnight, aren't you?" I said. "You haven't got to go back out today?"

Joe looked at me a moment silently.

"I haven't *got* to do anything," he said slowly, and I made a mental note to watch my expression in a place where independence is a guarded treasure.

The lumberjack climbed out of the back of the cavern and stretched his legs and arms.

"I'm off for the bunkhouse," he said. "We'll be lookin' for you, Joe, at supper. Plenty of empty bunks—only about seventy men on the job now. I'll be seein' you both around," and he started down the slope on the other side of the shack toward a long, low building indistinct against dark trees in the fading light.

"Just go right in," said Joe. "Somebody's always there."

I knocked on the door in front of me and a hearty voice shouted, "Come in." A man sitting at a table swung his chair round to look at me.

"Oh," he said, "you're the visitor we've been expecting. I'm the company clerk. Just put your duffel upstairs by the cot nearest the door."

"Upstairs" consisted of one high-roofed room furnished by lines of cots on either side. I dropped my duffel and went down.

"Have a chair by the stove," said the clerk. "Mr. Gould will be here pretty soon. It's 'most time for supper. Supper's at five-thirty and you'll want to turn in by eight because breakfast is three-thirty in the morning."

"For everybody?" I said, a little startled.

"Yep. The bosses work harder'n the men in this outfit. I've known Mr. Gould to work forty-eight hours without sleep sometimes when the first rains come."

"Does rain make it harder?"

"I'll say it does. We have to try to keep the logs from goin' out ahead of time. We don't want the ice to break up and the water to take our logs down until we've got 'em all hauled. We want it all done in one drive."

A door at the side opened and a sturdy blond unshaven man entered. He was coughing strenuously but he stopped in a moment and looked at me quizzically.

"You must be the fellow we're expecting," he said with a half-smile. "We want you to make yourself at home and ask all the questions you want to. I'm Gould."

We shook hands and I could understand the combination of respect and affection in the tones of the men who had spoken to me of the boss.

"Let's go over to supper," said Gould, and the three of us started down the slope toward the long, low building.

The mess hall, which we entered through a roofed-over porch, was a half story higher than the bunkhouse stretching out behind it. It was roughly but strongly made, with occasional rafters and upright pillars supporting the roof. The stoves and kitchen paraphernalia occupied all of the left half of it. On the other side a half-dozen long tables running perpendicular to the length of the hall and covered with oilcloth were all set for occupancy. From the crosspieces above us hung lighted gasoline lamps and enormous kettles and pots. Behind the stove three cooks, a woman and two men, were working frantically over wide, simmering caldrons from which steam and the appetizing odor of beef stew and vegetables arose.

We sat down on the long bench below the nearest table and one of the cooks brought us platters of food. Besides the stew, there were boiled potatoes and spinach. Slabs of white bread over an inch thick and piled high helped us get the pot liquor into our mouths. There were pitchers of coffee and big tin cups to drink it from. Ravenously we set to.

Then a door slammed and men piled into the hall from the bunkhouse. In an incredibly short time every place was occupied. Then there was silence. I had expected a roar of talk. All I heard was the occasional click of a fork against a dish, the bump of a platter returned to the table. I spoke of the quiet.

Gould laughed.

"These men are hungry," he said. "Wait until tomorrow night. You won't want to talk either. You'll hear plenty in the bunkhouse later. Now the main business is eating and everybody is tending to his own. Have some pie."

The pies were apple and they were golden brown, a little tart and flavored with just the right amount of cinnamon. I said so and Gould grinned. He called the cook and repeated my remark. The cook grinned, too.

"We're proud of the food here," said Gould. "As you see, we even bring in green vegetables over nineteen miles of snow. But the cook's masterpiece is apple pie. Everybody can have all he wants of anything."

The men began rising and strolling through the door into the bunkhouse.

"They can't be through already," I said.

"I guess you haven't been noticing the size of the loads on

their forks," said Gould. "I'm going on back to the office. I suppose you'll stop off in the bunkhouse for a while. Come on up when you want to. We usually turn in about eight."

"I'll take you back there," said the clerk. "Then I'll have to go to work for a while."

The bunkhouse was a story and a half high and about a hundred feet long. The bunks, about four feet wide, were built into it, a row of uppers and lowers on each side. No springs softened the slumber of their occupants. In the center was a stove and beside it was a high pile of short-cut logs. On the rafters above hung coats and shirts, drooping woolen union suits.

The men were gathered in little groups about some of the bunks near the stove. My fellow passenger of the afternoon approached.

"Hello," he said. "Come on over and sit down."

"You're in good hands. Burt'll take care of you," said the clerk. "See you later," and he left.

I sat on a log stool in a circle of about a dozen men.

"This is the American bunch," said Burt. "Next biggest is the Frenchies over there, then there's the Swedes and Austrians and Russians."

"Don't you ever join another bunch?" I asked.

"Tried it once but they all talked so funny I couldn't understand 'em. Hey, Elmer, give us that song you was startin'."

Elmer was long and lank and his blond hair was a tousled mat over his low forehead. "Shucks," he said uncomfortably, "that ain't no song fer company."

"This feller ain't company. Bet he knows a song or two himself."

"Well," said Elmer, "this song ain't polite enough to be sung anywheres else. You'd have to fix up the words quite a lot. Now you fellers all join in. Here's the first note. Now sing!"

"Ump pah, ump pah, ump-ta-de-ah-de-ah-h," they all sang and as they held the last note in a long singing crescendo Elmer began. His tune was the old *Reuben, Reuben, I've been thinkin'*, and this is the song with the words "fixed up" where possible without destroying the sense:

> My first trip up the Chippewa River
> My first trip to the American shore
> There I met a Miss O'Flanagan
> Commonly known as the Winnipeg Whore.
>
> She says to me I think I know you
> Let me sit upon your knee
> How'd you like to do some loving
> A dollar and a half's my regular fee.
>
> Some were singin', some were dancing
> Some were drunk upon the floor
> But I was over in the corner
> A-makin' love to the Winnipeg Whore.
>
> She was as slick as slippery ellum
> I didn't know what she was about
> Till I missed my watch and wallet.
> Holy Jesus! I cried out.
>
> Out came the whores and the sons-o'-bitches
> Up to the tune of forty or more
> You'd 'a' laughed till you split your britches
> To see me hightail out that door.

As the men roared into a final ump-ta-de-ah-de-ah-h-h, the other groups around the bunkhouse yelled and clapped.

"Hot stuff," said Elmer. "I don't usually go in fer that sort o' thing—but a jack that'd been around some taught me that. I like things a little more serious."

"Such as what?" I said.

"Well, now, I come from a little ways south o' here, country around Wilmurt and Morehouseville and Hoff-meister. Feller I know down there, name o' Dan Partello, helped get some fellers that had been wrecked in a plane out o' the woods in the middle o' winter. When Dan got back home he wrote a poem about it."

"Let's hear it," said Burt. "We ain't heard it more'n once a night since last winter."

Elmer dove across the bunk on which he had been sitting, reached into a cigar box on a shelf, and returned to sitting posture in one long graceful movement. In his hand were two frayed sheets of dirty white paper. Then he began to read loudly with sing-song inflections:

THE RESCUE

We folks in the Morehouse section
Were all in our homes secure
While outside a raging blizzard
Swept by with an angry roar.

There flashed through the night a message
That made hearth fires seem less warm,
"Plane down in the Adirondacks
Unable to ride the storm."

Next day in the snowbound country
Trails circled and crossed in vain.
Night came, and still held a secret,
The fate of the men and a plane.

Road-Monkey and Whistle-Punk

The dawn of a Sabbath morning
Broke radiant as burnished gold.
We thought only of those fellows
Out there in the biting cold.

All day were the airmen circling.
Their comrades were close, but where?
At dusk came the long-sought answer,
The course of a brilliant flare.

Misfortune had called to action
A man to be reckoned with,
Who'd give to the last full measure,
His name is pronounced "Dean Smith."

Our gang was soon brought together
And furnished as best we could
With blankets and wine and clothing
And, more than all else, some food.

Bub Palm and the three Partellos,
Hank Hart and the Kreuzers four,
Climbed over the first steep mountain
And hurried down Bochen's shore.

Up Salisbury Road we labored,
Then headed for old Hurelle,
Down that wild stretch of country
The going was simply hell.

The night bound us in with its fetters,
Our pace was painfully slow
With many a slip and stumble
And up to our knees in snow.

Listen for a Lonesome Drum

At length we came down the mountain
And crossed through a deep ravine
Where snow was so thick in the treetops
Our lanterns could not be seen.

Then up the steep side of Wilder
We struggled and gasped for breath.
Somewhere ahead in the darkness
Four fliers were facing death.

Dean came again and we signaled;
He turned and his motor's drone
While flying above his comrades
Told them they were not alone.

Our shouts and our barking pistol
Brought shots and a faint "O. K."
From men who had gone their limit
And knelt in the snow to pray.

We gathered round huddled figures
In cold that cut like a knife.
Our flasks and our fire reviving
That pitiful spark of life.

A pilot swooped with rations
Then gave his good ship the gun,
He circled once more then started
Toward home with his task well done.

The dawn of another morning
Was bright when that gallant crew
Who fought a good fight and won it,
Took leave of their frail lean-to.

"That's a good poem," said Burt.

"It was a cold trip," said Elmer seriously.

"Cold," said Burt, "but not as cold as one winter I worked here. I was in a camp about ten miles out and the mercury in the thermometer began goin' down so fast I stuck a driftpin through it to keep it from breakin' through the bottom o' the tube. Next morning I woke up on my bunk and I was right out in the snow with no roof over me. The mercury had pressed down so hard on that driftpin it turned the whole goddam camp over."

There was a long silence. Not by a single twitch of a muscle had any of my companions betrayed amusement or special interest. Only in their eyes there was a subdued light —as if each one waited an opportunity but did not want to appear eager to obtain it.

"You know how a deer sometimes'll follow a man into camp," said an elderly man with white drooping mustaches. "A deer is probably the curiousest of all the critters. Well, I seen a buck one mornin' and I sort o' got the idea he was followin' me. Jest as I got to camp I turned around and that deer dropped dead not three feet from me. His breath had froze all the way from his nose to the back o' my coat and he'd strangled to death."

"Speakin' o' freezin'," said Burt quickly before anyone could interrupt, "I guess you've heard how Ben Snyder tried to blow out his candle one night when he was goin' to bed. It wouldn't go out and finally he sees the flame was frozen. Next time he was in town he bought four dozen candles and when he got back he lighted 'em all. When the flames froze he broke 'em off and packed 'em in boxes and sold 'em for strawberries. Claimed he made about four hundred dollars that way."

Two of the groups near us were already in bed. Preparation for sleep seemed to consist of taking off boots, hat, trousers and shirt. I rose to go.

"I'll see you tomorrow," I said.

The men protested. They said they had a few things to tell me, but I was obstinate.

The snow crunched under my boots as I climbed the rise to the office and the air seemed to bite into my face. At the door I turned to look back. The lights in the low bunkhouse were already out and the stars were very bright above the dark trees beyond it.

The clerk was sitting by the stove reading as I went in.

"The boss is already in bed," he said. "He's worried because warm weather in February put us behind schedule and he's workin' hard to catch up."

"What does catching up mean?" I said.

"Well, you see we cut the trees in the late spring and summer. Then we peel 'em—they're easier to peel if the sap's still running in 'em. In the early winter we skid 'em to piles. That's the only operation not done by motors in this outfit. It takes a trained skid-horse to drag a log through the woods to a pile. You ought to see one of 'em work. A good horse doesn't need a man to tell him what to do. He'll sidestep a log rollin' on a downgrade as pretty as you please. And work a log loose that's hung up on a stump."

"What happens after you get 'em piled?"

"Then we load 'em on sled trains and the trucks bring 'em down to the river. That's what we're behind on. But we've got good men. We're catching up. We'll be ready in time for the spring drive."

"Where do you get the men?" I said.

"When an outfit's workin' jacks just turn up. Most of 'em

never work at anything else. You saw for yourself there's four or five nationalities in the bunkhouse but they're all alike in one thing—they're all jacks. They like the work, or they can't get away from it."

"Why can't they?"

"These jacks come in here and they have to work like hell. After they've been in the woods six months to a year they catch what we call spruce fever, crazy to get out—and they're sullen and hard to boss. Then they get stake-bound, savin' their pay instead of spendin' it here at the store on tobacco and chocolate and so on. When they've got a big enough stake, two or three hundred dollars, they start out of the woods. Sometimes they get as far as Utica, and the saloons and the women in Water Street get their money. Sometimes it's Ma's Place, a roadhouse near here. When we finish a job and lay off a lot of 'em for a month or so the word gets round somehow and the women and the liquor travel north to meet 'em before they've left Forestport. A week is a long time for a jack's stake to hold out. It's two or three days usually. Then they start back in."

"Does that happen to all of 'em?"

"I'd say to nine-tenths of 'em anyway. Did you see some Swedes over there tonight?"

"Yes."

"Well, I won't say which it was but I'll tell you a story about one of 'em and then we'll go up. He was somebody back in Sweden all right. He got sent over to America twenty years ago to study shipbuilding. I don't know how he got into the woods—just drifted in, I guess. He's been workin' for us for most of the time he's been in this country. I sort the mail and to this day he gets letters from Sweden with a fancy crowned crest on the paper. Well, a few years ago he was stake-bound for twelve months. All year he worked like hell and no overtime was too long for him. He had eight hundred dollars on his account here at the office. He told some of the boys he was goin' back to his folks in Sweden and for the last few weeks before he left you never saw a happier man. He danced around and laughed, and was just crazy with excitement over goin' home. One day he come by here and got his money and began walkin' down the outtrail singin' at the top of his lungs. Five days later I was comin' in in Joe's snowmobile when I saw him walkin' along toward the camp. I says, 'You want a ride back to work?' And he looks at me and says, 'God damn you. I won't work for you or nobody.' Well, he stayed in the bunkhouse but we didn't have to feed him because he couldn't eat for almost a week. Then one day I seen him out with a gang workin' and singin' at the same time. He's been at it ever since and he ain't had spruce fever or saved a nickel since. Let's turn in."

My sleep was troubled that night. I was unaccustomed to going to bed so early and kept waking up. About midnight the boss had a nightmare. I heard him yelling, heard his feet hit the floor and then saw him standing with waving arms in the circle cast by the clerk's flashlight. The clerk was yelling, too, to wake him up. The sight of the bewildered dreamer and the shouts were terrifying. Heads with staring eyes popped up from the cots along the walls. Still thrashing his arms about, the boss started toward me, the flashlight's circle following along with him and weirdly shadowing the walls. The clerk yelled again and jumped to head him off. I sat up, thoroughly frightened, just as the sleepwalker fell over my duffel bag and began a desperate struggle with it.

Then he awakened and stood up grinning sheepishly. In another minute he was snoring on his cot.

It seemed hardly a minute later that I heard a faraway bell ringing and the sound of voices in the room. Everybody was up and dressing. A lamp had been lighted and I saw by my watch that it was three o'clock. I dressed, a little embarrassed that I had worn woolen pajamas instead of sleeping in my underwear, and went down to the mess hall. Pots of oatmeal, pans of doughnuts, plates of big round pancakes, pitchers of coffee, of milk, of syrup, were on the tables. Before four o'clock the big trucks with tractors for back wheels and skis for front were starting off up the mountain grades dragging behind them long trains of empty "sleds."

"Hop up with the driver of one of these," said Gould. "Have your lunch at one of the camps near where we're operating. I'll run into you somewhere or see you tonight. Good luck."

For nine miles I watched the driver of the snowgoing truck work the heavy vehicle steadily up the side of the mountain. I did not talk to him for some time. Turning the wheel quickly to keep in the narrow track seemed to require all his attention. At last he said to me:

"I'm new at this. Most of us drivers are. Had a strike two weeks ago and the regular drivers left. I never worked on snow before this job."

"What did they strike for?" I said.

He looked at me a little contemptuously.

"Same old complaint—too much work for the pay."

"But they tell me this is a generous outfit," I said.

"Well, it is, most ways. But somehow or other they've made a rule that each one of us drivers has to make two trips to get a day's pay. Don't sound so hard—two eighteen-mile trips and your day's over. But these snow trucks break down every so often. They block the trucks behind and everybody loses. Time and again it takes a driver eighteen hours to make two trips and a few times I've got in with my second load around two o'clock in the morning—just about in time to start on the next day's work. The pay isn't bad, though, and I'm glad to get it."

The road had been getting steeper and his hands busier on the wheel and I did not question him further. Ahead of us I saw a huge pile of peeled logs cut into ten-foot lengths, and not far from it an open camp roofed over with evergreen boughs. A fire burned briskly just outside it. Two men beside the log pile greeted us with raised cant hooks.

"This is where my train is loaded," said the driver. "You'll find your friend Burt about a quarter-mile west in the hole."

"What's the hole?"

"It's a gully that's never been cut before. The boss is using Holt tractors to drag the wood out of there a load at a time. First time, they tell me, that logs have been dragged uphill from one watershed into another. Go have a look."

Burt hailed me with a long halloo as soon as I came in sight. He and his companion, a blond, blue-eyed, clean-shaven man of about fifty, had a sled about half-loaded. They had put short poles across the interval between a high log pile and their load and, with the aid of their cant hooks, were rolling logs over them. The load was growing rapidly.

"I meant to ask you last night," said Burt as I trudged up, "do you know where Yale College is?"

"Yes," I said.

"It's at New Haven, Connecticut," said Burt, "and my girl is a librarian at Yale College, by Jesus. I used to have a girl worth eighty-six thousand dollars but I give her up for this one. You've got to be pretty goddam smart to be a librarian at Yale College. She can act like a lady at all times."

"You have to be able to if you're a librarian at Yale," I said.

"That's right," said Burt, jabbing his cant hook into a heavy log and sending it down the two-pole runway. "You know she can appreciate things. I was thinkin' of her this mornin' when I come by a pond around four o'clock. There was one or two stars still shinin' and they shone up out of the ice, too. The east was gettin' light and the ice begun changin' color with it. It was beautiful, by Jesus, and I says to the Swede here, 'You can talk about your land of the midnight sun all you want to but this here beats it.'"

The Swede looked at us with clear blue eyes.

"It is almost as beautiful," he said slowly.

"He won't never give in," said Burt.

When I rode down the mountain beside the driver of another Linn snowtruck in the middle of the afternoon, a train of ten sleds piled high with logs stretched out behind us. I had had a lunch of hot stew and thick bread beside a blazing fire that did little to keep my fingers from stiffening with cold whenever I took off my mittens to manipulate my food. My driver was affable but he looked behind him anxiously at a jack standing on the back of the truck who seemed never to notice us but kept his eyes on the lifting and falling chain of log piles behind. I caught my breath as we arrived at the top of a steep grade and realized that we were about to descend it with the vast weight of the loaded sleds behind us. The driver stopped the train. I heard the jack behind us shouting loudly and an answering call from the middle of the downslope ahead. I suddenly noticed little piles of sand at regular distances along the slanting road and saw a man shoveling the contents of one of them into our path.

"We'll have to wait here until it's safe for us to start down," said the driver.

I was silent for a moment and the driver laughed and said:

"Don't worry none. Believe me, we won't go down here until that track is so slowed down that this engine'll have to pull hard to get the sleds to the bottom. I had my lesson the other day when I saw a driver at the foot of a slope lookin' as white as this snow and with his eyes bugged out like he'd seen a ghost."

"What happened to him?" I said.

"He had a train o' ten loads of heavy stuff the doodlebugs pulled out o' the hole. He come to a sand-hill and the road-monkey wasn't there, so he took a chance and went down anyway. After he got started five of his bull-bows broke and his loads began to buckle. Then the whistle-punk jumped and the driver give an exhibition of plain and fancy steerin' on the wildest ride of his life. He don't know how he got to the bottom alive and nobody else does."

"I wish I understood your language," I said. "It sounds like an interesting story."

He looked at me a moment and laughed again. "I forgot you don't know lumber talk," he said. "Well, doodlebugs are the Holt tractors that yank single loads out of the gully where Burt and the Swede are workin'. A sand-hill is a slope so steep it has to have sand spread on it, and the road-monkey is the fellow who spreads it. The bull-bows are the logs set between the loads to keep the sleds from running into each other and the train from buckling, and the whistle-punk is this fellow back of us here who has the job of seeing to it that the train is hooked up all right and watching it to see that we stop right away if there's any trouble."

"I understand it better now," I said as the road-monkey below us shouted and motioned us on. The driver threw in the clutch and we moved into the slope.

"How much weight is behind us?" I said.

"Ninety to a hundred ton."

"And how much does this truck weigh?"

"Ten ton."

"That driver you spoke of was an amateur at turning white and bug-eyed," I said. "Just have a look at me when we get to the middle of this slope."

The night before I left the woods a warm wind blew across the mountains, bringing heavy rain. Hour after hour the roof over our cots resounded to the pelting drops—sometimes in deep monotone and sometimes, during a sudden gust, in a swift, irregular crescendo. The boss worked all night and so did everybody else except the clerk and me. It was still raining when I left the mess hall at four in the morning and no one seemed to know whether the downpour had forced the calamity of an early drive. Joe Gordon stood beside his snowmobile shaking his head dolefully.

"If I hadn't said I'd take you out I'd be stayin' in to help."

"Have to meet a friend at McKeever before noon," I said.

The boss looked weary and grim when I said good-bye. As the snowmobile bumped along out of camp Joe cast a last glance at the countless logs piled on the ice surface below the road.

"This'll have to change to snow damn quick," he said, "or the logs'll go out."

"It must be quite a sight," I said.

"Yes, when the high water begins to carry 'em along, the lower logs shoot up from the bottom like they'd been fired from a cannon. There's a crackin' noise and a groanin' where they rub against each other. Then those in front really get goin' in the swift water. Some of 'em wing up on the banks and the jacks run along beside and shove 'em off. The real trouble comes when one of 'em wings up on a rock in white water and begins stoppin' others. That's what they call a center. Then the jacks get out a North River boat —you know, one o' them sixteen-foot, flat-bottomed craft with a round hull. Three men get in and two row while the jack in the prow uses his cant hook to catch onto the center and swing the boat into the eddy behind it. The jacks on the bank keep 'em from being swept downstream by holding onto a rope that's hitched to the prow. You know Pat Chisholm, that French foreman?"

"Yes."

"He's one o' the best white-water men there is but in last year's drive there weren't enough jacks on the bank to hold Pat's boat and he got carried over an eight-foot falls. Nobody killed but Pat claims you can see the ten holes his fingers made in a big rock just below the rim."

"I thought the jacks rode the logs down the river," I said.

Road-Monkey and Whistle-Punk

Joe laughed. "Ever try to ride a peeled log?"

"No."

"Well, don't. Time of ridin' and twirlin' logs is about gone. Some of our boys can do it but they don't take no chances on peeled logs that are slick as axle grease."

Coley was waiting at McKeever when I got there, and I left the snowmobile without regret. The air was growing steadily colder as we headed north and when snowflakes crowded down upon us I felt happy for the band of desperate workers I had left. The going was slow and we stopped off at the little hotel at Raquette Lake for lunch. We were standing in the barroom absorbing an unneeded appetizer when a big man entered and greeted us. His hair was gray and his stomach was large but he walked with the sure grace of a woodsman.

"We don't get many visitors up this way in the winter," he said.

"That's why we're here," I said. "We wanted to see what you people are like when you're not taking care of tourists."

"Well, I ought to know," said the big man. "I come here as a lad and I been here ever since. I'm Judge Dillon. That's my store next door. If I was goin' to describe folks around here I'd say they was law-abidin' but bullheaded."

"Have a drink with us," I said, "and we'd like to hear why you think so."

"Well," said Judge Dillon, "they're just stubborn. Had a big fight down at Forestport a few years ago. Lasted from a Friday until the next Wednesday 'cause nobody would give in. Practically every man in the neighborhood joined in on it at some time or other. Some folks'd go and fight

Adirondacks

for a while, come away for meals and go back and fight some more. Guess they'd still be there if they all hadn't got sort o' tuckered out.

"Then there's this bunch that cut a road through the woods up here when the Government told 'em not to. There's so many investigators in this section now, even the beavers just keep gnawing all the time and don't dare look around. That's all because we like to have our own way in these woods."

"I should think you'd get lonesome up here in the winter," I said. "Summer visitors must make this a gay place in the warm months. But now—isn't it a little dull?"

"I'll tell you about that," said Judge Dillon. "There's a little piece of poetry that says just how I feel. Maybe you can tell me who wrote it. It goes this way: 'From yonder ivied tower I watch the villagers around,' and it sounds like Gray's *Elegy* but it isn't. I'd say it's either a Whittier job or a Longfellow job. Anyway, it expresses my sentiments."

30

Troop B

THE SNOW WAS THICK ABOVE THE LAKE WHEN WE set out for our long drive north. Somewhere between us and the other side it became a curtain shutting off further sight in a welter of flakes over the lonely surface. As the hours went by the world seemed one vast monotony, an endless white highway lined by dark snow-tufted pines. Daylight was slowly fading as we passed through Tupper Lake;

the big hotel at Paul Smith's was a massive silhouette in a twilight waste; our headlights picked out a few snow-blanketed frame buildings at Whippleville; and not long after that we could see the lights of Malone.

The great gray barracks of Troop B, standing at the summit of a hill just outside the town, were spotted with vivid light. From the first-floor windows shafts of brilliance struck out into the darkness. With a happy feeling of relief we drove up to the side entrance where a trooper already awaited us.

"I'll put your car in the garage," he said. "Captain Broadfield is in his office."

Captain Broadfield was a big man and robust. At my first glimpse of him I discarded the legend a downstate trooper had told me—that to become a member of tough Troop B the applicant must lick its commanding officer.

"We're just the Rochester Country Club tonight," said the Captain, hitching his belt about his ample middle. "Four from that town have already gone to bed. You two make the half dozen."

"I brought Carmer up here to see your part of the country," said Coley. "He's going to write something about it."

"There's plenty of it," said the Captain, "and some of the people in it are pretty damned funny."

"I was telling him on the way up your story about the Frenchie who won the Chevrolet in a lottery," said Coley.

"What one was that?" said the Captain.

"You remember? He didn't have any furniture or electric lights or radio in his house, so he cut a hole in the side just big enough to let the car into his living room. Now he reads by the lights, listens to the radio and sleeps on the upholstery."

"That's Joe Dogue's house," said the Captain. "He's put in some improvements since then. He got some pipe and extended the exhaust around the room and up through the roof. That gives him heat and he's sitting pretty while his wife cooks his meals on the engine. And did I tell you about his being elected to the school board?"

"No," said Coley.

"First meeting the chairman says, 'We ought to have a cuspidor around here,' and Joe jumps up quick and says, 'I nominate Jean Giron for cuspidor for two years.'"

A door opened and a big blue-eyed man in a dark blue suit entered the office.

"Hi, Joe," said the Captain, "Meet a couple more of these Rochester country clubbers."

"I'm Lieutenant Lynch," said the newcomer as he shook hands. "I've been detailed to show you the country tomorrow."

"What he don't know about it, Eddie will," said Captain Broadfield. "Sergeant Eddie Scyro, general guardian of northern New York, will drive for you and see that you meet all the people he's been taking care of for the past few years. And that's plenty."

"We're pretty bushed after our ride," said Coley. "Mind if we turn in?"

"I've had a little supper set for you in the mess hall," said the Captain. "Go eat that. Lieutenant Lynch will show you where it is and assign you beds upstairs. Don't get up for reveille. You'd better eat breakfast around eight. Sergeant Scyro will have a car waiting for you whenever you're ready to start out. Good night."

The dormitory was big and airy, and Coley and I slept hard. I remember hearing first call and reveille and grinning to myself as I realized that I could hear them and disregard them with impunity. There was a clatter about twenty minutes later as the men returned from breakfast and I managed to get my eyes half-open long enough to see a crowd of tall bronzed men in dark gray shirts and purple ties, olive breeches and black puttees. As they made for the stairway to begin the day's patrols they hurried into jackets darker than their breeches, black Sam Browne belts and campaign hats circled by purple cords. Luxuriating in my idleness, I lay and listened to spouting streams of ingenious profanity that filled me with the joy most men have in being with their kind in barracks. The lumberjacks had been profane but, with all their poetic humor, their oaths were workaday compared with the wild flights of imaginative epithets I was hearing.

After the day had started a tall angular trooper came in and stood by the cot of a comrade who, I learned later, had been on duty the night before until long after midnight and had been excused from reveille.

"Get up," said the tall trooper calmly. "I've brought you some breakfast."

A tousled shock of blond hair appeared from under the blankets and slowly the sleeping one raised himself to a sitting posture.

"Wouldn't you know it would rain as long as I had to chase a runaway cow last night?" he demanded bitterly. "Now look at the goddam weather." Sunlight was pouring into the long high room and a soft breeze blew through the opened windows.

The tall fellow looked out at a blue sky in which white islands of cumulus drifted and began to declaim in a pleasant baritone:

I bring fresh showers for the thirsting flowers,
    From the seas and the streams;
I bear light shade for the leaves when laid
    In their noonday dreams.
From my wings are shaken the dews that waken
    The sweet buds every one,
When rocked to rest on their mother's breast,
    As she dances about the sun.

"Shut up," said the trooper on the cot. "What do I care about that when I can't find that ——in' cow?"

A well-set-up, stocky dark man came in and stood at the end of my bunk and grinned. I saw three chevrons on his arm.

"Sergeant Scyro," I said.

"Right," he said, "and if you fellows want breakfast and a chance to see something of the country maybe you'd better get up."

Coley and I rose and dressed, tried to make our cots neatly according to trooper regulations, and went down to breakfast realizing that we had failed.

Lieutenant Lynch in uniform was waiting at our table, his blue eyes quizzically alight.

"I heard you didn't make reveille," he said.

I sat with Sergeant Scyro and Coley sat with the Lieutenant as we started out. Already most of the snow through which we had come was melted from the roads and the air was mellow with the first warmth of spring.

The country north of Malone flattens toward the plain that borders the St. Lawrence River. Most of it is far from fertile as the little, desolate shacks of the farmers attest. It is rocky, scrub-filled, monotonous. Day after day our foursome visited the inhabitants of New York's northernmost borderland. It is a country of heartbreaking poverty, of ignorance and incredible shiftlessness, but it is also a land of ironic humor. Serious sympathy for these people, most of them French or of French antecedents, is somewhat impeded by their own satisfaction with their lot and by the fun they extract from a barren living.

I remember that we stopped first at the home of Cluffy and Zito and Mamma La Prad. Zito came out to meet us, his unkempt red mustache dripping a darker red tobacco juice. He pretended to be very indignant that troopers had dared to call at his place when he "hadn't done nothing," and he swore a great deal but he looked secretly pleased. So did Mamma who came out of the house, blue eyes blazing, white hair flying, to trade hearty insults with Sergeant Scyro, first in English and then as the exchange grew fiercer in a French whose meaning was the clearer for her contemptuously vulgar gestures. Lieutenant Lynch pointed out that though this family was poverty-stricken, each of the seven highly unpedigreed La Prad dogs in the yard wore a license tag. Mamma immediately mistook our economic observations for an interest in pets and displayed seven white rats in a cage before going into the kitchen to drive out a half-dozen pigeons and two bantam roosters for our inspection. Sergeant Scyro increased the conversational tension by telling how Zito's cow had got so thin that she seemed to be going to die of starvation, how Zito had refused to feed her when the troopers told him to, how the troopers had fed her and the poor thing, entirely unaccustomed to enough good food, had died at once from the shock.

"Goddam you, I'd 'a' killed you if I'd been there," said Zito.

"He would have, too," said the Sergeant.

"Where's Cluffy?" said Lieutenant Lynch.

"He's off haulin' wood," said Zito.

When we drove on, however, the Sergeant pointed out that a figure from behind the outhouse was joining the two who waved at us from the barnyard.

"I'll have to find out if Cluffy's been up to something," said the Sergeant.

Dick Martin owned two race horses, Worthy Orphan and Lee Volo. Just as soon as he unhitched them from the plow in the spring he would start racing them. He had a race track, judges, stand and all, on his farm. Every year he held his own fair and insisted on being furnished with troopers to handle the crowds, a detail much sought after by the members of Troop B who usually reported back to the barracks a little weak from repressed mirth. When we got to Dick's place, Dick was in a sulky behind Worthy Orphan who was trotting enthusiastically on the muddy track. Just in front of her a mule made the pace, galloping in heavy buckety-buck fashion as the heels and whip of a large woman in a voluminous black dress and high black shoes struck his sides. The group stopped as we approached.

"Goddam it," said Dick, "can't you get that mule to run faster than that?"

"He's goin' faster'n the horse, ain't he?" said the woman, displaying a mouth full of large gold teeth.

"Mountain-high Christ," said Dick. "If there was room to get by ye I'd 'a' lapped ye."

Lieutenant Lynch interrupted.

"Just came by to see if you're goin' to need that detail this year."

"I was thinkin' some o' havin' a dance instead," said Dick uncertainly, "but I ain't got it exactly figured out to a dead standstill."

"You ain't goin' to have no dance," said his wife, "races're bad enough."

"We'll send you the detail," said the Lieutenant, and we drove off.

The Recors sawmill was making a great clatter when we came by and one of the boys walked down to our car to point out some of its interesting mechanical portions taken with strict impartiality from one baby grand piano, one old Chevrolet, one Model-T Ford, one outworn treadmill. And as we approached Jim McGovern's place a tall, gaunt, big-jointed figure was lounging along the road toward us. The Sergeant stopped the car.

"Gentlemen," he said, "in this corner Mike LaPlante, the terror of the St. Lawrence country. When you fightin' again, Mike?"

"Soon's they can match me," said Mike, grinning through a grizzled mustache. "I'm keepin' in good training all right."

"How old are you now?" said the Sergeant.

"Around fifty-eight, I guess. I started box-fightin' when I

was fifty-six an' that was two years ago." He turned to Coley and the Lieutenant in the back of the car. "I lost my first fight," he said plaintively. "My footwork was slow—but it's better since I been trainin'."

"How do you train?" said Coley.

"I put on a bathin' suit," said Mike, "an' a pair o' rubber boots. Then I put a rope around my belly an' hitch it to a car and one o' the boys drives it for me. Five or six miles o' that does me a lot o' good."

"Well," said the Sergeant, "don't sign up with anybody unless you see me first. Don't want you to get gypped like you did last time."

Jim McGovern and his boy lived in a log house with a planked-up gable above it. A friendly police dog rushed out to greet us and we heard Jim yelling at him. In a moment Jim limped into sight, his weak blue eyes gleaming behind his glasses, his white mustache trembling above his working mouth. When he saw us he made us come in and watch the dog go through his tricks. Jim got more excited than the dog and sometimes his signals did not work, but we said he had a smart dog all right and that was what Jim wanted.

While we watched the tricks a tall, clear-eyed boy of about seventeen came down the ladder from the loft. He spoke to us pleasantly and after we had gone outside toward the car I asked him what he planned to do to earn a living.

"I'm plannin' to send him into the Navy," said Jim. "He can't get along and know anything here in these woods."

"What will you do then?" said the Lieutenant. "You need this boy."

"I'll get along all right with my dog," said Jim.

As we left, Lieutenant Lynch called my attention to many

holes in the plank door to Jim's house. "They were made by shots," he said. "We thought we had quite a mystery here once. The boy when he was a bit younger found a pile of old Nick Carter dime thrillers. He used to read 'em and then when his father was out of the house he'd tell his mother stories about the place being surrounded by desperate criminals. She was an excitable woman and she'd get out the shotgun and sit with it across her knees. The boy would listen at the window and when he shouted, 'There they are!' she'd let go through the door. It took us some time after we found the boy's books to convince his father and mother that the villains outside were only in the boy's imagination."

On our way home one afternoon toward the end of the days we devoted to our informal and incomplete census we pulled up by a shack so close to collapse it seemed not possibly habitable. But a man came out, leaving his door ajar, and leaned nonchalantly on the fence of his pigsty in which a single porker wallowed dismally.

"Why don't you sell that hog?" said Sergeant Scyro. "He won't get any bigger."

"I figure I got to keep one pig," said the man. "Might as well be this one."

"Well, why don't you clean up around here a bit," said the Sergeant, "and mop that floor in there?" pointing to the dirt-covered surface visible through the open door.

"I'd just as soon mop my floor," said the man, "but the water drops down through onto my potatoes in the cellar and makes 'em sprout."

The Sergeant looked at him intently. "A little good food wouldn't hurt you any," he said. "Better come by the barracks and have a meal with us soon."

"All right," said the man listlessly.

On our arrival at the barracks that day I rode on into the garage with the Sergeant. As we got out of the car I heard a vigorous squeaking that seemed to come from a box near a window.

"That's Ike the Second," said the Sergeant and he walked over to the box and picked several long angleworms from a tin can on a window sill. A large robin hopped out of the box and fluttered to the top of it where he scolded shrilly until the worms choked off further utterance.

"Did they tell you about Ike the First?" said the Sergeant. "He was much more of a bird than this one. We found him floppin' around the yard when he was a baby —just so much cat-bait. Guess his parents had lost him or been killed or something. We brought him up like you see we been raisin' this one. He used to fly all around the premises but he always showed up at mealtime and slept in that box. Well, one night he didn't come back and he wasn't around the next morning. Say, we put on a search like the Governor's baby had been kidnaped but it wasn't any use, we couldn't find him.

" 'Bout three days later a trooper was givin' testimony in a trial down at the Malone courthouse. It was a warm day and the window was open. All of a sudden there was a devil of a racket in a tree near the window and the next thing in flies Ike, lights on the trooper's shoulder and begins givin' him hell because he's hungry. He makes so much noise the judge says, 'You'll have to incarcerate this bird or I'll sentence him for contempt o' court.' So the trooper puts Ike in the men's room until the trial is over. When he goes to get him afterwards Ike has tried to get a drink out of a toilet and fallen in. He's pretty near drowned and madder than he ever was."

"Where is he now?" I said.

"That depends, I guess," said the Sergeant reflectively. "You see, our cook is mighty proud o' his meat pies. One day he cooked one so good he got to feelin' sorry for anybody that didn't have any. So he took a mess out to Ike and, bein' ordinarily a polite bird, Ike ate it. Then he died."

That night while I was sitting by the big fireplace in the reading room of the barracks Lieutenant Lynch approached bearing a large volume.

"The family album," he said, "known hereabouts as the *Book of Horrors*. So far you've seen how we patrol roads, help the poor when they get a raw deal and are kind to dumb animals. A trooper's life isn't very exciting. But every once in a while we find real trouble—and one of the first rules when we find it is to take a photograph of the scene of the crime before anything is disturbed."

The pictorial contents of the *Book of Horrors* tell such stories of murder and violence in lonely places as to fill the observer's heart with loathing and dismay. They need not be repeated here save for the mention of two strange tales: one, of the day when the troopers spread out in the woods to track "Sambo" (their pet name for a nameless giant), an insane, gorilla-like Negro who, armed and vicious, stood them off until, riddled with bullets, he was finally destroyed; and the other, of the cunning detective work of Lieutenant Lynch who, while examining a murder-suspect who was nervously chewing on matches, remembered that matches with chewed ends were scattered on the floor of the slain man's house, and thereby secured a confession.

"We are proud of our record on murder cases," said the Lieutenant. "We have solved the great majority of those we've handled. But sometimes on less important assignments the joke is on the trooper. I remember once we had the job of escorting milk trucks down a road blocked by strikers. We got into a little mix-up and in the middle of it I saw a farmer-striker who had fought his way to the top of a load yell at a trooper on the road below him. Just as the trooper looked up the striker turned a full twenty-gallon can of milk over on him. Then the striker jumped off the truck and ran and the trooper went after him. The farmer was so scared he ran right into a pool of water nearby, and began swimming for the other side. The trooper saw he couldn't catch him and in disgust he threw his police stick at him. He didn't think he was goin' to hit him but he did, right on the head and knocked him cold. Then the trooper had to go in and save him from drowning and get kidded for weeks about his two baths in one day."

"The best joke on a trooper that I've heard lately," said Sergeant Scyro, stretching himself comfortably on the divan, "was the time one of our game wardens got one of the boys to put on huntin' clothes and go with him to arrest some fellows who'd been takin' venison out of season. It took some time to find the camp and they got there just around dark. There was three men in the camp and they treated 'em fine, said they was just sittin' down to supper and made the warden and the trooper join 'em. They was both hungry as hell, and the venison steaks was mighty good, so they et and et. So did the other fellows. Every time anybody let up a bit the fellow in charge of the camp'd fill his plate up with venison. The trooper said it seemed like he'd et a whole buck all by himself. Well, jest as the trooper was polishin' off his last steak the warden tells the camp gang what he's there for, says he's sorry and all that but the law has to be obeyed. The fellow in charge o' the camp waits a while to answer, but after the trooper has swallowed the last mouthful he says sort o' slow-like:

" 'I wouldn't want to disappoint you fellows none, but your friend here has jest et up the last bit of evidence.' "

When I started for bed I found Captain Broadfield talking to Coley.

"I've got a couple tips for you," he said. "I don't know whether you'd be interested in 'em or not and they take you in opposite directions. Make this your headquarters, though, while you run 'em down. There's a story about a house over at Ogdensburg that everybody in this section talks about. I'd tell it to you myself but I think you'd get a better version of it further west. The other is that the woodsmen over Lake George way make quite a business of catching rattlesnakes."

"You take my car," said Coley. "I'll stay here and visit with the Captain while you work. He's thought up an entirely new angle on the business of catching fish."

"What's that?" I said obligingly.

"I'm developing a fish that will take only one kind of fly a secret kind I've invented myself. The rest of my scheme works out by a natural process of elimination. All the fish taking other kinds of flies will soon be caught by the thousands of other fishermen. That'll leave in the streams just the fish that'll take my fly and I'll be the only one who knows what that fly is. Logical, isn't it?"

"Perfectly," I said.

"Put that in your book," said Captain Broadfield.

31

Ogdensburg and the Florentine Fancy

THE STORY THAT THE PEOPLE OF THE NORTH COUNtry still tell about the house at Ogdensburg begins over a hundred years ago in the Italian city of Florence with the meeting of a boy and girl at a ball. That she was Ameriga, lineal descendant of Amerigo Vespucci, or that he was Ferdinand, Duc d'Orléans, son of King Louis-Philippe of France, meant little to either of them. But that they loved each other at first sight meant a great deal. A balcony, a garden, the silvered Arno slowly rolling into shadow as the moon dropped behind the hills, filled their hearts, as they have filled other hearts, and the daughter of the great house of the explorer escaped one night from her disapproving family and joyfully went to live in Paris with the son of the King.

Ferdinand had meant to marry Ameriga but the intervention of his father prohibited that. He had promised to love her always but it was not long before he had tired of her. When their love was at an end Ameriga could not bear the thought of a return to the place of its beginning. And so, with the courage of her exploring ancestor, she set out for the country which had honored him by taking his name. The settlement Duke Ferdinand had given her at their parting was almost gone; at home in Florence her family lived meagerly on a pension granted by Italy out of reverence for Amerigo; only the United States, land of opportunity, offered her hope of a happy existence.

At first the country proved itself worthy of her trust. After the social crudities of the administration of Andrew Jackson, Washingtonians were engrossed in creating a Capital society. Ameriga Vespucci lent it élan. She had moved in the company of princes and the country's snobs took her to their cold hearts. The courtly little Dutch President, Van Buren, found such obvious joy in her company that some even suspected his widower's heart had at last been touched. Daniel Webster, the senator of the Jovian brow and golden voice, found her charming. And Nathaniel Parker Willis, Beau Brummell of the Knickerbocker poets, darling of the nation's literary world, wrote:

TO AMERICA VESPUCCI:
> Blest was thy ancestor with a deathless fame
> When to this western world he gave his name;
> But far more blessed, methinks, that man would be,
> Fair scion! who might give his name to thee.

The life of a society belle in Washington was not inexpensive, however, and Ameriga knew that she must soon turn her popularity to some account. And so with infinite pains she drew up in her own handwriting and her own quaint expression a petition to the United States Senate that it allow her to become a citizen and, in recognition of the deeds of her illustrious forefather after whom its country had been named, that it grant her lands on which she might live.

Senator Benton, of New York presented the bill to the Senate and it was at once referred to the Committee on Public Lands. And then, though the senators looked with kindled gallantry on the petite, olive face with its imploring dark eyes gazing down on them from the balcony, the Committee found no precedent for granting the request and refused to recommend it.

The lovely Florentine was heartbroken. The friendly senators, looking on her tears with guilty embarrassment, dug into their pockets and made up a goodly sum which they tactfully presented not as charity but as their contribution to the memory of one of the world's great explorers. Ameriga gratefully received it and returned to Paris where she lived with her sister, the Vicomtesse Solen.

But her Washington friends did not forget her. The next two years saw great changes in American political life. Van Buren was defeated. Harrison was elected, only to die, and Tyler had become President. Letters came to Ameriga saying that with the new administration there was a chance that her hopes might be realized. Hastily she packed and took ship.

Her new campaign could not have begun more auspiciously nor ended more disastrously. For on the evening of the very day of her arrival in Boston the city celebrated with a gorgeous ball the visit of the Prince de Joinville, younger brother of the Duc d'Orléans. Clad in a gown the color of pomegranates, its long train sweeping statelily behind her,

her black hair falling in two long braids from under her red, gold-embroidered Greek toque, a heavy gold cord about her waist, Ameriga Vespucci entered the ballroom at Faneuil Hall on the arm of the Prince himself. Boston saw and worshiped, and all might have gone well with her and her plans had not a guest recognized her as the former mistress of the Prince's brother.

The next morning Ameriga was friendless, penniless, hopeless. There could be no grant from the Senate now, no generous collection in the name of her ancestor. America had turned from her in the name of righteousness and virtue. Of her old friends who had sought her society as a priceless favor only one came to her—John Van Buren, lovable, spendthrift, hard-drinking "Prince John," son of the former President of the United States—and he came to bargain.

Ameriga was too weary, too broken to haggle long. Soon she was once more a mistress—this time of an American prince who had outgrown his princehood and did not know it. Helplessly she traveled about with her restless lover, watching over him while he drank himself into insensibility, putting him to bed afterwards.

And now at long last the house at Ogdensburg shadows this story. For on a winter journey above Albany into Jefferson County, John Van Buren and Ameriga met George Parish, rich merchant of the north country. In the Brick Hotel at Evans Mills, popular legend goes, John, a little drunk, challenged Mr. Parish to a game of poker. When John's gold was gone he put up for a final hand his last possession against all that he had lost—and lost her, too.

And so George Parish drove his sleigh north to Ogdensburg and the fur robes that covered him covered Ameriga Vespucci.

The house to which he brought her had been for years the wonder of the St. Lawrence region. It was three stories high, its red brick walls towering above the humbler dwellings of the town, and it stood in the center of an estate that was enclosed by a stone wall, eight feet high. George Parish's uncle, David Parish, a Belgian banker, had had it built soon after the end of the eighteenth century. He had ordered the woodwork made in Rouen in France and had sent the artisans who created it to Ogdensburg to install it. Joseph Rosseel, his agent, had helped plan and execute the house, the stables, the courts paved with cobblestones, the gardens and the gardener's lodge, the circular tanbark track on which grooms exercised the horses.

The people of Ogdensburg soon heard the whispers that went around. And they proved themselves no less respectable and cruel than the Bostonians. A "fancy lady" could not come to live among them with impunity, they said. But Ameriga was protected now—by the high fortress of the house and the eight-foot wall about it. She chose not to subject herself to the snubs of her neighbors but to live within the circumscribed world George Parish had provided for her. She sought no friends in the north country—but she lived happily on the big estate, surrounded by comforts few of her neighbors could afford. Parish ordered whatever adornment she desired from Albany, from New York, from Paris. Her horses and her coaches were all that a feminine heart could desire. The fare provided by her chef was a treat for an epicure, and male epicures were not long in seeking her table. Though the wives of the town sat at home in a mood of flinty resentment, their husbands must for economic reasons if no other do business with Parish and be sufficiently "men of the world" to sup with him in his home. So eager gentlemen bent forward to catch the words of their clever, beautiful Italian hostess while George Parish smiled from his end of the long table.

Ameriga was living in a cosmopolitan world of gentlemen —she was the beloved of its richest and most distinguished citizen—and she was happier than she had been since those foolish days when, for a brief moment, she had believed she would be la Duchesse d'Orléans. Sitting in her sunny garden through whose gateway she could see the wide blue waters of the St. Lawrence, she could ignore ill-bred children running past and crying "fancy lady" with excitement and contempt in their shrill voices. Boats came into sight and vanished beyond far horizons, but the blood of the old explorer no longer complained within her. She was content, content for twenty years of living in her luxurious house with her kind, prospering lover.

It ended with merciful suddenness. She was getting to be an old lady, a little stout, a little wrinkled, but life was serene and secure. Then George Parish told her he must return to his lands in Europe, he was giving up his holdings in America—and her. She met his decision bravely, thanked him for his settlement of three thousand dollars a year, told him she would go again to live with her sister the Vicomtesse.

And after he had gone away she sent out the invitations for the only party the big house knew during the score of years she was its hostess. They went to the children of Ogdensburg and they were accepted—though many a serious conference preceded the parents' anxiously awaited decisions.

Children too old to need constant care found themselves unexpectedly accompanied on that sunlit day by mothers quite as excited as they at the opportunity of seeing what lay behind the eight-foot wall. Besides the wonder of the grounds themselves, there were floral arches, Japanese lanterns and, especially imported from New York, a magician. Most impressive of all were the oranges served among the refreshments—tropic fruit that most of the guests had never seen before. The prisoner of the Parish house was so happy in the joy of the children that the good people who had long been her jailers were at last moved to friendly tolerance. A kindly minister spoke their gratitude—and the party was over.

The next day Ameriga left Ogdensburg on her lonely journey back to France. In Paris she was welcomed by her sister and she lived peacefully there, though her letters show that her memories tortured her, until in a few years she died.

The Parish house, its interior remodeled elegantly in oak after the elaborate manner of the eighteen-nineties, still stands. It is known to Ogdensburg and visiting tourists as the Remington Art Memorial and it houses a collection of the paintings and sculpture of Western subjects by the late Frederic Remington, one of America's most popular artists at the turn of the century. Just a few of Ameriga's lovely possessions—her portable writing desk exquisite with inlay and some of the dainty articles of her toilet—are kept in the room that was hers. If in some ghostly state she has found a way to return across the ocean to her American home, I know she must be puzzled by all the rearing bronze bronchos, and the paintings of cowboys galloping over the endless yellow desert, but I am quite sure she is not afraid.

32

Rattlesnake Hunter

THE DARK, WINDING ROAD THROUGH THE ADIRON-dacks, splashed here and there by spring sunlight, guided me past lake after lake, high summit after high summit. I saw Saranac, then Placid, and I turned south at Elizabethtown, preferring the tree shadows of the Schroon Lake road to the more open highway that rims the waters of Champlain and Lake George. A few minutes after I had left Schroon, I took a dirt road that seemed to lead southeast toward my destination. It was steep and it branched often. Soon I realized that I had in all probability taken a wrong turn and I looked eagerly ahead for human aid.

It seemed to have materialized in a lank, middle-aged fellow in overalls and black shirt who was hoeing dispiritedly at a rocky patch of earth near the road. His jaws were moving rhythmically, and occasionally he spat a yellow stream toward the blade of his hoe.

"Can you tell me how to get to Bolton's Landing?" I said.

He stopped work, leaned on his hoe-handle and regarded me solemnly.

"Well," he said, "if I was goin' to Bolton's Landing, I wouldn't *start* from here."

I laughed, but his weather-seamed face did not change expression.

"There must be a way," I said.

"Take the next turn left. That'll bring you into Padan-Aram. Ought to help some."

"I suppose you're glad of a warm day," I said. "Your farming season can't be long in this northern part of the state."

"Only lasts about fifteen minutes," he said very seriously, "and *they* seem to come around lunchtime."

When I first saw Bill Clark he was down in one of his back lots mending fence. I had parked my car close to the edge of the narrow, winding road that leads over the mountains back of the lake and I had reached his porch, littered with pails, baskets, milk pans, bits of old machinery and ears of seed corn before he saw me. He waved then and came slowly up the rise toward his little house.

"Yesterday was my Sabbath," he said, "so that's why you catch me workin' on your Sunday."

"I don't mind," I assured him hastily. "I just wondered if you wouldn't take me out to hunt rattlesnakes with you."

He smiled and his mouth spread to each side of his face—paralleling the lines about his blue eyes. His squat figure was firmly planted on the stony soil.

"Don't get many requests like that," he said. "Folks don't care much about catchin' snakes. But I guess I could oblige you. When c'n ye go?"

"I'm ready any time," I said.

"Ain't no time like the present," said Bill. "We may be a little late startin' since it's near nine o'clock but maybe we can pick one up before very long, certainly before dark."

"One'll be enough," I said. "I just want to see how you do it."

Bill stepped to the wall of the porch and picked up a long stick with some sort of metal contraption on the end.

"You see this," he said impressively; "this is what's known as the Bill Clark rattlesnake tongs. I do practically all my snake catchin' with it. Fifty years ago I used to use a forked stick—or my hands—but by and by I invented this an' it's the best thing for takin' a rattler that I know."

"How does it work?" I said.

"Well, it's really a broomstick with a wire run through eyelets along the side. They's a handle at your end and at the business end it's got a pair of steel jaws like pincers an' they work the same way. When I see a rattler I get up on him and get his neck between them jaws. Then I pull on the handle an' the jaws close on his neck, an' I've got him. I usually carry a basket to put him in because he might be a her and have five or six little ones down her gullet. I git jest as much bounty for little rattles as I do for big ones. But if I'm in a hurry I jest put my foot on his neck and jerk his head off with the tongs. Then I bury the head under a stone and go ahead. Well, I reckon I'm ready. Here's a pair o' tongs fer you."

We put the tongs in the back of the car and started driving south along the west shore of the lake.

"How much can you make out of one average-size rattlesnake?" I said.

"Well, now, that depends," said Bill. "We used to get three dollars a rattle regardless o' size. Then they reduced it to a dollar 'n' a half, but now it's back up to two-fifty. Then there's all the oil you can try out of him. May amount to three-four dollars' worth."

"Oil?" I said.

"Sure. Rattlesnake oil. Good for what ails ye, whatever it is. Drugstores buy it an' these doctors that goes out with a tent and an Indian through the country sells lots of it. Mighty good for rheumatism—makes ye soople. Feller I know says he knew a man wunst used too much of it—got so soople he couldn't stand up."

His blue eyes sought mine in kindly seriousness.

"I take it the female rattler carries her young in her gullet," I said sternly.

"Yep. But they ain't no way o' tellin' unless ye take her home an' put her in a box an' wait fer 'em to crawl out. Then we can get bounty fer all the little rattlers. That's a damn sight better than doin' like a rattlesnake feller on the other side of the lake did a couple years ago. He broke the big rattles in two an' tried to collect bounties fer both ends. He's still in the penitentiary."

We were crossing the southern end of the lake now. The great cliffs on the east side were looming above us and the water at their feet was very blue. Far to the north green islands seemed to be floating on the still surface.

"I like livin' back from the water," said Bill suddenly. "A lake always looks better when you come up on it. Here's where we stop an' hit a trail."

Through an upward slanting field we strode, tongs dragging behind us, then climbed along a creek bed until we reached a wooded ridge.

"There ought to be some in the rocks at the end of this ridge," said Bill.

"Isn't this business a little dangerous?" I said.

"Ain't been struck in fifty years."

"Yes, but suppose there's more than one at a time."

"More than one!" He struck his thigh with his open palm. "Guess I ain't told ye 'bout the time round ten years ago when Dal Pratt an' I was huntin' on this very ridge. We was separated. Pratt had gone on up the mountain an' I come into a little rocky ravine not much bigger'n a minute and there, by God, was all the rattlesnakes in this whole Adirondack country a-sunnin' 'emselves. They'd jest come out o' their winter dens an' was gettin' ready to move to their summer ones. Five hundred to a thousand rattlers, by God, a-turnin' and twistin' there in the sun an' all of 'em singin' so's you could hear 'em a half-a-mile."

Bill's eyes gleamed, his face seemed contorted with joy. I imagined that he was counting up the grand total of rattles and rattlesnake oil in terms of dollars.

"I called to Pratt an' he heard me and come along the mountain to the edge of the ravine. He jumped down on a boulder just beside my shoulder an' then not payin' any attention landed right beside me an' there we both was with all them rattlers raisin' hell around us. I seen Pratt's eyes sort o' flicker so I says to him, I says:

" 'If you be scared you better git back up thar on that rock.'

" 'Waal,' he says, sort o' slow an' careful, 'I be.' "

Bill waited for this monosyllabic expression of emotion to sink in, his eyes twinkling. Then he said, "I sure was a fool to use my shotgun that day. I got seventeen on the first shot and I got about seventy-five that morning—but I could of got the whole lot if I'd took my time and used these here tongs."

We had come to a pile of dark rocks and Bill began poking around under them with the tongs. Once he turned one

· 369 ·

over, looking expectantly at the spot beneath while I stepped back and felt frightened. At last he said:

"We'll rest here a bit," and sat down on a rock. Fearfully I sat beside him.

"Why can't you breed rattlesnakes?" I said. "Then you wouldn't have to go to all this trouble and you'd get your bounty and oil just the same."

"I thought o' that," said Bill reflectively. "Fact is I tried it once. I got a lot o' rattlers an' put 'em all in a box all winter and all spring an' nothin' happened. Didn't get no little rattlers at all. Then Henry Hall, friend o' mine lives down in the town o' Lake George, come by and he says, 'Ye won't git no little ones unless you put a blacksnake in there.' So I put a blacksnake in there and by God it wan't no time 'fore there was six little fellers crawlin' around. So I'd say it would be my conclusion after fifty years o' huntin' rattlers that the blacksnake is the papa rattler."

"I didn't know they ever mated," I said.

"Oh, sure. One mornin' I seen a big blacksnake come out from under a rock and a rattler followed him out and they mated right there—you know how they do—twistin' and turnin' sort of like they was dancin'. Well then, I'm damned if he didn't get back under that rock and bring out another rattler and mate with her, and then he went back again and when a third rattler come out I jest went on about my business."

"You haven't told me why you aren't breeding black-snakes with rattlers to get more rattlers," I said.

"Well, that was Henry's fault, too, really. He seen I had some luck, so he tried it. He put some blacksnakes and rat-tlers in a big wire cage and kept 'em there a long time. But nothin' happened. So he kept 'em a couple o' months more and still he didn't get none and somehow he got to blamin' it on the female rattlers. Henry's house is right plumb on the street in Lake George an' one mornin' his wife woke up and there sits Henry in the doorway with his shotgun on his knees.

" 'You goin' huntin'?' she says.

" 'Nope,' says Henry.

" 'What you plannin' on?' she says.

" 'I'm figgerin' on shootin' the first female that comes down the street.'

" 'You can't do that,' she says.

" 'I'm goin' to,' says Henry.

"Well, then she screamed an' some men come in an' satcheled onto Henry an' by God they had to take him to the crazy house. He's sane enough 'bout everything else except females but he's bound to take a shot at the first one o' *them* he sees. So they have to keep him locked up. He's up there now."

Bill pulled some sandwiches and two bottles of milk from his basket and we ate and talked a while. Then we dozed off and mid-afternoon had come before we felt like continuing our quest. Neither of us expected it to have so sudden an ending.

For as Bill rose, the rock on which his feet rested tilted slightly. From under it came a prolonged buzz not unlike the note of a cicada but lower and harder. The shambling ease of the old man vanished. With one quick movement he kicked the rock over and there beneath it in a writhing coil lay a snake. His head was already moving back making ready to strike. His mouth was open very wide and his eyes were darkly gleaming beads above it.

"See if you can catch him by the neck," said Bill and I

pushed my tongs awkwardly forward. As I pulled the wire handle the rattler struck and his head lunged up the pole, the jaws at the bottom catching him toward the middle of his body. Again he struck, coiling about the steel teeth that held him, his dripping fangs reaching halfway up to my rigid hands while I stood paralyzed, gazing at him.

"Hold tight," said Bill sharply, and I heard the sharp click of his tongs as they bit into the snake just behind the head.

I must have had sense enough to loosen my hold then, for I remember Bill's raising the twisting burden and turning away from me. Then he had the snake firmly held, his right hand close up to the head, and he was stuffing it into a wicker fish-basket lined with felt and hung by a strap over his shoulder.

"Well, that's one," he said.

"I was too scared to do a good job," I said miserably.

"It takes practice," said Bill, "but you weren't in much danger. I was ready to hit him if he got too close to ye. A rattler ain't much of a fighter. One lick and he gives up and runs. Looks like we might find some today. Blamed if I didn't think that C.C.C. camp had driven most of 'em back into the mountains."

"No," I said, "I've had enough."

Bill followed me down the trail in reproachful silence. Finally he said:

"I reckon you'll want this one killed so's you can show it to your friends. We better stop and kill it now, for it takes a rattler a long time to die."

"How long?" I said.

"Depends—but my son and me cut the heart out of a big one once and laid it on a rock in the hot sun. It was beatin' forty-seven times a minute then and when we come back three hours later it was still beatin'—twenty-three times a minute."

"You'd better keep it," I said as we reached the car and climbed in. "Perhaps it's a female carrying a lot of little ones."

"Perhaps," said Bill pessimistically, and then we both lapsed into a long silence as we rolled along the side of the lake. The sun was out of sight somewhere beyond Bill's house and its rays were almost level as they struck against the rock cliffs on the eastern shore. The water below them seemed covered with a golden sheet.

We were approaching Bolton's Landing when Bill spoke again.

"Sometimes," he said, "the rattlers cross the lake."

"Ever see 'em?" I said.

"Sure," he said. "Lots of times. They take the little ones down their gullets and set out. You can see the mother snake's head above the water and she keeps her tail out, too. You can hear it rattlin' away—sort o' like an outboard motor. In the spring o' the year, in the moonlight, it makes a mighty pretty sight."

Listen for a Lonesome Drum

MANY OF THE SUPERSTITIONS OF THIS NORTHERN COUNTRY originated with its French inhabitants. One of the most poetic of these is the belief that if one hears a *chanson des voyageurs* sounding from high in the air he will know that he is hearing the song of Frenchmen who, living away from their native land, became so homesick that they sold their souls to the devil for the privilege of being immediately returned to their loved ones. In *chasse-galères,* tublike boats that sail swiftly above the treetops, these damned souls sing as they journey home.

In these north woods, too, one may sometimes come upon a man who has great charm but fierce eyes and pointed ears which will betray to the close observer that he is really a *loup-garou,* a wolf in the form and guise of a man. Many a luckless wanderer has made the discovery of the true nature of his companion too late for human aid.

A falling star, to these French residents of York State's northern border, is a soul which is selling itself to the devil. If one makes the sign of the cross while the star is still falling, he will save a falling soul from damnation.

When smoke goes straight up from the chimney a frost will soon arrive.

When snow blows from the trees a cold snap is on its way.

When you hear a fox barking a storm is coming.

If a loon is "hollering," there will be a storm tomorrow.

If a loon is flying, there will be a change of wind.

The tall tales of this section would not be complete without the story of the old woman who threw a kettleful of boiling water at her cat. On its way it froze into a solid ball of ice that knocked the cat into the middle of next week.

Part Seven

Storm Country

Schoharie Valley

I cannot tell how the truth may be;
I say the tale as 'twas said to me.

From *The Lay of the Last Minstrel,* by Sir Walter Scott

33

They Sang
the Murdered Bride

DESPITE ITS MAJOR OUTPUT — AN ESTIMATED
twelve hundred million lollypop sticks a year the town of
Berlin, Rensselaer County, New York, does not immediately
impart an impression of gay indulgence. Its modest frame
and brick houses are a ragged scatter along the Little Hoosac
River which has cut a deep valley between the Taghanick
and Petersburg mountains, and the motorist rolling through
the town's business section on U. S. Route 22 remembers it,
if at all, for long white two-story wooden structures, the
roofs of which extend over second-floor porches which shelter similar porches below.

The lines of these houses are severe and their recessed
windows catch little light. An aura of gloom appears to have
settled about them, as if tragic events leave psychic after-
effects. Behind these walls more than a hundred years ago
a few Berliners lived out a melodrama which ended in a
murder so shocking that it drew the fascinated attention of
the people of the entire northeast, treating them alternately
to such cold shudders of horror and such warm flushes of
pathos that they developed a condition constraining them

to burst into dolorous song. No crime in the state's history has inspired more ballad-narratives or more execrable verse, and country folk of Canada and of all the eastern states from Maine to Virginia still sing them.

At about the time that Henry Green came of age in 1844, four things happened that were memorable to him for the short time in which he was yet to have a memory. His store burned down, the Baptist Church expelled him for getting drunk, he was arrested for rescuing a friend from the custody of a constable, and he lost his girl.

The inhabitants of Berlin, three hundred odd, did not, however, look upon these separate incidents, or even their sum total, as indicative that Henry was a disreputable character. Indeed, his community standing, if affected at all, was enhanced. The Greens had been among the first families to settle in the valley. They were highly respected, well-to-do people and when, after Henry's widowed mother had taken him and his sister to live fourteen miles west in Troy, her son came back to Berlin and bought a store, his old neighbors greeted him happily. It was true that after the store burned some residents were mean enough to point out that its business had not been good and that after cursory investigation the insurance company of which Henry's uncle was a director had paid up with notable promptness, but there was no actual proof that the fire had not been accidental.

As for Henry's trouble with the Baptists, all the non-Baptists were inclined to agree with an opinion later expressed under oath by Henry's Aunt Rhoda Streeter—"Among the Berlin Temperance people, drinking at all is considered too much." Besides, Henry had admitted his guilt and his plea for reinstatement had been granted.

Taking a prisoner away from a constable was in the year

of 1844 a commendable enterprise when the prisoner, like this one, was in trouble over payments to that extractor of feudal rents, Stephen Van Rensselaer, Lord of Rensselaer Manor. Such unfortunates were looked upon by good country folk as honest men persecuted by a tyrant. There can be no doubt that the majority of Berlin's citizens considered Henry's penalty—a fine of 125 dollars—an outrage, and that they felt Henry had acted in the interests of justice when, disguised as an Indian Chief, he had led eleven of Berlin's young men, clad as braves of lesser rank, to rescue Schuyler Jones from the clutches of Constable John Nichols.

Parting with Alzina Godfrey, moreover, may well have improved Henry's reputation among the very folk who had condemned his drinking, for one of the more godly members of Berlin society expressed the general opinion of his kind when he said he looked upon the pretty, rich and vivacious girl as "something of a high-flyer."

More compensatory than all these facts that helped Henry Green to look with complacence on his past was an artistic event of considerable magnitude in Berlin. A troupe of traveling players arrived in town on December 31 and presented on that day, New Year's Eve, and the evening of January 1, 1845, a dramatic work, "The Reformed Drunkard" (possibly a pirated version of P. T. Barnum's "The Drunkard," first produced the same year), which clearly outlined the horrors from which the Baptists had saved Henry. Among the actors of the company were a young girl, Miss Mary Ann Wyatt, and her brother David.

Mary Ann had been born in Thornton, New Hampshire, she told Mrs. Ferdinand Hull at whose comfortable house she stayed, and she had been a worker in the cotton mills of Lowell, Massachusetts, until the opportunity of becoming an actress in a holy cause had presented itself. The wandering Temperance performers had played four nights at Washington Market in Troy a month before their Berlin engagement, and the good people of Hancock, Massachusetts, would be their next audience. After that they would be coming back to York State for engagements at Lebanon Springs, New Lebanon, and the Hudson River towns of Malden, Valatie, Coxsackie and Kinderhook.

Apparently the Berlin performances were so good that they caused a disproportionately large number of their audience to succumb to the lure of the stage. By the time of the New Lebanon show, four Berliners, including Henry Green, had joined the company and found opportunities for their talents. At first Henry's only participation was the singing of appropriate songs but he was soon given a role to play and when, in early February, the company presented "The Reformed Drunkard" at Kinderhook, actors Mary Ann Wyatt and Henry Green were exchanging unsimulated love-looks across the narrow stage. In his daytime walks with them through the old Dutch town, David Wyatt noticed his sister's hand no longer sought its accustomed resting place on his sleeve but nestled in the bend of Henry's arm. Each of his companions had begun praising to him the virtues of the other and David was not surprised when his sister asked him if he would approve her marrying Henry. The young man replied that he had nothing against Henry, a high encomium in his native New Hampshire and an honest answer though perhaps justifiably influenced by his having noted the sleek horse and smarter cutter which had brought the prospective bridegroom across the snowy roads from Berlin. Moreover, the troupe, unsuccessful in its recent engagements, had decided to disband after the Kinderhook performance and no doubt David felt that his sister's marriage to a young man reported by fellow-townsmen in the company to be of family and property would be advantageous.

For the last time then, on February 7, the little company recited the moralistic and sententious dialogue of "The Reformed Drunkard." The next morning, the date of the wedding having been set for February 17, Henry sped to Berlin to invite to it his best friends. There, with a lover's emphasis, he told his friend, Alson Niles, that he would rather have Mary Ann if she was not worth a change of linen than Alzina with all her wealth. Thinking on this apparently so overcame him with ardor that he raced back to Stephentown where he had left his fiancée. He arrived on Sunday, February 10, and that day, at his loving insistence, he and Mary Ann were wed in Stephentown's Christian Chapel by Elder Spoor.

The newlyweds arrived in Berlin on Tuesday evening and were soon thereafter ensconced in the home of Ferdinand Hull where Mary had stayed before. Berliners were not surprised that Henry's mother arrived from Troy on Wednesday and sent word that she wished to see her son at the Denniston and Streeter Tavern. They already had the feeling in their bones that the elder Mrs. Green would protest her boy's alliance with a penniless traveling player but they were grateful, nevertheless, to the Tavern's maid-of-all-work, Polly Ann Boone, for placing an attentive ear at the keyhole of a closed door in order to be able to confirm their surmise.

Henry busied himself when not with his mother in making up for the disappointment of his friends who had been asked to attend his wedding by inviting them to go on a St. Valentine's Day sleighride the next day to celebrate the already accomplished event. The merry party set out in a big hay-strewn wagon-box-on-runners at noon and, though sleighing was not very good on the winding river road, they made a leisurely journey to Cooley's Tavern at Hoosick Corners about eleven miles north. It was on this jolly excursion that Alzina Godfrey, according to local tell, said that she had meant to marry Henry herself, or a sentence of similar meaning—the natural and jocose remark of a girl who had once been courted by the bridegroom of another. Laughing Alzina, perhaps a little piqued that the wedding had taken place so soon after the sentimental hours of midsummer, could not have known then nor could any of her companions, not even Henry himself, the awful change which, once the words were said, had begun in his mind.

At Cooley's the gay companions warmed themselves and ate hearty. Mary Ann said she was cold and not feeling well and she went into the kitchen and drank some ginger tea. She felt better after that but on the drive back to Berlin, while the rest of the party sang to the accompaniment of the jingling sleighbells on the horses, she said she was still not in good health.

The next morning at about seven o'clock when young Dr. Rhodes was having his breakfast in a room adjoining his office, he became aware that Henry Green had noiselessly entered the office door and was standing by his medicine cabinet. Henry said he was unwell and the doctor gave him some large soft brown pills which, if taken four at a time, might prove cathartic. Soon thereafter Henry offered pills similar in size, color and shape to his wife who swallowed six of them, though protesting that her indisposition was slight and she needed no medicine. Immediately Mary Ann felt very much worse.

They Sang the Murdered Bride

Saturday morning the bride decided to stay in bed. Her solicitous husband apparently felt that he could leave her side, for he appeared at Denniston and Streeter's Store where the usual Saturday noon crowd had gathered. While standing in conversation with friends who were making the usual joking remarks to a new bridegroom Henry suddenly exclaimed, "A rat! No—a mouse," and pointed to a shelf saying one or the other of these animals had run behind the cinnamon bag. None of his companions had seen this happen but Henry assured them it was true and asked Dan Denniston why he did not put arsenic on the shelf to poison such rodents. A discussion of the safety of such an action followed and Henry asked how much arsenic it would take to kill a human being and was told probably not more than could be held on the end of the blade of a jack-knife.

Early in the afternoon Henry returned to the bedside of Mary Ann and gave her a glass of water into which he had mixed a white powder which he said was soda. He left the house and shortly thereafter Mrs. Hull found Mrs. Green retching violently and desperately ill. She immediately called Emerson Hull, elderly physician to the Green family, and he prescribed for the patient and departed.

The doctor had hardly closed the door when attentive Henry was back at his wife's bedside, this time with a glass of water into which he had stirred a white powder which he said was cream of tartar. Mary Ann had no sooner downed it than she felt terrific pains in her stomach which continued for some time, causing her to gasp that she felt as if she were burning up. Henry helpfully presented a glass of water and wine for her relief and just before giving her the mixture he took from his vest pocket some white powder which he sifted into the glass, saying that it was "a little flour."

Dr. Hull had made a tentative diagnosis of cholera morbis and during that Saturday night made several visits to his patient. Henry had decided to sleep on a cot in the corner of the sick room in order to be instantly available. This he proved to be for when Julia Whitford, acting as night nurse, went downstairs to make some tea around two o'clock he rose and gave his wife another white powder. He also sifted white powder into the chicken soup and into the "crust coffee." Julia Ann Whitford was puzzled when she returned and heard from young Mrs. Green that her husband had given her a powder. Two papers of powder which Dr. Hull had left were still intact. She saw a granular white substance in the chicken soup and a horrible and incredible suspicion seized upon her. She told it to Mrs. Hull and the two women collected the white stuff from the soup bowl. When Dr. Hull came in the morning they gave it to him and found that there was no necessity for telling the old physician what was in their minds. He took the powder to the kitchen at once and placed a portion of it on the hot stove. It gave off a smell like that of garlic—and he knew that burning arsenic was said to smell so.

The day that followed was one of steadily mounting horror. Through the upstairs bedroom where Mary Ann lay passed a procession of kindly, worrying women—some volunteering to spell the tired nurses, some paying calls of sympathy and good will. But a secret word was passing among them and their faces when they looked on Henry were white and drawn, their lips compressed, their eyes glittering. He made no move that was not recorded in the memories of Julia Ann Whitford, Pamelia Ann McLaughlin, Polly Ann

They Sang the Murdered Bride

Boone, Mary Ann Brimmer, Jemima Crandall, Sophronia and Rhoda Streeter. Standing in fluttering clusters in corners just off the stage where the tragedy was still playing they were a kind of Greek chorus disturbing the air of the old house with the terrible urgency of their whispering. Yet Henry Green pursued his direct and indefatigable way. By mid-afternoon he was understandably without the white powder he had distributed so freely. He borrowed a key to Denniston and Streeter's Store from unsuspecting elderly Barzaleel Streeter, saying he wanted to get some oats for his horse, and by four o'clock he was again beside his wife.

"Come, Mary Ann, it is four o'clock and it is time to take your medicine."

"I do not want to take it just now."

"The doctor said you must take it at four."

"I can't take it, Henry."

At this moment David Wyatt spoke up asking his sister if she thought she was being given too much medicine and the girl groaned and replied pointedly, "Yes, too much already."

When Barzaleel Streeter went into the store at five he noticed that the arsenic jar had been moved from its accustomed place.

At about this time in a downstairs room, Dr. Hull was telling David Wyatt in low tones that Mary Ann should be informed that she would soon die. David went at once to his sister saying "Mary, the doctor thinks you can't live."

"Must I die," said Mary Ann, "and not see my mother?"

Then she turned to her husband and said the words which were to give her strange immortality among the jigging fiddles, the wheezing pedal-organs, the twanging jewsharps at church sociables and farmhouse shindigs. They appear in no less than seven still-current ballad-versions of her pathetic story.

"Henry," she said, "have I ever deceived you?"

"No," said Henry.

Soon Mary Ann asked Dr. Hull if she might speak to him and in a voice just above a whisper told him of her belief that the white powders that Henry had put into her food and drink had poisoned her. The doctor at once summoned another witness, Barzaleel Streeter, to listen to her but the old man heard only a few sentences before Mary Ann's voice faded into silence.

On Monday morning at about eleven, a group of stern-faced citizens, including Doctor Hull, met at Elder Joseph Rogers' watchmaker's shop. Once more the powder collected by the women was produced. Rogers furnished a microscope and some arsenic he had once purchased and after careful examination those present decided that the two powders were alike in texture. The men tried heating the powders separately on iron and on copper surfaces but they could not definitely agree that they smelled an odor like that of garlic. At about the time they had finished their simple experiments they heard that Mary Ann Wyatt had died. A half hour later, enterprising Allen Streeter, village carpenter, applied to Henry Green for the job of making his wife's coffin and Henry's answer gave evidence that already the attitude of his friends and relatives had wounded him.

"As long as the people have suspicions on me I shall order nothing and pay for nothing and so that ends it." Nevertheless Allen Streeter got the job.

Tuesday afternoon in the Baptist Church, Coroner Betts and a coroner's jury met for the unpleasant business of the autopsy. Beside Dr. Hull stood a stranger whose presence made all realize that justice was taking the first step of its inexorable advance. Dignified and distinguished Dr. James Christie of Troy assisted at the removal of the stomach and aesophagus of the body with the purpose of taking these parts to Troy for analysis by the great doctors on the faculty of Rensselaer Polytechnic Institute. As a result of the jury's action then the coroner ordered the arrest of Henry Green on the charge of murdering his wife and the suspect was soon on the road to Troy in the humiliating charge of Constable Nichols from whose grip he had but recently snatched anti-renter Jones.

The trial, set for July 7, was one of the great events in Troy's history. So important were Henry's family connections and so active had they been in his behalf that the state took unusual efforts to see that impartial justice be done. Four judges, the Honorable Amasa J. Parker presiding, sat on the bench. John Van Buren, handsome, red-bearded Attorney-General of the State and son of former President Martin Van Buren, aided District Attorney Townsend for the prosecution. Henry's moneyed relatives had employed in his defense four of the most able and expensive lawyers of the region. By the time that court opened, the general talk was that Henry would be acquitted or pardoned.

The courtroom was crowded with spectators, "many of them females," when Henry Green entered. He was clad in a black suit as befitted a recently bereft widower but wore a jaunty weed in his hat, and the reporters present remarked on his prepossessing appearance.

While the prisoner sat stonily through the long hot hours

of the afternoon the prosecution conducted its case patiently and well. The great doctors from the college testified that they had found arsenic, much of it, in the stomach that Dr. Christie had brought to them. Dr. Hull and Barzaleel Streeter told of Mary Ann's deathbed accusation. And the women who had watched at the bedside recited in careful detail what they had seen. Try as it would, the defense could find no weakness or uncertainty in the testimony of Henry Green's sorrowful but uncompromisingly truthful old friends and close relatives. For twelve days the trial went on and the best that Henry's attorneys could do as it neared its end was to introduce witnesses to establish the prisoner's good character, to state that he sometimes had sudden fits, and to declare that it was unthinkable that a bridegroom should murder his bride so soon after their wedding.

Judge Parker's charge to the jury was brief and impartial. He told the twelve men they must not be influenced by pity or by attempts to operate on their minds "by local appeals and prejudices." When court convened on July 19 at three o'clock, the jury had reached the verdict of guilty and Judge Parker sentenced Henry Green to be hanged on the 10 of September. Hanged he was to his great surprise (he had so confidently expected reprieve that he refused to join a prisoner whom he helped to escape). The execution was private inside the jail but even so the Troy Citizens Corps was commanded to parade outside to keep order among the two to three thousand citizens who jammed Ferry Street from noon until four o'clock waiting for the moment when he would cease to be.

The news that Henry had confessed his crime to the two ministers of Troy who were to accompany him to the gallows had been released the day before, and there was considerable cynical and ironic comment among the crowd on the report that he had said, when asked by the men of the cloth if he had thought of suicide, "Oh no, I would not do that for I could not be forgiven that sin after death."

"I was riding with a lot of girls to Hoosick," Henry told the clergymen in the confession, later published, "and something said to me on that ride, with what happened going and returning, induced me to commit the crime." He added regretfully that he had not known at the time that the contents of the stomach could be analyzed after death.

Henry did not report "what happened going and returning" on the sleighride except to say it aroused his wife's "suspicions and jealousy." Perhaps the sort of delicacy that kept both prosecution and defense from calling the high-flying Alzina to the witness stand during the trial prevailed upon all knowing witnesses to refrain from telling what encouraging favors she had bestowed on the confused bridegroom during the fateful sleighride.

Henry climbed the steps of the scaffold, a clergyman on each side, at three-forty. The baritone that had been lifted in temperance songs when he had been courting the lovely itinerant Mary Ann Wyatt sounded above the voices of the fifty witnesses as all joined in singing *Rock of Ages Cleft for Me*. After the prayers of the ministers and Henry's own short plea for divine mercy the trap was sprung.

Already the country folk of the regions near Troy, their imaginations stimulated by Henry's long wait for execution, had been pleasurably stirred into the beginnings of song. On the back page of a transcript of the testimony, hastily published at popular demand by the *Troy Budget* in the week after the end of the trial, had appeared a sentimental over-literary poem entitled *Mrs. Henry G. Green*. It began:

> She stood upon the Temp'rance Stage
> 'Mid scenes of rare display

and continued with a long description of Mary Ann Wyatt's charms, including a neck of "parian marble fair" before it got down to the business of telling the story of her murder.

From this the rural song-makers characteristically borrowed such lines as they chose and then made up the rest. Their first inspired choice of a tune was an old Irish folk-melody and soon feet thumped to the strumming of guitars and voices roared out the "come-all-ye" first stanza of *The Ballad of Henry Green*.

Come listen to my tragedy, good people, young and old
I'll tell you of a story, twill make your blood run cold
Concerning a fair damsel, Miss Wyatt was her name
She was poisoned by her husband, and he hung for the same.

Greatly pleased with the results of their creative labors the people set to work to make more songs from the inspiring material—and *Mary Wyatt* and *The Murdered Wife* were soon furnishing incredibly mawkish words for their singing. Collectors who search isolated country communities with notebooks and recording machines have turned up many tuneful relics of Mary Ann's melancholy history, none, however, omitting the substance of the lines:

> But ere her gentle spirit fled
> She called him to her side—
> "Oh, Henry, have I e'er deceived?"
> "No," coldly he replied—

· 390 ·

and almost all folk-soloists who know one of the many versions still insert sobbing sounds as they carol:

"Now Henry has deceived me—how my poor heart is
    wrung!
But when I'm dead and buried don't have poor Henry
    hung.
Now I have forgiven him—" she turned upon her side
"In Heaven meet me Henry!" and she sweetly smiled
    and died.

In Berlin today old-timers tell that forty years after her death the remains of Mary Ann Wyatt were moved in order to make room for building lots. When the coffin was lifted from the grave, the story goes, the top boards burst open and disclosed only a mass of long, reddish-gold tresses. Instantly then, as the air touched it, the thick veil disappeared leaving only a bald and grinning skeleton in which the teeth shone so like perfect jewels that the diggers divided them among themselves as souvenirs. Be it said to the credit of the good people of Berlin that when the remains were reinterred they saw to it that at their expense a stone memorial was erected on which is engraved the legend:

This monument is erected by the Citizens of Berlin in memory of Mary Ann Wyatt, wife of Henry G. Green who was married Feb. 9, 1845 and on the 14th day of the same month was poisoned by her Husband with arsenic without any real or pretended cause.

Beautiful, intelligent and virtuous, she was wept over by the community, and the violated law justly exacted the life of her murderer as a penalty for his crime.

With these words carved in granite and with their songs do the people of the lollypop-stick capital remember the young temperance player and her bridegroom.

34

Behind the Helderbergs

IN THE SOUTHERN SECTIONS OF YORK STATE THERE are valleys whose high walls arrest the clouds and hold them for long periods. Naturally the lowland intervals are fertile, not only because of the rivers which have caused them but also because the lingering clouds frequently drop their burden on the fields they shadow. And people dwelling among these fields have come to love the hieroglyphics of lightning on the murky surfaces overhead, the sullen after-rumbles of thunder ricocheting from the steep hillsides.

Of all the valleys-under-the-clouds none has a more separate and independent life than that of the Schoharie. Shut off on the south by the Catskills, on the east by the Helderbergs—those "shining mountains" over which its first white settlers came—on the north by the York State hills that are soon to flatten into the levels of the Mohawk plain, the hollow cut by the winding Schoharie Creek has long been a haven for refugees from a world grown difficult.

The Mohawk chief, Karighondontee, exiled from his tribe for marrying an Algonquian woman, found asylum beside

Schoharie water and it was not long before other banished Indians joined him. Soon he was chief of an outlaw tribe, living contentedly in a rich earthen bowl over whose edges few men found their way.

Several generations of Indians had passed before, in the early years of the eighteenth century, the Palatine Germans, fugitives to England from the border wars of France and Germany and thence exported by British colonizers to the banks of the Hudson, wearily descended the last of the Helderbergs into the alluvial reaches below. The Indian outlaws received them kindly as fellow refugees and soon little German settlements sprang up—Middleburg and Weisersdorf and Schoharie. These towns—because main lines of travel do not cut through their environs, because their streets are shut off from the bustling metropolitan world by natural barricades—have kept more of the atmosphere of colonial America than any others in York State.

I know of no pleasanter travel experience than to set out by the old south road from Cobleskill, to come over the brow of the intervening mountain and to see Middleburg lying at the far end of the valley beside the shining stillness of the wide creek. Now I know from having spent many days there that on my way down I shall meet a horse and buggy and a man riding a horse before I cross the bridge into town and hear the clangor that issues from the open doors of the blacksmith shops. Many of the people of the region have never surrendered to the folly of going faster than is necessary. Horses are still very much a part of life in Schoharie County, so much so, in fact, that in the town of West Sand Lake the Association for Mutual Protection Against Horse Thieves is still a thriving band—though most branches of

Old South Road from Cobleskill

this once-famous organization of vigilantes have been in-
active for many years.

I hope I shall always arrive at Middleburg in time to see
the train on America's shortest railway, the Middleburg and
Schoharie, start on its daily trip up the valley. It is an expensive journey, five cents a mile for the five miles to the
end of the line at Schoharie, but, as residents gleefully point
out, it is really cheap since you get a longer ride for a quarter
than anywhere else; indeed, it sometimes takes half a day.
They also tell of the traveling salesman bumping along in
the passenger coach who suddenly felt the train gliding
smoothly and looked out the window to discover that for
the last few moments it had been running off the track. The
train is usually quite short—a milk car and a passenger coach,
both drawn by a tiny Edison locomotive which its depre-
cators say "can't quite pass for a watch." From the hillsides
the whole thing looks like a small boy's toy. Once, I was
told, a carload of green lumber was coupled on and the
whole valley worried for fear the engine would not be able
to pull it out of a sag down toward the middle of the run.
Fortunately, said my informant, it took so long to get that
far that the wood had dried out light and the engine managed to get it up to the station. From Schoharie another
railroad, quite independent of the M. & S. and just a half-
mile longer, makes connection with the Delaware & Hudson
at Schoharie Junction. Residents along their course are very
proud of the two railroads covering in total a stretch of only
ten miles. They say you cannot find that situation anywhere
else in the United States.

The people of the Schoharie Valley are still predomi-
nantly blond, due probably to the fact that the chief mixture
of blood has been with the Dutch and the English. Their

industries are mostly agricultural: dairying, fruit growing and hop growing (once the main industry and now returning to popularity). They are healthy and for the most part they live comfortably. More in their food than in any other way do they betray their Teutonic origins, particularly in the back country where farmers with German and Dutch names live in homes as neat as those which their ancestors left to cross the Atlantic.

Roll-it-gies, a favorite for which their butchers get frequent orders, are an elaboration on tripe. They are made by first allowing lime to eat out the mucous membrane lining of a cow's stomach. The stomach is then soaked in buttermilk and cut in large ovals. These are stuffed with strips of cheap beef boiled until it is so tender a rye straw can be run through it. The resultant bundle, about the shape of a football, is vatted in vinegar until it is cured and reasonably sour. It is then ready for slicing. Slices are baked or fried brown, and eaten with delight.

A favorite drink is buttermilk pop, made from browned crusts of bread and browned butter stirred in a kettle with buttermilk added gradually. Still other delicacies include summer sausage (made from the second stomach of a pig, stuffed with sausage and soaked in brine), blood pudding, liverwurst, scrapple, headcheese, pigs' feet, "apron strings" (noodles), Training Day gingerbread (though the military reason for its title is forgotten), and apple dumplings (for which an average individual consumption is reported as fourteen at a sitting). On some farms cider boiling is still an annual custom. Before dawn the fires begin to burn under big fifty-gallon brass kettles just outside the orchards, and the scent of the boiling juice of Tallman Sweets is pungent all day through the sharp autumn air. The thick syrupy liquid resultant from the boiling is kept in stone jars and used as a sauce throughout the winter.

Most of the other folk customs result from the social shindigs occasioned by the hop harvests. Before prohibition nearly every farm in the valley had its big hop house, calculated not only to store the crop but to house a large group of helpers during the picking season. Now that hop growing is being taken up again, some of these buildings have been renovated. Housewives once more hoard food and pile quilts in readiness for the time when gay bands of pickers invade the valley. In motor trucks they descend on the farms to pick the hops, eat much, sleep little and dance hard on the hop-house floor while the fiddler calls the figures and pitches into *The Devil's Dream* and *The Fisher's Hornpipe*. All the boys know that if they kiss a girl through one of the loops in the hop vines she will always be faithful, and everybody knows that if the worms on the hop vines have silver spots the harvest will be light but if the worms have gold spots the crop will bring a great price.

The pickers sleep under intricately patterned patchwork covers, for the farm women have always made their own quilts. Here are Albany Pavement and Dove-in-the-Window, Rose of Sharon and The Album, Nine-Block Piecework, Star and Compass and Double Irish Chain. After the picking season they will make a garish kaleidoscopic carnival tossing on all the clotheslines of the valley.

Schoharie people are happy in their isolation and the solidarity it has given them through the generations. They are intensely loyal to their section and to their country. They have always sent more than their share of recruits to the national wars and they point to the record with satisfaction tinged with slight embarrassment caused by memories of their treatment of the recorder. No one may live long in the valley without hearing the story of George Warner, its self-appointed historian.

Warner had served very acceptably in the Northern forces during the Civil War, and he rejoiced that his grandfather had fought against the British crown. Many years after he had come home from the Union Army he began to brood over the fact that the country had no account of the names and careers of his ancestors and those other brave men who had left their farms beside the creek and on the hill slopes to risk their lives against the British in 1775 and 1812, against the Mexicans in 1846, against the Confederates in 1864. Immediately he set to work to repair the deficiency and after a long period of indefatigable labor he succeeded. Feeling sure that his neighbors would take as much pride in the chronicle as he did, he mortgaged his farm for thirteen hundred dollars to pay for publication and set out to sell his volumes at three dollars apiece. But three dollars is a lot of money to many a farmer and George Warner was a touchy man. "Do you want to buy my book?" he would ask, and if the farmer scratched his head a bit or said something about times being hard and maybe he had better wait until next hog-killing time, George would clap his hat on his head and march off muttering. Then no amount of apology, not even an offer of the money in cash, would soften him. The man had insulted him and his history and he could never have a copy come hell or high water.

Time went on and only a few of the books were sold. George Warner realized that before long he would be no more of this world. One day the Baker boys who lived on the next farm saw him digging near the brook that ran down one edge of his property. When they asked him what he was doing he was surly and said something about making a cistern. Then one of the boys coming home late at night saw a lighted lantern on the earth pile beside the dug hole. The next day the lantern and the pile were both gone. The hole had been filled in.

When George Warner died he asked on his deathbed that his body be wrapped in an American flag, that he be buried when sunset flamed across the valley, that his grave be unmarked. But friends are often indifferent to the dead. No one offered a flag to enfold the old soldier. And nature, indifferent too, provided a dreary drizzle from the Storm Country's gray ceiling on the morning he was buried. Only his last request was honored.

When the dead man's effects were disposed of no one found any books. It was some years before the Baker boys, suspecting the reason for the hole beside the stream and the light at midnight, told Mr. Truax, the new owner of the Warner farm, what they had seen. Diggers found the books in the hole, placed backs downward so that the brook water might seep into the leaves and destroy them. The diggers spread them out in a sunny field to let them dry. Many turned as hard as stone. Then, not suspecting their value to county historians, Mr. Truax had them put in the top of his hop house. Years later his little girl told her history teacher about them and they were discovered for the last time. Now the few that are readable are treasured in Schoharie and state libraries. The last one to be sold brought many dollars more than three. And not long ago the American Historical Society publicly honored George Warner, but not over his unmarked and unknown grave.

Behind the Helderbergs

More tragic, however, than the tale of the unappreciated historian is the drama of the Sloughters. Before the American Revolution one of the English governors of the province bore the name Sloughter. He was so cruel and unjust in the eyes of the Palatine settlers that they came to use his name as an epithet. Incredible as it seems, the term is still in such use today and young people of the region have told me that their mothers made a practice of washing out their mouths with soap whenever they spoke it. A farmer near Middleburg told me when I pressed him for a meaning, "Well, I should say Sloughter means a no'count son-of-a-bitch, only more so."

Unhappily the term has another meaning, too. On the west side of the Schoharie and about two miles south of Middleburg, Vroman's Nose, a round cliff-sided mountain, stands alone in the middle of the valley. Almost under its eastern rim a little road winds westward along the banks of Lime Kiln Creek. Where the stream splatters down the rocks of its narrow ravine are the ramshackle dwellings of a strange group of people. Like the Calcboguers of the Genesee country, they are poor, neglected, underprivileged, in many ways antisocial, but always loyal to each other when they face outsiders. The people of Schoharie county call them Sloughters. A few years ago they were dominated by a fierce old woman, Polly Scrom, and to this day the ravine on whose banks they live is known as Poll's Holler. Poll's Lib and Lib's Poll, each almost as well known as the old woman herself, bring the generations of her posterity down to the present.

I talked with a Sloughter in the yard of his mountain home. His hair was curly and bushy, his figure wiry, his clothes were patched picturesquely. His eyes were dull and he seemed not to hear much that I said. But when I happened to praise his long-eared dog, I was surprised to see light come into his eyes, nervous force into his gestures as he informed me that the animal was part bloodhound and the best coon dog in the valley. Then, as if ashamed of letting himself go, he became wary and sullen and I left him.

Once in a great while a Sloughter comes into Middleburg. Barefooted he wanders the streets of the little town, open-mouthed he examines new buildings and new automobiles. Then he wanders back the valley road toward Vroman's Nose. In a community nature has shut off from the rest of the world he and his kind are most segregated.

I liked living beside the Schoharie. It was fun driving to a square dance at Livingstonville and rolling back beside the gleaming pools of the swamp which I learned to call the "vlaie," or wandering along the fragrant street called Clauverway, or attending a church supper which an elderly Lutheran informed me should be called a "kintecoy."

I was told that no one brought up beside the creek with its border of white stones will ever forget it and that all who have left their old homes there will try to return before they die. No beer, the Schoharie people said to me, is so good as that made from the hops that climb the army of poles striping the flat lands around Middleburg, no milk is so sweet as that which comes from Schoharie dairies, and no Northern Spy apple is really a Northern Spy unless it grew from the limy soil of Schoharie orchards. They said there are over a hundred families in Schoharie County living in the very same houses their ancestors built over a hundred years ago. The Schoharie Valley, they concluded, is a little country by itself, separate and prideful.

Behind the Helderbergs

THROUGHOUT THE STORM COUNTRY AND EAST OF IT ALONG the Susquehanna River the name of John Augustus Caesar Darling is a household word. Born at Shandalee near Sand Pond and Livingston Manor, John Darling first distinguished himself at an early age by driving his plow, drawn by his two pet steers, right through a great six-foot high stump. The plow split the stump all right and he got through but the two halves, springing back together again, caught his shirt and tore it off his back.

A little later on a foggy morning John set his ladder up against his house and climbed up to shingle his roof. After he got through the sun came out and he discovered he had laid the shingles on the fog forty feet above the roof.

John Darling was best known for his exploits in the sugar bush. His sap pans weighed a ton apiece. One day while he was in the bush he saw three mosquitoes as big as airplanes and singing twice as loud making straight for him. He just had time to tip one of those ton pans over himself before they arrived. They started right in boring through the iron bottom with their bills and all three of them had got through it and were prodding around for him when John Darling got a good idea. He had his ax with him and he just split all three bills in two and then pressed each half back up against the iron surface over him. The result of that was that the last he saw of those mosquitoes they were heading off over the treetops toward Binghamton and they were taking his sap pan with them. He never did get it back.

Once a year, just before summer came, John Darling would walk to town and go to a barber and get a shine, haircut and shave. He always had the barber collect his whiskers into big gunny sacks and he took them home to his old woman. She would throw them in the kettle and boil them and in that way she always salvaged seven or eight gallons of maple syrup that had got stuck on them during the buckwheat-cake season.

One of the old sows on John Darling's farm was run over by a truck and her hind legs were cut off. So John made a rolling truck and fastened it under her hindquarters and she got along all right that way. When she farrowed, though, every little pig of her litter was born with a little truck where his hind legs ought to be.

York State had a tremendous amount of snow one winter —so much that the drifts hadn't melted by midsummer. One Fourth of July, according to John Darling's tell, he was out in a field mowing when a big stag jumped a fence near him and landed in a snowdrift so deep he got stuck in it. John said it was just a moment's work for him to run over and cut the stag's throat with his scythe, and that he and his family had venison all through the summer. This story is questionable, to say the least, for people in Dryden who should know tell me that this incident happened to my own great-great-great-grandfather, Edward Griswold, who told it whenever he could get anybody to listen to him—and he was a churchgoing man. This fact seems to me to cast a considerable doubt on John Darling's veracity.

35

Hill Waters

THE CLOUDS WERE LOW AND DARK, ALMOST TOUCH-
ing the points of the Gothic towers of Cornell University,
and lightning was casting sudden glows on twisting curtains
of gray mist when I came to the top of a hill and looked
down across the dull, green waters of Lake Cayuga to Ithaca.
The Storm Country was living up to its name.

"Let me remind you that you were born in that country," my sister had said when I left her in Geneseo that
morning. "Our father and his father and all his grandfathers
as far back as the Revolution lived there. And remember,
if you write about it, to bless it as the only place you and I
ever knew where we could be sure of having buckwheat pan
cakes every morning for breakfast."

My visit in Ithaca will not be forgotten. As the days
reached summer length I climbed the city's friendly hills
to knock at many doors and to hear much about the free-
thinking, imaginative, amusing people who live among the
Finger Lakes. Sometimes I drove among the hills, never
wearying of the vista I learned to expect, a sudden stretch
of glinting water lying between high green slopes. I came
particularly to know the idyllic life that centers about the
shores of little Owasco where the summer residents traipse
merrily from home to home each evening, eating and drink-

ing their fill all through the vacation months, stopping at their own houses only to sleep and, about once in two weeks, to feed the crowd as it migrates toward them.

Most often, however, when darkness had settled I found myself seated on the broad veranda of an old frame inn close to the ripples of Lake Cayuga. A few friends from the Cornell faculty sat with me and the tall beer pitcher on the table needed replenishing from time to time. One evening we talked shop, for I had spent a decade in college teaching, and I learned that Cornell has kept the independent tradition of its own section though it is one of the most cosmopolitan of all American colleges. "We have kept rules and regulations for both faculty and students down to a minimum," one of the professors said to me, "and the policy seems to work though the community contains people from nearly every country."

I remembered his remark the next day, a Sunday, when on a drive westward toward Olean I came upon the pleasant little coeducational college of Houghton and heard a sermon based on the premises that all human beings are born with a sinful nature, that the Old and New Testaments are inspired and inerrant, that the world may expect the personal, premillennial and imminent return of Jesus and that at about that time will begin the everlasting happiness of the saved and the everlasting conscious suffering of the lost.

These somewhat Calvinistic views led me to a request for a college handbook in which I read, among many others, the following regulations:

> Students addicted to the use of either tobacco or alcoholic liquors are requested not to register until they

have tried and found that they can abstain. The use of either is strictly forbidden.

Among the games of skill, the use of pool and billiard tables, and among the games of chance, the playing of cards is forbidden.

We are firmly convinced that dancing is a great evil, and that it has caused the loss of character of many. Neither dancing nor attending private or public dances is allowed.

We believe that the theater is detrimental to a high standard of morals and is not suitable amusement for a Christian man or woman. Non-resident students under twenty-one will not be permitted to attend moving pictures. . . .

The suits worn by students participating in athletics shall consist of the standard suits determined by the college [these include basket-ball uniforms in which the shorts reach to the knee]. . . . No other suits may be substituted. . . . All dresses shall have sleeves. Stockings are to be worn at all times [by girls] including all athletic functions.

After seven o'clock in the evening all women are required to be in their rooms unless they have received special permision . . . to be out.

It is understood that only high-class radio programs are to be selected.

Freshmen shall not spend more than two afternoons a week, sophomores three, juniors and seniors four with members of the opposite sex.

The rules relating to tobacco and alcohol, profane and obscene language, gambling, public dances . . . athletic dress, apply to the married students and the home students the same as they apply to non-resident students.

People have their own ideas in York State—and stick to them. It is hard to realize that Cornell and Houghton, so far apart in educational theory, are but a comparatively few miles from each other.

On another evening I asked my faculty friends to tell me the story back of the fact that the brain of a murderer named Ruloff is preserved in alcohol and displayed to the public gaze in the science museum of the university. They told me the story and obligingly offered others that are popular folk tales of the region. In the following weeks I heard these same tales recounted many times by various kinds of people.

36

The Tale of the Murderous Philologist

THE SCHUTTS WERE DRIVING ALONG THE TOWPATH one day and there walking beside the canal they saw a bright-faced young man who looked tired and hungry. They stopped and asked him about himself and he said his name was Edward H. Ruloffson, his home was Hammond River near St. John in New Brunswick, Canada, and he had come to the States to start his career. The Schutts were good people, so they took him into the wagon and they drove him home to Dryden. He turned out to be such a smart young fellow and so handy around the place they just kept him and sent him to school. It was only a short time before he had learned as much as the teacher knew, changed his name for some reason or other to Ruloff, and had a good job working in the drugstore. The Schutts got to be quite fond of him. So did their daughter Harriet, and the first thing the old folks knew he'd up and married the girl. Then the happy couple moved over near Ithaca to a farm not far from Rogue's Harbor.

At first they seemed to be getting along all right. They had a baby, a little girl, and Ruloff was working steadily. Then one night folks nearby heard them quarreling. Some people say it was because he wouldn't let her go back to Dryden to visit her folks.

The next morning about ten o'clock Ruloff was over at the Robertson place, across the road from his own, asking for the loan of a horse and a democrat wagon because he wanted to take a box of books into Mottville. Tom Robertson said it was all right and when he saw Ruloff trying to lift a big wooden box onto the democrat he walked out and gave him a hand. It was mighty heavy, Tom said afterwards, but he knew books were heavy so he didn't suspect anything.

Just as Ruloff took up the reins from the whip socket some school children who were out for noon recess asked for a ride and he let them climb up the back wheel and ride on top of the wooden box. Tom saw them pass over the top of the hill, the children playing on top of that box, and he said later he wouldn't forget it to his dying day, especially after he'd found out that almost certainly the corpses of Ruloff's wife and little girl were under the wooden cover they played on.

No one ever saw the box again. When people missed Mrs. Ruloff, her husband said she'd gone away to visit relatives in Ohio. Somebody told the Schutts about it over in Dryden but before any of them could get to Ruloff's place he had gone away and left no address. One of the Schutt boys started out on the trail and he caught up with his brother-in-law at Buffalo. Ruloff convinced young Schutt that he was on his way to join Harriet in Madison, Ohio, and persuaded him to go along as far as Cleveland by way of Lake Erie. Just before the boat left the dock, Ruloff gave young Schutt the slip and got off, leaving the boy to make the trip alone.

Strangely enough, Ruloff was on the boat dock at Cleveland when Harriet's brother returned from Madison where he found no trace of his sister. This time Ruloff said his wife had disappeared and he didn't know where she was. With apparent willingness he returned to Ithaca where an aroused countryside saw to it that he was arrested and tried. Since the death of his wife could not be proved, the most serious crime for which he could be indicted was abduction. That was sufficient, however, to bring him a sentence of ten years in Auburn prison.

Ruloff enjoyed those ten years. The prison library was well supplied with Greek and Latin classics and finally people who had discovered his interest in languages brought him other volumes. His mind was sharp and retentive and he knew more about languages than most scholars in America when he was released.

Unfortunately for him his old neighbors' minds were also

retentive and as the time for his liberation drew near their wrath surged up again.

No sooner had the prisoner been set free than he was rearrested for the murder of his child. The trial of this case occasioned a Court of Appeals judgment famous in American jurisprudence: "Absence in and of itself is not sufficient in a criminal case to establish death." Even while the court was debating this "corpus delicti" decision, however, Ruloff was escaping. He had won the affection and loyalty of the jailer's son, Albert Jarvis, and the two of them were bouncing along snowy roads behind a team of galloping black horses.

No one knows why Ruloff gave himself up a few months later. Perhaps he had advance knowledge of the Court of Appeals decision. At any rate, he surrendered himself while the judges were still debating and was immediately lodged in the Ithaca jail. But the escape cost him more dearly than he was for a long time to realize. The extreme cold of that winter night froze off the big toe of his left foot, a fact that was to have its sinister influence after many years had passed.

But Ruloff had overlooked an immediate danger. One day many citizens of Ithaca and Dryden received a printed poster which read as follows:

Shall the Murderer Go Unpunished?

Edward Ruloff will soon gain his freedom unless prompt and effective measures are taken by the people to prevent it. . . .

Shall these things be? Shall this monster be turned loose to glut his tiger appetite for revenge and blood? . . . In the name of humanity, in the name of the relatives of the murdered wife whose heartstrings have been lacerated by the fiend in human shape, in the name of the murdered wife and child, whose pale ghost calls to you from the silent tomb to do your duty, we ask you, shall the murderer go unpunished? . . . Will you allow this man who bears the mark of Cain upon his brow to go forth in this community and add fresh victims to the grave? No, you will not! You cannot!

We call on those who wish justice done to the murderer to meet at the Clinton House in Ithaca on Saturday, March 12, 1859, at 12 o'clock noon. It will depend on the action you take that day whether Edward H. Ruloff walks forth a free man or whether he dies the death he so richly deserves.

At the meeting scheduled on the poster plans were made for constructing a battering ram and raiding the prisoner's cell. The ram was completed on the very day that Sheriff Robertson got wind of the conspiracy and spirited Ruloff away to Auburn prison for safekeeping. So great was the mob's disappointment that Sheriff Robertson lost his job at the next election.

Little is known of the twenty years of Ruloff's life between his escape and the sequence of strange events which led to his death. Young Albert Jarvis, the jailer's boy, stayed with him, believing in him implicitly, and a man named Dexter joined them. It is said that the three committed various crimes, mostly burglaries, in New England and that Ruloff served short sentences in various prisons for his part in them. When, however, he posed in a New Hampshire town as an Episcopal minister, graduate of Oxford, while he planned the robbing of the town bank, an irate judge sent him to prison for ten years. He escaped after three months.

Ruloff had not forgotten his scholarly gifts when he left Auburn. On the contrary, he had developed them until he could speak fluently in Hebrew, Greek, Latin, French and German. Gradually his interest in philology supplanted his taste for crime and for several years he lived in New York city, first in Delancey Street and later on Third Avenue, as a studious, industrious, well-behaved citizen. During his first prison term he had begun work on a volume showing the common origin of all languages. This he entitled *Method in Formation of Language* and pushed to its conclusion as rapidly as his painstaking scholarship would allow. He convinced his two associates-in-crime that the publication of the work would be an event of such importance in the book world that it would not be necessary for any of them either to work or to steal again, and both of them were overjoyed when Ruloff told them he expected to get financial backing for his project at a convention of the American Philological Association at Poughkeepsie in 1867.

The distinguished faculty of the new college founded at Poughkeepsie by Matthew Vassar and the visiting philologists from other American seats of learning were greatly impressed at their meeting by one Professor Edouard Leurio who presented his erudite theories in a manuscript— *Method in Formation of Language*. Not one of them suspected as he listened to the suave flow of the professor's sentences that the speaker was a convicted felon, the probable murderer of his own wife and child, a masquerader under an alias, a scholar whose learning had been acquired in an institution of reform rather than of education. But when the professor asked for money to enable him to publish his contribution they politely informed him that there were neither precedents nor funds for such an enterprise.

Ruloff left Poughkeepsie in a towering rage. Jarvis and Dexter were taken aback. They had supposed the publication of the work a certainty. Now they began to doubt its worth, and their leader decided on a last desperate venture to obtain for his researches their rightful recognition before the world.

One dark midnight soon thereafter three burglars entered the Halbert Shoe Store in the city of Binghamton, New York. Two clerks, Burrows and Merrick, who were sleeping on the premises, gave battle and one of them, Merrick, was mercilessly shot to death by the leader of the bandits. All through the early morning hours Burrows and a posse of townspeople sought the criminals. When sunlight came two of the latter were plainly visible floating lifeless on the clear waters of the Susquehanna. Their bodies were so bruised that many thought they had been beaten unconscious by the man whose murderous crime they had witnessed before they were thrown into the deeps of the river to drown.

About midnight of that day an officer accosted a courteous elderly gentleman who was carrying a brief case and whose only irregularity of conduct seemed to be that he was crouching in an uncomfortable position in an outhouse near the city limits of Binghamton. The gentleman willingly accompanied the constable to the sheriff's office where he explained that he was a traveling scholar somewhat embarrassed by a lack of funds. The sheriff at once apologized for delaying him and the benignly smiling gray-haired student had turned to go when a man whose memory had been groping back through twenty years noticed a depression in the left shoe of the sheriff's guest, just over the big toe.

"Aren't you Ruloff?" said the man.

"Yes," said the scholar promptly and he went on to talk of the injustices that had been done in the past to a man whose only interest was in the classics and philology. He spoke so charmingly and convincingly that he was soon shaking hands with the sheriff and the other men in the office and they were all bidding him Godspeed.

He had been on his way again an hour or so before investigators at the scene of the murder reported that one of the burglars had left behind a pair of shoes, the left of which showed a distinct indentation over the big toe. Frantic pursuers soon caught the fugitive who was walking briskly along the railroad tracks in a direction away from Binghamton.

Soon, though Ruloff defended himself at his trial with all his famous cunning, he was reposing behind prison walls again reading and rereading his favorite poem, *The Prison of Chillon*, sending out appeal after appeal that his life might be spared in the interests of classical learning. A popular movement to secure him a reprieve gained such momentum among the sentimental and the pious scholarly that it would have succeeded had it not been for the insistence of New York's Governor Hoffman that the law take its course.

But Ruloff was executed, hanged on a sunny, mid-May morning at the last public hanging in Binghamton. I talked with a farmer who saw it and he told me that when they asked Ruloff if he wanted a minister to pray for him on the scaffold he said no, but if they wanted one up there to pray for the crowd it would be all right with him. And when the hanging was delayed a little past eleven o'clock in the morning, which was the time set, he complained, saying, "Hurry it up. I want to be in hell in time for dinner." The hanging was unusually gruesome, the farmer said, because with characteristic bravado, Ruloff had put his right hand in his pocket before the trap was sprung. The fall jerked the hand free, he said, but Ruloff, still apparently conscious, put it back in his pocket.

After he was dead his body was displayed in its coffin outside the prison for a while. Then authorities from Cornell took it to extract the brain which they preserved in alcohol and displayed at the university. Scholars later stated that it weighed almost seven ounces more than the average, a half ounce more than that of the great Thackeray, five ounces more than that contained in the massive head of Daniel Webster.

No sooner had the body been buried than with the speed of modern tabloids sensational books began to appear purporting to reveal the truth about Ruloff and his crimes. *The Veil of Secrecy Removed* (published in Binghamton) stated that it was "The Only True and Authentic History of Edward H. Ruloff," but *The Man of Two Lives,* published by the American News Company in New York in 1871, also claimed itself reliable. As a matter of fact, no one has ever known definitely what happened to Ruloff's wife and child, though for a long time there was a rumor that the child was alive and dwelling in Pennsylvania. And no one has ever known what went on inside the massive convoluted brain at which curious visitors now stare without remembering.

WHEN OLD BILL CAME TO TOMPKINS COUNTY HE PRE-
tended he was deaf and dumb. He had a peddler's wagon
filled with wares to suit housewives and a lot of medicines
guaranteed to cure whatever was ailing the patient. He did
a land-office business all over the countryside, for few women
could resist the appeal of his tall, powerful body, his shining blue eyes, his even-toothed smile, and the pathos of his
affliction.

Bill liked the Moravia section so much that he decided
to live there. He bought a house, grew a beard, and gradually let people forget the old notion that he could not talk
or hear. As a matter of fact, he could talk a fellow's ear off
and frequently did when he got to lecturing about alcohol
and the havoc it could cause when taken into the human
system.

The Moravia people were glad to have Bill around for a
while. He was an amusing man and a nearly perfect shot
with a rifle. One of his ways of attracting a crowd to his
medicine-selling was to set up a dummy with a pipe in its
mouth and then stand off two hundred paces and break
the pipe stem with a bullet. One day at the Cortland Fair
he shifted his aim and shattered a pipe in the mouth of a
bystander. Everybody enjoyed that except the bystander

who stayed mad even after Old Bill had given him ten dollars to get a new pipe.

But people living near Moravia and Dryden and McGraw were losing horses in the night and it was not long before their suspicions turned toward Old Bill. They knew he was frequently away on long trips. They saw lights at night in the ravine near his house. Although their own animals never turned up again after they had been stolen, sometimes farmers living on unfrequented roads would see little herds of strange horses being hurried along by some of Old Bill's younger associates.

Gradually it became known that Old Bill was in a position to sell good Virginia horses to Tompkins County farmers who had recently been bereft of their nags, and that in Virginia he was offering sound York State horses to farmers whose livestock had been illegally depleted. Feeling grew very strong against the medicine peddler, but no one could prove any of his actions illegal. A young man tried to spy on him and Old Bill trapped him in a cave and kept him there overnight. The gang of horse thieves grew more dangerous and more defiant of the law. Then Bill tried to make a jury believe that the young man who had spied on him was a thief. He was getting on very well when one of his henchmen in the witness box unexpectedly betrayed Bill's dishonest practices, and the jury, forgetting their duties for the moment, hurdled the rail of the jury box and made for the defendant. Old Bill reached the window ahead of them and a moment thereafter residents of the city of Auburn witnessed an unusual sort of steeplechase in which a bearded man of over six feet kept a small but satisfactory distance between himself and the baying pack, made up of twelve good men and true. They chased him over the county line, so the legend says, and he never came back.

A BLONDE GIRL, HER EYES BLUER THAN THE LAKES OF HER native Italy, sang one night long ago before an opera audience in Madrid. When the performance was over a stalwart young man stormed down to the edge of the stage that he might look up into the singer's face. From the nearest box a dark, proud don applauded enthusiastically, a fact not unnoted by his wife who sat behind him and lifted her fan to conceal the glances of hatred she directed at him.

A few weeks later the stalwart young man lay in his grave, his body pierced and bloody from many a dagger thrust, while the don and the Italian artist were on the high seas fleeing from Spanish justice and the vengeful family of the humiliated woman.

When the fugitive couple came to America they at once set out with a band of trappers for the interior. Their party came one day into a region of lakes as small and blue as distant Como and Maggiore, and there the blonde girl begged her lover to stay. He built her a gray stone house in a secluded ravine that led down to Seneca Lake and, knowing the persistence of his enraged countrymen, he ordered constructed a tunnel beneath the earth from the cellar of the house to a point on the lake where he always kept a boat moored.

The couple had two years of happiness before the anticipated night came when riders shouting Spanish oaths surrounded the house and called on its occupants to come out. Quickly the don led his mistress and their Indian servants to the tunnel entrance and they began to make their way toward the lake. But the Spaniards discovered their way of escape and followed them closely. Just as they reached the end of the passage the don, not realizing that the girl in despair had turned to meet their pursuers, released through a mechanical device the keystone of the arch over their heads. Only he and his Indian servants were left alive as the heavy walls crashed inward.

In a Roman monastery, so the story goes, the wandering, despairing don finally found such rest as the world can give to men like him, and there he died. He lies buried under a slab on which his brother monks carved the simple inscription, "Fra Bartolomeo, 1817." And in a ravine three miles south of the York State city of Geneva lie a few gray stones, once part of the strong walls of a house built by a Spanish murderer for a sweet-voiced Italian girl with yellow hair.

37

Lyme Gallagher
to Rosy Bone

ROMEYN BERRY, CONSTANT WANDERER OF TOMP-
kins County's dirt roads, was at the wheel on my last day in
the Storm Country. When he called for me in the morning,
his white knickers immaculate, his elderly checked sport coat
displaying here and there a nonchalant rip, a hat the shape
of a sun helmet but made of the same checked wool as the
coat topping off his six feet of generously massed structure—
I knew that I had found a companion of distinctive quality
and personal integrity.

We took the road to Dryden by way of Ellis Hollow.
There Peleg Ellis, veteran of the War of 1812, grown
crochety with years and daft with rum, used to drill a regiment of moonbeams under the illusion that they were men,
shouting his orders out on the night air, standing with folded
arms as the battalions passed in review to the beat of a
regimental drum. Folks who live near by say that on some
nights when the moon is clear a voice from the hollow still
barks commands and a drum answers, just as invisible drums
are beating in every York State region.

This section has been settled a long time and it has kept its salty American place names: Land of Canaan, Lyme Gallagher, Frog Huddle, Padlock, Tobeytown, Fiddler's Green, Rogue's Harbor, Teetertown, Rosy Bone. On the Jim Mack road we passed many a century-old house which boasted, close under the eaves, small windows covered by elaborately designed grilles. Romeyn Berry said folks call them lie-on-your-stomach windows because a person has to stretch out on the floor of the attic, avoiding the close slanting roof, in order to see out of them. Many of the grilles are of wrought iron but the most interesting, he said, are imitations carved from wood by artistic farmers who could not afford metal.

In contrast to the old houses, he pointed out the neat new home of Jerry Fidler, Ithaca barber, who had proved his right to associate with a Yankee heritage by insulating his walls against the cold with the hair he had cut from the heads of patrons over a period of twenty years.

One dark little cloud was in the blue sky as we approached Dryden and it suddenly let go with a sharp torrent of rain that ceased in five minutes. We saw a farmer standing, hay rake in hand, beside the road. His wet shirt was sticking to his broad chest and the hay spread at his feet glistened with raindrops.

"Hard luck," I said.

He looked at us.

"If I was a God," he said evenly, "I'd *be* a God and not a damn fool." He turned and walked off toward his barn while Romeyn Berry and I spoke of Job's poetic parallels to this outburst, and I remembered that my father had told me that in this region, where he was born and reared, men had for generations asserted their right to think as they pleased, even about the Almighty.

In the center of the town of Dryden on the wall of an old white frame building, which owns a pillared gallery extending out over the sidewalk, is a sign which reads THE SPIT AND WHITTLE CLUB. On the benches beneath it we sat and waited for the mail with a group of pleasant idlers, the oldest of whom said that as soon as he got through waiting for the morning mail he began waiting for the afternoon. I was amused by their complete matter-of-course acceptance of my companion's costume, which I had thought a bit bizarre for such journeying and therefore inclined to lose us the confidence of people we wanted to talk to. It was evident that in Dryden a man wore what clothes he had and nobody thought anything about it.

It was a short time before I heard the story of Dryden's meanest man. He had a mortgage on a poor man's cow, I was told, and he went around to foreclose it, taking a boy along to lead the animal to his barn. The owner wasn't there but his wife, her children tagging at her skirts, made such a piteous plea for her babes' sustenance that the hardhearted forecloser burst into tears. The boy had already started to lead the cow away but on seeing his employer's emotion he also wept and started to bring her back.

"You take that cow on home," said Dryden's meanest man. "I'll do the cryin' around here."

Under the shade of the vines that trailed from the over-hanging gallery I also heard and put together stray pieces of the history of the band of fifty Pilgrims who had entered Dryden more than a hundred years ago in big wagons laden with tents and drawn by four-horse teams. Their belief allowed them to eat only such food as they sucked through goose quills while standing erect, and they considered it God's will that they should not make use of tables, chairs or beds. Their chief idiosyncrasy of dress was a large square of white cloth sewed to the back of each coat, "a mark for the Devil to shoot at." Each night they all went promiscuously to bed together in a large communal pile of straw and each morning, yelling "like a parcel of wolves," they went through a physically violent ceremony of "driving the Devil from camp." Though they won some converts in the county, they were coldly treated by most of the citizens of Dryden and they finally packed up their caravan and started it rolling toward the island in the Mississippi River on which their strange cult ended its existence.

We left Dryden reluctantly but not before someone had told us about the farmer ventriloquist who used to scare his hired men half to death by causing a cow to speak up suddenly to her milker, saying, "Go easy, you son-of-a-bitch, or I'll kick your ribs around your spine." Noon found us devouring huge portions of ham and eggs and slabs of salt-risin' bread, our plates resting on the checkered tablecloths of Card's Country Store in Slaterville.

In the afternoon we found in an old neglected cemetery the grave of one of my ancestors. A healthy elm tree grew directly in front of the headstone. The inscription said he had been a soldier and that he lived from 1750 to 1853.

"When did he come to this region?" said Romeyn Berry.

"When he was about fifty," I said.

"If you could talk to him," said my friend, "you would know what makes upstate what it is. In the last fifty-three years of his hundred and three he saw people take hold on this land and this land take its hold on them. He knew those crazy fanatics. He saw the Dutch like himself marrying the

English. He could make your job a lot easier if he could talk to you."

"My grandfather knew him well," I said, "but all that I can remember his saying about him is that he was 'a pretty crabbed old man.' "

"American history is short," said Romeyn Berry, "when we can speak of talking with a man who knew a soldier in Washington's army."

The afternoon sunlight was waning when we passed the town of Richford lying at the end of a long hill down which, local historians report, the stagecoach trumpeter used to signal the number of passengers aboard by blowing as many blasts on his horn. Then dinner for the lot would be ready when the stage clattered up to the tavern.

We stopped before the thoroughly unattractive exterior of a little church in Moravia and, as I waited while my companion sought out Father Stevens in a nearby house, I wondered why we had come.

Father Stevens was a stout, ambling, clean-shaven man whose frankness and lack of illusion appealed to us both. He had little to say at first, merely unlocked the front door and let us precede him into the church. Yellow light was streaming in the west windows and we three were silent a long time. The whole church was aflower with wood carving of such delicacy, such exquisite tracery, such simple, graceful design that it filled us with wordless delight. Over font and lectern and chancel and choir ran vines and blossoms in never-repeated wooden patterns.

"The saints," said Father Stevens, pointing to life-size figures carved in darker and redded wood, "we imported from Oberammergau. The rest of the work has been done here, mostly by Charlie Hall."

"How did it happen?" I said.

The good Father sighed.

"You see, I'm not much of a preacher; if I were I would not be rector of a small church in a rural district. Naturally I wanted my church to have some of the distinction which my sermons fail to give. So when Charlie showed me what he could do with knives and wood a few years ago I decided we would use his handiwork for that purpose."

"And who is Charlie?" I said.

Father Stevens sighed again.

"He is a native York Stater. From the time he was a small boy he's had a knife at work on wood. But he has been a little hard to handle. Just when we're getting a good job done he's likely to run off, disappear completely, leaving me to get it finished as best I can. Time and again I've said to him, 'Charlie, you're doing fine, here. People have begun to appreciate your work. You're beginning to get orders from outside the church. If you'll just settle down and tend to business steadily you'll become an important, well-to-do citizen of this community.' Then Charlie says, 'Yes, Father. I realize all that and from now on I'm going to stay here and amount to something.' That resolution may last him a few months—but sooner or later he's off again, no one knows where. He's gone now—and he left us in such a situation that I'm inclined not to let him work in the church any more."

We strolled about, enchanted by the exquisite details through which each flower differed from its neighbor even when it was of the same variety. The Tyrolean carvings seemed heavy and graceless beside this upstate artistry.

"This is part of our native tradition," said Romeyn Berry, "the tradition of the skilled artisan. There's that Madison County gunsmith you've told me about, Risley. And not far from him I happen to know lives a furniture maker, Sam Franklin, who does as perfect a job, beveling and joining and all, with a Colonial highboy as did ever a colonist; and over in Westmoreland lives a blacksmith who can do more artistic work with a piece of hot iron on his anvil than all the wrought-iron factories. It's the same way all over the state. We like to make things and we make them well. This church is completely in character with the country it serves."

As we stood in the doorway taking one last look at the lovely, intricate profusion, it seemed to me, however, that the church represented more than a feeling for craftsmanship. It symbolized in one way or another most of the characteristics of upstate people—their Yankee practicality in the realm of practical things, their love of their natural surroundings, their appreciation of elaborations of fancy, and their ecstatic surrender to mystic influences which they have felt through generations of living in this spirit-pervaded land.

Author's Note

IN THIS BOOK I HAVE TRIED TO INTERPRET THAT land which is generally designated by residents of New York City as "upstate." Since the metropolis of Greater New York is in reality a separate city-state bound to upstate only by a few political and governmental ties, I have not written of it or of the sections in its sphere of influence.

I have described the events narrated here substantially as they occurred. A few characters are disguised to save them serious embarrassment.

My hearty thanks to all the people who appear in these pages. They and hundreds of others have aided me generously. I cannot fail to express particular gratitude to the following sharers of my adventures whose names do not appear in the chronicle: Mr. and Mrs. Sidney Homer of Bolton Landing, Mr. and Mrs. Samuel Hopkins Adams of Auburn, Professor Alexander Flick, State Historian, of Albany, Dean Charles M. Ogden of Cornell University, Paul Williams of Utica, Dudley Gordon of Chautauqua, Dr. Arthur Parker of the Rochester City Museum, Mr. and Mrs. Howard Henderson, Mr. and Mrs. Oscar Kuolt, Mr. and Mrs. Willard Eddy, Mr. and Mrs. William Earl Weller of Rochester, Guy Comfort of Perry, Richard Ellsworth of

Canton, Professor Harold W. Thompson of Albany State Teachers' College, Mrs. Walter Henricks and Mrs. Charles H. Beaumont of Penn Yan, Chauncey Rickard of Schoharie, Mr. and Mrs. Robert Drummond of Kenwood, Charles W. Wenborne of Brocton, Mrs. Stanley Mock of Batavia, Dr. and Mrs. Henry W. Titus of New Rochelle, Mr. and Mrs. Robert Warner of Silvermine, Connecticut, Mr. and Mrs. Arden Norton Sr., Ray Pollard and James Hall of Cobleskill, Miss Hazle Smith of Geneseo, Miss Lucy Teresa Gilhooley of Alexander, and all my Indian friends who helped with cheerful though sometimes puzzled enthusiasm.